May all your v...

*[signature]*

Nov 07

# Valuation for Financial Reporting

## Fair Value

## Measurements and Reporting,

## Intangible Assets, Goodwill and Impairment

# VALUATION FOR FINANCIAL REPORTING

## Fair Value Measurements and Reporting, Intangible Assets, Goodwill and Impairment

MICHAEL J. MARD
JAMES R. HITCHNER
STEVEN D. HYDEN

John Wiley & Sons, Inc.

For general information on our other products and services, or technical support, please contact our Customer Care Department within the United States at 800–762–2974, outside the United States at 317–572–3993 or fax 317–572–4002.

Wiley also publishes its books in a variety of electronic formats. Some content that appears in print may not be available in electronic books.

For more information about Wiley products, visit our Web site at *http://www.wiley.com*.

***Library of Congress Cataloging-in-Publication Data:***

Mard, Michael J.
   Valuation for financial reporting : the determination of fair value for audited intangible assets / Michael J. Mard, James R. Hitchner, Steven D. Hyden. — 2nd ed.
     p. cm.
   Rev. ed. of: Valuation for financial reporting / Michael J. Mard ... [et al.]. c2002.
   Includes bibliographical references and index.
   ISBN 978–0–471–68041–3 (cloth)
  1. Intangible property—Accounting.  2. Goodwill (Commerce)—Accounting.  I. Hitchner, James R.  II. Hyden, Steven D.  III. Title.
   HF5681.I55V348 2007
   657′.3—dc22

                                      2007002517

Printed in the United States of America

10  9  8  7  6  5  4  3  2  1

*To our families*
*near and far*
*young and old*
*those that have come to us recently*
*those that have gone before us*
*we love you and thank you.*

*To Pam, Seph, Joe, and Shelley, Mom and Dad:*
*Thank you for your love and support, which make*
*this book possible.*

*—Mike Mard*

*To my three children, Jason, Michael and Deborah.*
*I couldn't be more proud of you.*
*To Karen, with love,*
*you make all we do so much better.*

*—Jim Hitchner*

*To my loves, Maria and Amy:*
*Your support means everything.*

*—Steve Hyden*

# Contents

# Preface

The second edition of this book is about fair value in financial reporting, with primary emphasis on fair value, its measurements and reporting, and the valuation and impairment analysis of intangible assets and goodwill. Chapter 1 discusses the objectives of financial reporting and the recent Financial Accounting Standards Board (FASB) Statement of Financial Accounting Standards (SFAS) No. 157, *Fair Value Measurements*, from the perspective of the valuation specialist. In addition, Chapter 1 describes work done by academic researchers on the relevance of fair value accounting.

This book is designed to bring practical implementation guidance to what is now a challenge for CFOs, auditors, and other CPAs in the private and public sectors. Because of the requirements for financial reporting of intangible assets and goodwill, auditors and valuation analysts will not only have to focus on determining the fair values of assets in accordance with SFAS No. 157 and SFAS No. 141, *Business Combinations* (and its upcoming replacement), they also must assess on at least an annual basis whether impairment of those assets has occurred in accordance with SFAS No. 142, *Goodwill and Other Intangible Assets* and SFAS No. 144, *Accounting for the Impairment or Disposal of Long-Lived Assets*. This book will explain the valuation aspects of the new financial reporting requirements, including how to identify the distinguishing characteristics of goodwill and identifiable intangible assets, determine if impairment has occurred, and employ specific methods to assess the financial impact of such impairment.

In later chapters, readers are provided a detailed example of a business combination in which tangible and intangible assets are identified and the values measured. A detailed example of an impairment analysis is also provided. The case study covers the determination of fair value or assets and reporting units under SFAS Nos. 141, 142, 144, and 157.

Significant issues related to SFAS No. 142 are addressed, including treatment of previously identified but unbooked intangible assets subsumed in goodwill, what constitutes a reporting unit, and how to handle synergies resulting from the business combination and subsequent impairment.

We have included two sample valuation reports, a checklist for data gathering, and a work program designed to guide the valuation analyst through the maze of methodologies that may be employed in the determination of the value of intangibles. We have also included an analysis of the valuation industry's reporting standards with cross-referencing among the various organizations. In-process research and development (IPR&D) receives special attention, with the inclusion of the American Institute of Certified Public Accountants (AICPA) Model Audit Program that delineates procedures to be considered when auditing a business combination transaction that may include the purchase of IPR&D.

This book does not cover in any detail the financial reporting disclosures required by generally accepted accounting principles (GAAP). We believe such matters to be corporate and audit decisions. Our goal has been to provide a concise and understandable explanation of the regulatory and conceptual issues underlying fair value measurements in business combinations and impairment testing. The authors hope that this second edition, retitled *Valuation for Financial Reporting: Fair Value Measurements and Reporting, Intangible Assets, Goodwill and Impairment,* will help clarify the relevant pronouncements and provide practical implementation guidance.

# Acknowledgments

To Deanna Muraki, thanks for taking our raw writings and turning them into a finished product. To Faye Danger, thanks for your diligence and for keeping us on the straight and narrow.

We also thank John DeRemigis, Editor, Judy Howarth, Associate Editor, and Dexter Gasque, Senior Production Editor, for providing Wiley's formidable support. Our partners and staff deserve special thanks for keeping the wheels turning while we were elsewhere engaged.

We thank the following contributing authors:

Michael A. Crain, CPA/ABV, ASA, CFA, CFE, for his contributions to Chapter 1.
Donald P. Wisehart, ASA, CPA/ABV, CVA, MST, for his contribution to Chapter 4.
David Ellner, CPA/ABV, for his assistance in preparing the sample reports in Chapter 4.

We wish to thank our reviewers for their many comments and suggestions for improving this second edition: *Darren S. Cordier*, CFA, Business Valuation Advisors, LLC; *Alfred King*, CMA, Marshall & Stevens; *Nicholas J. Mastracchio, Jr.*, Ph.D., CPA, University of South Florida; *Raymond D. Rath*, ASA; *Jacqueline Reck*, Ph.D., University of South Florida; and *James S. Rigby, Jr.*, CPA/ABV, ASA, The Financial Valuation Group.

Special thanks is also given to the American Institute of Certified Public Accountants (AICPA) and the Financial Accounting Standards Board. Portions of various documents, copyrighted by the AICPA, Harborside Financial Center, 201 Plaza Three, Jersey City, NJ 07311-3881, U.S.A., are reprinted with permission. Portions of various documents, copyrighted by the Financial Accounting Standards Board, 401 Merritt 7, P.O. Box 5116, Norwalk, CT 06856-5116, U.S.A., are reprinted with permission. Complete copies of the documents are available from the AICPA and the FASB.

MICHAEL J. MARD
JAMES R. HITCHNER
STEVEN D. HYDEN

# About the Authors

**Michael J. Mard, CPA/ABV, ASA,** is a managing director of The Financial Valuation Group (FVG) in Tampa, Florida. FVG is a national financial advisory firm specializing in valuation and litigation services. Mr. Mard is founding president of The Financial Consulting Group, a national association of professional service firms dedicated to excellence in valuation, litigation, and financial consulting. He has Bachelor's and Master's degrees in accounting from the University of South Florida. He holds the American Institute of Certified Public Accountants (AICPA) Accreditation in Business Valuation (ABV) designation and is an Accredited Senior Appraiser (ASA) with the American Society of Appraisers.

Mr. Mard has been a full-time business appraiser and expert witness for more than 23 years, specializing in intangible assets, specifically intellectual property. He has developed analyses that have been reviewed and accepted by the Securities and Exchange Commission (SEC), major accounting firms, the Internal Revenue Service (IRS), and the courts. Mr. Mard has provided expert testimony in both federal and state courts related to intangible assets, intellectual property, business damages, marital dissolution, shareholder disputes, and IRS matters.

Mr. Mard is lead author of *Driving Your Company's Value: Strategic Benchmarking for Value*, co-author of *Financial Valuation: Applications and Models* (both 1st and 2nd editions), and co-author of *Financial Valuation Workbook* (both 1st and 2nd editions), all published by John Wiley & Sons. He is co-author of AICPA's three-part self-study video course series on SFAS No. 141 and 142 on business combinations, intangible assets, and goodwill impairment. Mr. Mard has co-authored 20 courses and published more than 60 articles. He has been a presenter, speaker, and instructor more than 70 times.

Mr. Mard is very active at state and national levels, with an emphasis on business valuation standards and intellectual property valuations. He has served on numerous committees and task forces of the AICPA, Florida Institute of Certified Public Accountants, American Society of Appraisers, and the Financial Accounting Standards Board (FASB), including serving on the FASB's Valuation Resource Group. He has received the AICPA Business Volunteer of the Year Award and has been inducted into the AICPA Business Valuation Hall of Fame.

**James R. Hitchner, CPA/ABV, ASA,** is a managing director of The Financial Valuation Group in Atlanta, Georgia, and a founding member and president of The Financial Consulting Group.

Mr. Hitchner has more than 29 years of professional experience, including 27 years in valuation services and two years in real estate development. He was with Phillips Hitchner Group, Inc. for seven years and was also partner-in-charge of valuation services for the southern region of Coopers & Lybrand (now Pricewaterhouse-Coopers), where he spent more than nine years. He was also employed as a senior appraiser with the national appraisal firm American Appraisal Associates, in both the financial and industrial valuation groups.

Mr. Hitchner is editor/co-author of *Financial Valuation: Applications and Models* (both 1st and 2nd editions) and co-author of *Financial Valuation Workbook* (both 1st and 2nd editions), all published by John Wiley & Sons. He is co-author of the AICPA three-part self-study video course series on SFAS 141 and 142 on business combinations, intangible assets, and goodwill impairment. He is editor-in-chief of the *Financial Valuation and Litigation Expert* Journal (*www.valuationproducts.com*), a bimonthly journal presenting views and tools from leading experts on valuation, forensic/fraud, and litigation services.

He has been recognized as a qualified expert witness and has provided testimony on valuations in numerous state and federal courts. In the valuation area he has co-authored more than 20 courses, taught more than 50 courses, published more than 50 articles, and has made more than 100 conference presentations, including for AICPA, the American Society of Appraisers, the National Association of Certified Valuation Analysts, the Institute of Business Appraisers, and numerous state CPA societies. He has also been a faculty member teaching valuation courses for judges for the National Judicial College and the Flaschner Judicial Institute.

He is an inductee into the AICPA Business Valuation Hall of Fame, two-time recipient of the AICPA Business Valuation Volunteer of the Year award, and current member of the AICPA task force on Business Valuation Standards. He has a Bachelor of Science degree in engineering from the University of Pittsburgh and a master of business administration degree from Rider University in New Jersey. He holds the AICPA Accreditation in Business Valuation (ABV) specialty designation, and also is an Accredited Senior Appraiser (ASA) with the American Society of Appraisers.

**Steven D. Hyden, CPA/ABV, ASA,** is a managing director of The Financial Valuation Group in Tampa, Florida. Mr. Hyden is also president of Hyden Capital, Inc., an affiliate providing merger and acquisition advisory services. Mr. Hyden has been a full-time business appraiser and expert witness for more than 20 years, specializing in intangible assets, including intellectual property. He has developed analyses that have been reviewed and accepted by the SEC, major accounting firms, the IRS, and the courts.

Mr. Hyden is co-author of *Financial Valuation: Applications and Models* (both 1st and 2nd editions) published by John Wiley & Sons. He has published numerous articles, co-authored and taught multiple valuation courses including an A&A CPE course on SFAS No. 157, and was guest expert for the AICPA Continuing Professional Education video course series "Valuation of Intellectual Property."

Mr. Hyden has a Bachelor's degree in marketing from Syracuse University and an MBA from Pace University in New York. He is a CPA and holds the AICPA Accreditation in Business Valuation (ABV) specialty designation. Mr. Hyden also is an Accredited Senior Appraiser (ASA) with the American Society of Appraisers and currently serves on the Appraisal Institute Task Force.

# About the Website

This book, *Valuation for Financial Reporting: Fair Value Measurements and Reporting, Intangible Assets, Goodwill and Impairment*, includes a USPAP-compliant PowerPoint format of the report sample presented in Chapter 4. Please visit the supporting Web site to view this sample report at:

www.wiley.com/go/mardvaluation2e

# Valuation for Financial Reporting

## Fair Value

## Measurements and Reporting,

## Intangible Assets, Goodwill and Impairment

# Chapter 1

# Fair Value Measurements and Financial Reporting[1]

*Five years after Enron, corporate financial reporting stands at a crossroads. One route leads deep into the lightly charted terrain of "principles-based" reporting, where thousands of rules and regulations would be replaced by a relative handful of guiding precepts. The norm in Europe, this would be terra incognita of the most profound sort for American companies. Proponents argue that the unceasing torrent of new standards and regulations is creating an unworkable system. Foes counter that if the existing rules failed to prevent corruption and provide transparency, a system based on vague pronouncements is doomed to fail. The alternative path entails a continuing series of changes to the status quo that would undoubtedly increase complexity even as they attempt to improve transparency and accountability. No issue underscores these concerns more dramatically than fair-value accounting, in which assets and liabilities are marked to market rather than recorded at historical cost. The degree to which fair-value accounting is embraced (or not) will have a major impact on the very nature of corporate finance. In short, Sarbanes-Oxley was just a warm-up for what lies ahead.*

—Ronald Fink
"Think reporting has changed since Enron? Just wait."
*CFO Magazine*, September 1, 2006

## OBJECTIVES OF FINANCIAL REPORTING AND THE CURRENT ENVIRONMENT

In order to understand the historical and ongoing changes in generally accepted accounting principles (GAAP) surrounding fair value accounting and fair value measurements, one needs to grasp the basic objectives of financial reporting. Accounting standard setters strive to meet these objectives in their pronouncements, which through the years have been consistent—to provide users of financial statements the most meaningful information to inform their investment decisions. As the environment has changed, we have seen changes in the type of information standard setters consider most meaningful.

One of the sources of U.S. accounting literature that discusses the objectives of financial reporting is Statement of Financial Accounting Concepts No. 1, *Objectives of Financial Reporting by Business Enterprises,* published by the Financial Accounting Standards Board (FASB) in 1978. Two key points are:

1. Financial reporting is intended to provide information in making various types of decisions (e.g., investment, credit, resource allocation, management performance).
2. The objectives of financial reporting are affected by the economic, legal, political, and social environment.

The FASB and the London-based International Accounting Standards Board (IASB) are currently working on a joint initiative called the Conceptual Framework project. The goal of this multiyear project is to provide a foundation for the future development of accounting standards by the FASB and IASB. Both of these boards have goals of developing accounting standards with the following attributes:

- Principles-based
- Internally consistent
- Internationally converged
- Lead to financial reporting that provides the information needed for investment, credit, and similar decisions[2]

Phase A of the Conceptual Framework project is pending at the time of this writing, and the two boards have substantially completed their considerations of the objectives of financial reporting. An interim report of this phase said the following about the objectives:

> In the Boards' existing frameworks, the overriding objective is to provide information that is useful to present and potential investors and creditors and others in making investment, credit, and similar resource allocation decisions. The Boards' discussions of the objectives of financial reporting and decisions reached to date are based on that overriding objective.

> The Boards made the following decisions about the objectives of financial reporting:

> As with the existing frameworks, the Boards' converged framework should be concerned with general purpose financial reports that focus on the common information needs of external users. The framework should identify the primary users as present and potential investors and creditors (and their advisors), rather than focus only on the information needs of existing common shareholders. Later in the project, the Boards will consider whether financial reporting also should provide information to meet the information needs of particular types of users, such as different kinds of equity participants.

> General purpose financial reporting should provide information about the entity to the external users who lack the power to prescribe the information they require and

therefore must rely on the information provided by an entity's management. The entity's management also will be interested in that information. However, because management has the power to obtain the information it requires, any additional information needs of management are beyond the scope of the framework. Similarly, additional information needs of particular users (for example, a credit rating agency or a principal lender) that may have the power to prescribe the information they require are beyond the scope of the framework.

General purpose financial statements should provide information that is helpful to users in assessing an entity's liquidity and solvency, which is consistent with the overall objective of providing decision-useful information to a wide range of external users. This does not mean, however, that the information provided in the financial statements should focus on meeting the information needs of particular types of users that use the financial statements primarily or only to help them assess an entity's liquidity and solvency.

Stewardship or accountability should not be a separate objective of financial reporting by business entities. The Boards agreed that the converged framework should clarify that financial reporting information consistent with the primary objective would include financial reporting information useful for assessing management's stewardship. The Boards agreed to continue with the original plan to issue a due process document for Phase A before consideration of prospective financial reporting information. The Boards agreed that the due process document should indicate that the Boards will consider prospective financial reporting information in a later phase, specifically Phase E—presentation and disclosure, including the boundaries of financial reporting.[3]

Since the 1990s, financial reporting has been moving away from measuring certain assets and liabilities at historical cost and more toward fair value. Currently, GAAP requires (or allows) a mixture of both types of measurements as well as other measurement types. Although financial reporting is unlikely to entirely get away from mixed attributes, the accounting standard setters in the United States and internationally are expanding their emphasis on fair value accounting because they believe it provides more relevant information to users of financial statements.

Reforms that started with the Sarbanes-Oxley Act of 2002 stimulated U.S. accounting and auditing regulators and standard setters to take action. The primary U.S. organizations involved in these reforms are the U.S. Securities and Exchange Commission (SEC), the FASB, and the U.S. Public Company Accounting Oversight Board (PCAOB), which are attempting to strengthen financial reporting as well as increase public confidence in the capital markets. The reforms caused these entities to rethink principles and regulations affecting financial reporting, the capital markets, and the overall economy. The SEC, FASB, and PCAOB are currently working both independently and jointly to make significant changes to the system that relies heavily on financial reporting. The FASB, under Chairman Robert H. Herz (recently re-appointed to a second five-year term), has undertaken an aggressive agenda to reduce the complexity of accounting standards and improve the transparency and usefulness of financial reporting for investors and capital markets. These issues are international in scope, as they affect both the U.S. and global economies.[4]

To highlight the universal appeal of these goals, in 2002 the FASB and IASB entered into a memorandum of understanding called the *Norwalk Agreement*. The two boards committed to use their best efforts to make their existing financial reporting standards fully compatible as soon as practicable and to coordinate their future work programs to ensure that once achieved, compatibility is maintained.

Proponents of fair value accounting in financial reporting say such accounting standards make financial information more relevant and improve transparency of companies to stakeholders. Historically, accounting information focused on presenting information based on the cost of acquiring assets and the expiration of those costs. This type of accounting measurement was largely relevant to investors and creditors in the past, because in many instances one could reasonably assess the value of shares or quality of the collateralized assets based on the company's book value. Exhibit 1.1 shows that the price-to-book-value ratio of the Dow Jones Industrial Average (DJIA) stock index generally ranged from 1.0 to 2.0 between 1950 and 1990. By the 1990s, investors were, knowingly or unknowingly, increasingly placing substantial value on the intangible assets of companies. As Exhibit 1.1 demonstrates, the price-to-book-value ratio of the DJIA reached 8.2 in 2000, which reflects substantial value being placed on intangible (largely unbooked) assets by investors. Since then, this ratio has decreased, but it is still higher than it was in the past.

Critics of fair value accounting claim that the measurements are too subjective, too complex, and unnecessarily increase volatility of earnings. Accountants and auditors make many of these criticisms, as do some managements. Despite these criticisms, the accounting standard setters are moving toward fair value measurements to make financial reporting more relevant to users.

One can classify the key parties in financial reporting as preparers, auditors, and users. Preparers are primarily management of companies in possession and control of the underlying financial records. Auditors in the United States are certified public accountants (CPAs)[5] who are licensed by state government agencies, and perform

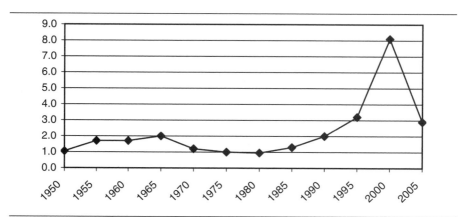

**Exhibit 1.1**   Price-to-Book Value Ratio of Dow Jones Industrial Average Stock Index[6]

verifications on the preparers' financial reporting by following auditing standards or regulations. One commonly thinks of external users of financial information as existing and potential investors and creditors and their advisors. Management are also users of their financial information, but financial accounting standards place little focus on these users because they have control over the underlying accounting records.

When fair value measurements are necessary for financial reporting, preparers may have valuation specialists on their staff or hire outside consultants to provide the measurements. Auditors may rely on valuation specialists in their firms as technical resources and reviewers in the audit process.

More emphasis on fair value measurements in financial reporting provide opportunities for valuation specialists willing to study and become competent in this area. Because this area involves GAAP, a background or understanding in accounting and auditing can help the valuation specialist understand the meaning and implications of fair value accounting literature.

Valuation specialists are being held to an increasingly higher level of performance. Many auditors are now familiar with best practices literature on fair value measurements, such as *Assets Acquired in a Business Combination to be Used in Research and Development Activities: A Focus on Software, Electronic Devices, and Pharmaceutical Industries* (New York: American Institute of Certified Public Accountants, 2001) (The IPR&D Practice Aid) and *Valuation of Privately-Held-Company Equity Securities Issued as Compensation* (New York: American Institute of Certified Public Accountants, 2004). Statement of Financial Accounting Standards, *Fair Value Measurements*, refers to the IPR&D Practice Aid ((SFAS) No. 157, footnote 10). Even though this practice aid was written for specific industries, many auditors now view the procedures it describes as best practices across other industries.

Many auditors now expect valuation specialists to analyze management's key assumptions underlying a financial forecast used to develop fair value measurements. The IPR&D Practice Aid recommends this step as one that should normally be performed by the specialist. In addition, auditors may want valuation specialists to provide alternative valuation methodologies to evaluate the reasonableness of fair value conclusions, such as creating a business enterprise analysis of an acquired business.

As a result of stricter auditor independence rules and more scrutiny from accounting regulators, companies are frequently hiring valuation specialists to perform fair value measurements required by GAAP. Most companies hire outside valuation specialists when they do not have internal resources to perform fair value measurements. Auditors will perform their audit tests on the valuation work of the specialists, whether internal or external. These activities require new relationships and coordination among the preparers, auditors, and valuation specialists.

Valuation specialists who were trained to perform analysis under *fair market value* will need additional education and experience if they are to successfully practice in the world of fair value. First, they need to understand the nuances that differentiate fair value from fair market value. It is beyond the scope of this book to discuss the various standards of value, but there is ample published literature on the subject. Additionally, valuation practitioners need a thorough understanding of the relevant accounting literature.

Valuation specialists who enter this service line must be willing to work in an accounting environment, which presents challenges above and beyond those found in the theoretical valuation world. They must understand and use accounting standards and best practices that apply to fair value measurements, be able to work with auditors, and stay current with the relevant accounting literature.

# STATEMENT OF FINANCIAL ACCOUNTING STANDARDS NO. 157, *FAIR VALUE MEASUREMENTS*

The FASB is the U.S. accounting standard setter for anyone reporting under GAAP. It is the standard setter because the U.S. Securities and Exchange Commission effectively recognizes the FASB for establishing GAAP applicable to publicly registered companies (subject to additional SEC requirements). Therefore, the fair value accounting literature issued by the FASB is effectively a regulatory accounting standard.

The FASB continues to move ahead with an agenda that includes fair value accounting. In 2006 it issued Statement of Financial Accounting Standards No. 157, *Fair Value Measurements* to take affect for financial statements issued for fiscal years beginning after November 15, 2007 and interim periods within those fiscal years.

## SCOPE

SFAS No. 157 establishes a framework for making fair value measurements and requires additional disclosures about the measurements. The pronouncement does not establish any new areas in financial reporting where fair value accounting is required. Rather, it interacts with other accounting literature that requires or permits fair value measurements—with some exceptions (paragraph 2). Appendix D of SFAS No. 157 lists accounting pronouncements within the scope of the standard as of the issuance date. It amends 28 Opinions, Statements, Interpretations, and other official pronouncements previously issued by accounting standard setters and applies to another 39 pieces of accounting literature. Appendix 1.1 to this chapter lists the pronouncements impacted by SFAS No. 157. Appendix 1.2 lists the literature specifically excluded from application of SFAS No. 157.

## FAIR VALUE

SFAS No. 157 provides a single authoritative definition of *fair value* for financial reporting. It defines fair value as:

> Fair value is the price that would be received to sell an asset or paid to transfer a liability in an orderly transaction between market participants at the measurement date.[7]

Fair value for financial reporting is one of five standards of value in the business valuation body of knowledge. The others are fair market value, investment value, intrinsic value, and fair value (under state statutes) in dissenting shareholder matters.

Fair value for financial reporting is different from fair market value. Characteristics of fair value in business combinations under GAAP and best practices include:

- Valuation methodologies specified in the accounting literature and/or acceptable to the auditors;
- Generally established on an asset-by-asset and a situation-by-situation basis;
- Typically a control value;
- The fair values of individual assets do not include a specific buyer's unique synergies unless such synergies are also those of "market participants";
- The additional purchase price paid in a business combination due to a synergistic component is recorded as goodwill and subsequently will be subject to impairment testing under SFAS No. 142;
- The total fair value of all assets acquired is always reconciled (adjusted) to the purchase price in a business combination or to a market participant's price;
- In the absence of quoted market prices, the technique used to estimate fair value would be the method producing a fair value best approximating quoted market prices;
- Includes tax amortization benefits;
- Transaction costs are not deducted;
- Considers the highest and best use of market participants in the principal (or most advantageous) market to establish the valuation premise (in-use or in-exchange);
- Considers a reporting entity's credit standing;
- Requires the use of market participant assumptions in accepting management's prospective financial information (projections); and
- Relies on but does not define active market.

## Fair Value Hierarchy

In SFAS No. 157, the FASB specified a hierarchy approach to determining fair value. The pronouncement defines a hierarchy[8] in the development of fair value measurements as follows:

*Level 1.* Inputs are observable market inputs that reflect quoted prices for identical assets or liabilities in active markets the reporting entity has the ability to access at the measurement date.

*Level 2.* Inputs are observable market inputs other than quoted prices for identical assets or liabilities in active markets the reporting entity has the ability to access at the measurement date. Level 2 inputs include the following:

- Quoted prices for similar assets or liabilities in active markets
- Quoted prices for identical or similar assets or liabilities in markets that are not active; that is, a market in which there are few transactions for the asset or liability, the prices are not current, or price quotations vary substantially either over time or among

market makers (e.g., some brokered markets) or in which little information is released publicly (e.g., a principal-to-principal market)

- Market inputs other than quoted prices that are directly observable for the asset or liability; for example, interest rates, yield curves, volatilities, and default rates that are observable at the commonly quoted intervals
- Market inputs that are not directly observable for the asset or liability but that are derived principally from or corroborated by other observable market data through correlation or by other means (market-corroborated inputs); for example, inputs derived through extrapolation or interpolation that are corroborated by other observable market data

*Level 3.* Inputs are unobservable market inputs; for example, inputs derived through extrapolation or interpolation that are not able to be corroborated by observable market data. Unobservable market inputs shall be used to measure fair value if observable market inputs are not available, thereby allowing for situations in which there is little, if any, market activity for the asset or liability. However, the fair value measurement objective remains the same; that is, an exit price from the perspective of a market participant (seller). Therefore, a fair value measurement using unobservable market inputs within Level 3 shall consider the assumptions that market participants would use in pricing the asset or liability, including assumptions about the amount a market participant (buyer) would demand to assume the risk related to the unobservable market inputs used to measure fair value. The reporting entity's own data used to develop the inputs shall be adjusted to exclude factors specific to the reporting entity if information is available that indicates that market participants would use different assumptions.

## Entry Price Versus Exit Price

SFAS No. 157 describes fair value from the perspective of an exit (sale) price rather than an entry (purchase) price.[9] The price is determined based on the amount required to exchange the asset or liability in an orderly transaction between market participants. Exchange means to sell the asset or transfer the liability at the measurement date. An orderly transaction assumes exposure to the market for a period prior to the measurement date to allow for marketing activities that are usual and customary. An exit price is based on a hypothetical transaction from the perspective of a market participant who holds the asset or owes the liability. Therefore, the objective is to determine the price that would be received to sell the asset or paid to transfer the liability at the measurement date, which makes it an exit price.

## Principal (or Most Advantageous) Market

The exit price is to be considered from the perspective of market participants in the principal (or most advantageous) market for the asset or liability.[10] A fair value measurement is based on a transaction assumed to occur in the principal market for the asset or liability. The principal market is the market with the greatest volume and level of activity for the asset or liability. The most advantageous market is the market that would provide the highest price for an asset and the lowest for a liability. The principal market trumps the most advantageous market. If there is a principal market for the asset or liability, the fair value measurement shall represent the price in that market (whether that price is directly observable or otherwise determined using a valuation technique), even if the price in a different market is potentially more advantageous at the measurement date.

## Transaction Costs

The pronouncement states the price shall not be adjusted for transaction costs because transaction costs are not an attribute of the asset or liability.[11] They are specific to the transaction and represent the incremental direct costs to sell the asset or transfer the liability. However, any transportation costs are included in the fair value measurement.

## Market Participants

SFAS No. 157 defines market participants for purposes of fair value measurements.[12] They are buyers and sellers in the most advantageous market for the asset or liability. Market participants are also:

- Independent of the reporting entity
- Knowledgeable (having all relevant information, including obtaining information through usual and customary due diligence)
- Able to transact
- Willing to transact (motivated but not compelled)

## Highest and Best Use of an Asset

A fair value measurement of an asset assumes the highest and best use of the asset from the perspective of market participants, regardless of how the company actually intends to use it.[13] It also requires considering that the use of the asset is:

- Physically possible
- Legally permissible
- Financially feasible

Highest and best use is based on the use of the asset and generally results in maximizing the value. As such, the valuation premise may be either:

- *In-use*, which would provide maximum value through its use in combination with other assets as a group, such as a group of nonfinancial assets
- *In-exchange*, which would provide maximum value on a stand-alone basis, such as some financial assets

Importantly, the fair value of an asset in-use is determined based on the use of the asset together with other assets as a group (consistent with its highest and best use from the perspective of market participants), even if the asset that is the subject of the measurement is aggregated (or disaggregated) at a different level for purposes of applying other accounting pronouncements. This requirement may result in different aggregation assumptions from those used for impairment analyses under SFAS No. 142 or SFAS No. 144.

## Applicability to Liabilities

For a liability, a fair value measurement assumes a transfer of the liability to market participants. For the determination of price related to the transfer of a liability, nonperformance risk must be considered and must be the same before and after the assumed transfer. Nonperformance risk is the risk of not fulfilling the obligation and includes (but may not be limited to) the reporting entity's own credit risk.[14]

## Initial Recognition

When an asset is acquired or a liability is assumed in an exchange transaction, the transaction price represents an *entry price* to acquire or assume. By contrast, fair value measurement after acquisition or assumption is a function of the hypothetical price to sell the asset or paid to transfer the liability and is thus an *exit price*.[15]

## Valuation Approaches: Market, Income, and Cost

SFAS No. 157 also discusses that the valuation techniques used to measure fair value should be consistent with the market approach, income approach, and cost approach.[16] The measurement objective is to use a valuation technique (or a combination of techniques) appropriate for the circumstances but maximizing the use of market inputs.[17]

Fundamentally, value is a function of economics and is based on the return on assets. The cost approach represents the things owned or borrowed. The income approach quantifies the return these assets can be expected to produce. The market approach merely reflects the market's perceptions of the things owned and borrowed or their expected returns.

For the determination of fair value measurement, the *cost approach* is based on the current replacement cost—the amount that at the measurement date would be required to replace the service capacity of the asset. It is based on the cost to a market participant to acquire or construct a substitute asset of comparable utility, adjusted for obsolescence whether physical, functional, or economic.

The *income approach* uses valuation techniques to convert future amounts to a single present amount and is based on the value indicated by current market expectations about those future amounts. Although SFAS No. 157 says it does not apply to SFAS 123R (accounting for employee stock options and other share-based payments), SFAS No. 157 still includes present value techniques such as option-pricing models, binomial models, and the multiperiod excess earnings method.[18] Importantly, present value techniques originally presented by the FASB in Statement of Financial Accounting Concepts No. 7 have been included in SFAS No. 157 as Appendix B. This means those present value techniques are now Level A GAAP.[19] Appendix B of SFAS No. 157 discusses two methods for present value calculations:

1. Discount rate adjustment technique, *which is the traditional method whereby the denominator incorporates all risk elements related to the single cash flow being discounted*
2. Expected present value technique, *which is a function of the probability weighted average of all possible cash flows discounted at a risk-free rate. There are two methods*:
   a. *Adjusting the expected cash flows for systematic (or market) risk*
   b. *Not adjusting the expected cash flows for systematic risk, but instead including the risk adjustment in the discount rate*[20]

The *market approach* uses prices of market transactions involving identical or similar assets or liabilities. Remember here the fair value hierarchy: Level 1 is identical assets or liabilities and Level 2 is similar assets or liabilities. Therefore, the market approach may be either a Level 1 or Level 2 determination. Further, matrix pricing is considered consistent with the market approach. This applies to debt securities that do not rely exclusively on quoted prices for the specific securities, but rather rely on the securities' relationship to other benchmark quoted securities.

## Inputs: Observable and Unobservable

Inputs refer broadly to the assumptions that market participants would use in pricing the asset or liability and can be of two types:

* *Observable inputs* are based on assumptions market participants would use and be independent of the reporting entity
* *Unobservable inputs* are based on the entity's own assumptions about the assumptions market participants would use based on the best available information[21]

Fair value measurements require maximizing observable inputs and minimizing unobservable inputs.

## Active Market

The FASB has provided the following, rather vague, definition of active market:

An active market for the asset or liability is a market in which transactions for the asset or liability occur with sufficient frequency and volume to provide pricing information on an ongoing basis.[22]

As stated previously, Level 1 inputs are observable market inputs that reflect quoted prices for identical assets or liabilities in active markets.[23] In explaining its reasoning for referencing quoted market prices, the FASB cited paragraph 57 of SFAS No. 107:[24]

The Board concluded that quoted market prices provide the most reliable measure of fair value. Quoted market prices are easy to obtain and are reliable and verifiable. They are used and relied upon regularly and are well understood by investors, creditors, and other users of financial information. In recent years, new markets have developed and some existing markets have *evolved from thin to active markets*, thereby increasing the ready availability of reliable fair value information (emphasis added).

Further, the FASB affirmed:

... that its intent was not to preclude adjustments to a quoted price if that price is not readily available or representative of fair value, noting that in those situations, the market for the particular asset or liability might not be active. To convey its intent more clearly, the Board clarified that *in those situations, the fair value of the asset or liability should be measured using the quoted price, as adjusted, but within a lower level of the fair value hierarchy* (emphasis added).[25]

While it is clear that the FASB recognizes the distinction between a thin and an active market, it chose not to provide a clear definition of active market. While the literature fails to provide a specific definition or objective measures for determining whether a market is an active market, it would seem an active market would take into consideration the following:

1. Narrow range for bid/ask prices
2. Homogeneous asset
3. Significant trading volume
4. Liquid (obvious, but needs to be said)
5. Observable (again, obvious)
6. Level of activity. A mathematically related definition would speak to bid/ask spreads, volume of activity compared to total float or shares outstanding; that is, an active market could handle a certain volume with a limited impact on price given a limited time frame.

Whether a market is sufficiently active to satisfy the derivation of price deemed "quoted price" will be a matter of judgment and will likely vary from reporting unit to reporting unit.

## SUBSEQUENT EVENTS

In an effort to obtain the most relevant price available, even if it is after the measurement date, the FASB is allowing subsequent events to determine such price.[26]

As the Board observes, in some cases significant events might occur after the close of a market but before the measurement date, which will defeat the previously determined quoted price such that it might not be representative of fair value at the measurement date. Examples given include principal-to-principal transactions, brokered trades, or announcements. As a result, the FASB stated:

> ...the reporting entity should not ignore information that is available at the reporting date (for example, a large change in the price in another market after the close of the principal market in which the asset or liability trades). The Board agreed that entities should establish and consistently apply a policy for identifying those events that might affect fair value measurements. However, if a quoted price is adjusted for new information, the fair value measurement is a lower level measurement.[27]

## SECURITIES OWNED AS AN ASSET AND BLOCKAGE DISCOUNTS

The FASB focused on securities owned as an asset and the unit of account (paragraphs C79–80). It considered whether the unit of account for a block position that trades in an active market is an individual unit or a block. The fair value measurement price consequently would be a function of the price either reflecting or not reflecting the blockage factor (generally, a depression of value resulting from the size of the position traded). After considering its own previous pronouncements on this issue (principally SFAS Nos. 107, 115, 124, 133 and 140) and many comments from users and providers, the FASB decided to not allow blockage adjustments.

> In particular, the Board emphasized that when a quoted price in an active market for a security is available, that price should be used to measure fair value without regard to an entity's intent to transact at that price. Basing the fair value on the quoted price results in comparable reporting. Adjusting the price for the size of the position introduces management intent (to trade in blocks) into the measurement, reducing comparability.[28]

Therefore, SFAS No. 157 precludes the use of blockage discounts in fair value measurements and eliminates the exceptions of using blockage as provided in previous pronouncements (i.e., SFAS Nos. 107, 115, 124, 133, and 140). The unit of account for an instrument that trades in an active market is the individual trading unit.

Specific terms used in SFAS No. 157 are defined in Appendix 1.3.

## RESTRICTED STOCK

The fair value of restricted stock must be determined based on whether market participants would consider the effect of the restriction. For example, a publicly traded stock restricted under Rule 144 or similar rules of the SEC would be adjusted to reflect such restrictions if the restriction is an attribute of the security and would transfer to market participants.[29]

# ACADEMIC RESEARCH ON THE RELEVANCE
# OF FAIR VALUE ACCOUNTING

During the 1980s and 1990s, researchers conducted numerous empirical studies on the relevance of fair value accounting. The timing coincided with the public debate on the appropriate accounting standard for financial instruments. The FASB had added this topic to its agenda in 1986, and the subject later became controversial. Financial institutions opposed a change requiring them to account for their financial assets at fair value. Alternatively, banking regulators and others claimed the accounting standard for financial instruments at the time did not provide users with relevant information, and changes to the standards were necessary. Proponents of fair value accounting argued that assets, liabilities, and earnings based on fair values, rather than on historical costs, provided more relevant information to users. Former SEC Chairman Richard Breeden testified in 1990 before the U.S. Senate's Committee on Banking, Housing, and Urban Affairs, saying he believed that market-based data is the most relevant financial information. He also advocated a move to fair value accounting for all public companies and financial institutions. (The debate on fair value accounting continues even today.)

In 1990 and 1991, the FASB issued two accounting standards that focused on information disclosures of financial instruments: SFAS No. 105, *Disclosure of Information about Financial Instruments with Off-Balance-Sheet Risk and Financial Instruments with Concentrations of Credit Risk,* and SFAS No. 107, *Disclosures about Fair Value of Financial Instruments.* In 1993, the FASB issued SFAS No. 115, *Accounting for Certain Investments in Debt and Equity Securities*, which changed how firms accounted for and reported on securities they held for investment. The firms most affected by these accounting standards were financial institutions such as banks and thrifts. SFAS No. 115 required firms to measure the fair values of financial instruments that were to be traded or available for sale. The standard made some changes to debt securities but did not address all of the financial reporting issues. Under SFAS No. 115, banks and thrift institutions report the fair values of these financial instruments on their balance sheets and gains or losses from the change in fair values in their income statements.

Financial disclosures required by banking regulators and accounting standard setters provided academic researchers with rich data for empirical studies on the relevance of fair value accounting to investors. The research primarily explored two areas. First, researchers examined the association between the stock prices of financial institutions and the net assets of those firms when their financial instruments were measured at fair value. Second, studies tested the relation between investors' gains and losses from owning bank stocks and the banks' own profits and losses using the securities' fair values.

Research using bank and thrift data revealed that accounting for financial instruments at their fair values rather than historical costs improves the relevancy of financial reporting. Selected research on the relevancy of fair value accounting is described as follows.

## BANKS: BALANCE SHEET RELEVANCE

A journal article by Mary E. Barth (the Barth Study)[30] studies the relevancy of fair value accounting to investors. It examined two different accounting measurements, historical cost and fair value, on the same financial statement components. Prior research had not found strong evidence on the relevance of fair value accounting. Researchers argued that management errors in estimating the fair values of assets were the primary cause for earlier findings. These earlier findings were based on studies that examined multiple industries and cross-sectional differences, which may have led to findings of weak evidence.

In contrast, the Barth Study examined the relevance of fair value accounting in a single industry: banking. The study investigated how financial-instrument assets measured at fair value and the related securities gains and losses are reflected in bank stock prices compared with historical cost measurements, to determine which is more relevant to investors for valuing bank stocks. The Barth Study examined U.S. banks whose financial data appeared on the 1990 Compustat Annual Bank Tape. The financial statement data covered periods from 1971 to 1990. The investment assets in the banks in this study averaged about 15% to 20% of total assets. The average differences between historical cost and fair value were large: 37% of the book value and 57% of the market value of equity.

The Barth Study showed that financial-instrument assets measured at fair values provide statistically significant explanatory power over historical costs in the share prices of banks. The study also found that the historical costs of financial instruments provide no significant explanatory power incremental to fair values. The Barth Study concluded that using fair values to measure financial instruments appeared to be relevant to investors in valuing bank equities.

## BANKS: INCOME STATEMENT RELEVANCE

The Barth Study found inconsistent results on securities gains and losses. The significance of any explanatory power of securities gains and losses based on fair value measurements beyond historical costs depended on the statistical model used. Models that offered explanatory power were not robust. Some models revealed that fair values offered no statistically significant explanatory power. However, historical costs always provided explanatory power beyond fair values.

Barth argued that the evidence suggested that the inability of fair values to offer any incremental explanatory power was a result of management errors in estimating the securities' fair values. (Valuation errors are still a principle argument of those who are generally opposed to fair value accounting.) Measurement errors are a larger percentage relative to securities gains and losses than they are to the securities fair values, causing a greater relative impact. Barth acknowledged this argument was unverifiable. The Barth Study concluded that using fair values to measure gains and losses of financial instruments did not appear to be relevant to investors in valuing bank equities.

In contrast, a journal article by Anwer S. Ahmed and Carolyn Takeda (the Ahmed/Takeda Study)[31] studied the same issues as the Barth Study but controlled for the effects of interest rate sensitivity on other assets and liabilities (on-balance sheet). The Ahmed/Takeda Study found securities gains and losses using fair values have incremental explanatory power over historical costs. These findings suggest the inconsistent results in the Barth Study may not be attributed to securities' fair value measurement problems and arguably offer evidence that fair values to measure gains and losses are relevant to investors in valuing bank stocks.

## CLOSED-END FUNDS: BALANCE SHEET AND INCOME STATEMENT RELEVANCE

A journal article by Thomas J. Carroll, Thomas J. Linsmeier,[32] and Kathy R. Petroni (the Carroll et al. Study)[33] studied a sample of 143 closed-end funds using data from 1982 to 1997. They argue that closed-end funds offer better evidence on the relevance of fair value accounting than other financial instruments. One reason the authors offer is that substantially all of the assets appearing on the financial statements of funds are reported at their fair values. (Liabilities in the funds are negligible.) The Carroll et al. Study also argues that the broader types of investments owned by funds offers better evidence than other financial instruments. This data allowed the researchers to perform additional tests on usefulness based on varying degrees of *reliability* of fair value measurements.

The Carroll et al. Study found a statistically significant association between stock prices of the funds and the funds' investments when they were measured with fair values after controlling for historical costs. It also found a significant relation between stock returns and the investment gains and losses. The research suggests that securities measured at fair value are relevant to investors in valuing stocks of closed-end funds.

The authors of the Carroll et al. Study also tested their hypothesis across different fund types and compared the results to one another. Tests included funds with publicly held equities from G7 countries and those with equities other than those publicly held from G7 countries. The results across all fund types showed a statistically significant association between fund stock prices and the fund investments using fair values. The Carroll et al. Study argues that the findings suggest the need to express all securities at their estimated fair values, including those that are traded in thin markets, such as private or non-G7 markets.

## ENDNOTES

1. Michael A. Crain, CPA/ABV, ASA, CFA, CFE, is a contributing author to this chapter. Crain is Managing Director of The Financial Valuation Group in Ft. Lauderdale, Florida, and Chair of the American Institute of Certified Public Accountants Business Valuation Committee.

2. Financial Accounting Standards Board, FASB Project Update, *Conceptual Framework—Joint Project of the IASB and FASB*, Objectives, Revisions: December 1, 2006, www.fasb.org/project/conceptual-framework.shtml.

3. Ibid., and Financial Accounting Standards Board, Financial Accounting Series, Preliminary Views, *Conceptual Framework for Financial Reporting: Objective of Financial Reporting and Qualitative Characteristics of Decision-Useful Financial Reporting Information*, July 6, 2006.

4. Presentation by FASB Chairman Robert H. Herz to the American Institute of Certified Public Accountants' National Conference on Current SEC and PCAOB Reporting Developments, December 6, 2005.

5. Alternatively, chartered accountants in some other countries.

6. The authors thank Charles Morris, CFA, of Morris Investment Counsel, Atlanta, GA, for providing the data used to prepare this graphic.

7. Financial Accounting Standards Board, Statement of Financial Accounting Standards No. 157, *Fair Value Measurements* (2006), at 5.

8. Ibid., at 22–31.

9. Ibid., at 7.

10. Ibid., at 8.

11. Ibid., at 9.

12. Ibid., at 10–11.

13. Ibid., at 12–14.

14. Ibid., at 15.

15. Ibid., at 16.

16. Ibid., at 18.

17. Ibid., at 21.

18. Ibid., at 18.b.

19. Accounting standard setters have classified accounting pronouncements and other publications into a hierarchy (or levels).

20. Financial Accounting Standards Board, Statement of Financial Accounting Standards No, 157, *Fair Value Measurements,* (2006), Appendix B.

21. Ibid., at 21.

22. Ibid., at 24.

23. Ibid., at C66.

24. Ibid., at C66.

25. Ibid., at C68.

26. Ibid., at C70.

27. Ibid.

28. Ibid., at C79.

29. Ibid., at A28·A29.

30. Barth, Mary E, "Fair value accounting: Evidence from investment securities and the market valuations of banks," *The Accounting Review* 69 (January 1994), pp. 1–25.

31. Ahmed, Anwer S., and Carolyn Takeda, "Stock market valuation of gains and losses on commercial banks' investment securities: An empirical analysis," *Journal of Accounting & Economics* 20 (1995), pp. 207–225.

32. Thomas J. Linsmeier was appointed as a member of the Financial Accounting Standards Board in 2006.

33. Carroll, Thomas J., Thomas J. Linsmeier, and Kathy R. Petroni, "The reliability of fair value versus historical cost information: Evidence from closed-end mutual funds," *Journal of Accounting, Auditing and Finance,* 18 (1) (2003), pp. 1–24.

# References to APB and FASB Pronouncements (FASB SFAS No. 157, APPENDIX D)

D1. This appendix lists APB and FASB pronouncements existing at the date of this Statement that refer to fair value. Those pronouncements that are amended by this Statement are indicated by an asterisk.

1. Opinion 18, *The Equity Method of Accounting for Investments in Common Stock*
2. Opinion 21\*, *Interest on Receivables and Payables*
3. Opinion 28\*, *Interim Financial Reporting*
4. Opinion 29\*, *Accounting for Nonmonetary Transactions*
5. Statement 13\*, *Accounting for Leases*
6. Statement 15\*, *Accounting by Debtors and Creditors for Troubled Debt Restructurings*
7. Statement 19\*, *Financial Accounting and Reporting by Oil and Gas Producing Companies*
8. Statement 23, *Inception of the Lease*
9. Statement 28, *Accounting for Sales with Leasebacks*
10. Statement 35\*, *Accounting and Reporting by Defined Benefit Pension Plans*
11. Statement 45, *Accounting for Franchise Fee Revenue*
12. Statement 60\*, *Accounting and Reporting by Insurance Enterprises*
13. Statement 61, *Accounting for Title Plant*
14. Statement 63\*, *Financial Reporting by Broadcasters*
15. Statement 65\*, *Accounting for Certain Mortgage Banking Activities*
16. Statement 66, *Accounting for Sales of Real Estate*
17. Statement 67\*, *Accounting for Costs and Initial Rental Operations of Real Estate Projects*
18. Statement 68, *Research and Development Arrangements*
19. Statement 84, *Induced Conversions of Convertible Debt*
20. Statement 87\*, *Employers' Accounting for Pensions*
21. Statement 98, *Accounting for Leases*
22. Statement 106\*, *Employers' Accounting for Postretirement Benefits Other Than Pensions*

23. Statement 107*, *Disclosures about Fair Value of Financial Instruments*
24. Statement 114, *Accounting by Creditors for Impairment of a Loan*
25. Statement 115*, *Accounting for Certain Investments in Debt and Equity Securities*
26. Statement 116*, *Accounting for Contributions Received and Contributions Made*
27. Statement 124*, *Accounting for Certain Investments Held by Not-for-Profit Organizations*
28. Statement 126, *Exemption from Certain Required Disclosures about Financial Instruments for Certain Nonpublic Entities*
29. Statement 133*, *Accounting for Derivative Instruments and Hedging Activities*
30. Statement 136*, *Transfers of Assets to a Not-for-Profit Organization or Charitable Trust That Raises or Holds Contributions for Others*
31. Statement 138, *Accounting for Certain Derivative Instruments and Certain Hedging Activities*
32. Statement 140*, *Accounting for Transfers and Servicing of Financial Assets and Extinguishments of Liabilities*
33. Statement 141*, *Business Combinations*
34. Statement 142*, *Goodwill and Other Intangible Assets*
35. Statement 143*, *Accounting for Asset Retirement Obligations*
36. Statement 144*, *Accounting for the Impairment or Disposal of Long-Lived Assets*
37. Statement 146*, *Accounting for Costs Associated with Exit or Disposal Activities*
38. Statement 149, *Amendment of Statement 133 on Derivative Instruments and Hedging Activities*
39. Statement 150*, *Accounting for Certain Financial Instruments with Characteristics of both Liabilities and Equity*
40. Statement 153, *Exchanges of Nonmonetary Assets*
41. Statement 156*, *Accounting for Servicing of Financial Assets*
42. Interpretation 9, *Applying APB Opinions No. 16 and 17 When a Savings and Loan Association or a Similar Institution Is Acquired in a Business Combination Accounted for by the Purchase Method*
43. Interpretation 23, *Leases of Certain Property Owned by a Governmental Unit or Authority*
44. Interpretation 24, *Leases Involving Only Part of a Building*
45. Interpretation 45*, *Guarantor's Accounting and Disclosure Requirements for Guarantees, Including Indirect Guarantees of Indebtedness of Others*
46. Interpretation 46 (revised December 2003), *Consolidation of Variable Interest Entities*
47. Interpretation 47, *Accounting for Conditional Asset Retirement Obligations*
48. Technical Bulletin 84-1, *Accounting for Stock Issued to Acquire the Results of a Research and Development Arrangement*
49. Technical Bulletin 85-1, *Accounting for the Receipt of Federal Home Loan Mortgage Corporation Participating Preferred Stock*

**50.** Technical Bulletin 85-5, *Issues Relating to Accounting for Business Combinations*

**51.** Technical Bulletin 85-6, *Accounting for a Purchase of Treasury Shares at a Price Significantly in Excess of the Current Market Price of the Shares and the Income Statement Classification of Costs Incurred in Defending against a Takeover Attempt*

**52.** Technical Bulletin 86-2, *Accounting for an Interest in the Residual Value of a Leased Asset*

**53.** Technical Bulletin 88-1, *Issues Relating to Accounting for Leases*

**54.** FSP FAS 115-1 and 124-1, *The Meaning of Other-Than-Temporary Impairment and Its Application to Certain Investments*

**55.** FSP FAS 143-1, *Accounting for Electronic Equipment Waste Obligations*

**56.** FSP FAS 144-1, *Determination of Cost Basis for Foreclosed Assets under FASB Statement No. 15 and the Measurement of Cumulative Losses Previously Recognized under Paragraph 37 of FASB Statement No. 144*

**57.** FSP FAS 150-1, *Issuer's Accounting for Freestanding Financial Instruments Composed of More Than One Option or Forward Contract Embodying Obligations under FASB Statement No. 150*

**58.** FSP FAS 150-2, *Accounting for Mandatorily Redeemable Shares Requiring Redemption by Payment of an Amount that Differs from the Book Value of Those Shares under FASB Statement No. 150*

**59.** FSP FAS 150-3, *Effective Date, Disclosures, and Transition for Mandatorily Redeemable Financial Instruments of Certain Nonpublic Entities and Certain Mandatorily Redeemable Noncontrolling Interests under FASB Statement No. 150*

**60.** FSP FAS 150-4, *Issuers' Accounting for Employee Stock Ownership Plans under FASB Statement No. 150*

**61.** FSP FIN 45-2, *Whether FASB Interpretation No. 45 Provides Support for Subsequently Accounting for a Guarantor's Liability at Fair Value*

**62.** FSP FIN 46(R)-2, *Calculation of Expected Losses under FASB Interpretation No. 46(R)*

**63.** FSP FIN 46(R)-3, *Evaluating Whether as a Group the Holders of the Equity Investment at Risk Lack the Direct or Indirect Ability to Make Decisions about an Entity's Activities through Voting Rights Similar Rights under FASB Interpretation No. 46(R)*

**64.** FSP FIN 46(R)-5, *Implicit Variable Interests under FASB Interpretation No. 46*

**65.** FSP FIN 46(R)-6, *Determining the Variability to Be Considered in Applying FASB Interpretation No. 46(R)*

**66.** FSP FTB 85-4-1, *Accounting for Life Settlement Contracts by Third-Party Investors*

**67.** FSP AAG INV-1 and SOP 94-4-1, *Reporting of Fully Benefit-Responsive Investment Contracts Held by Certain Investment Companies Subject to the AICPA Investment Company Guide and Defined-Contribution Health and Welfare and Pension Plans*

# Pronouncements Excluded From SFAS No. 157

SFAS No. 157 does not apply under accounting pronouncements that address share-based payment transactions. These include:

1. APB Opinion No. 25, *Accounting for Stock Issued to Employees*
2. FASB Statement No. 123 (revised 2004), *Share-Based Payment*
3. FASB Statement No. 148, *Accounting for Stock-Based Compensation—Transition and Disclosure*
4. FASB Interpretation No. 44, *Accounting for Certain Transactions Involving Stock Compensation*
5. FASB Technical Bulletin No. 97-1, *Accounting under Statement 123 for Certain Employee Stock Purchase Plans with a Look-Back Option*

# Glossary

This glossary contains definitions of certain terms identified by the authors that are used in SFAS No. 157, *Fair Value Measurements.*

| Term | Definition | Paragraph |
|------|-----------|-----------|
| Asset Group | An aggregation (grouping) of assets that forms the basis for applying the *in-use* premise. | Paragraph 6 |
| Blockage Factor | The size of the position relative to trading volume | Summary |
| Entry Price | The price paid to acquire the asset or received to assume the liability | Paragraph 16 |
| Exchange Price | The price in an orderly transaction between market participants to sell the asset or transfer the liability in the market in which the reporting entity would transact for the asset or liability, that is, the principal or most advantageous market for the asset or liability | Summary |
| Exit Price | The price that would be received to sell the asset or paid to transfer the liability | Paragraph 16 |
| Fair Value | The price that would be received to sell an asset or paid to transfer a liability in an orderly transaction between market participants at the measurement date | Paragraph 5 |
| Fair Value Hierarchy | Prioritizes the inputs to valuation techniques used to measure fair value into three broad levels | Paragraph 22 |
| Highest and Best Use | The use of an asset by market participants that would maximize the value of the asset or the group of assets within which the asset would be used | Paragraph 12 |
| Level 1 Inputs | Quoted prices in active markets for identical assets or liabilities that the reporting entity has the ability to access at the measurement date | Paragraph 24 |
| Level 2 Inputs | Inputs other than quoted prices that are observable for the asset or liability, either directly or indirectly | Paragraph 28 |
| Level 3 Inputs | Unobservable inputs for the asset or liability; the reporting entity's own assumptions about the assumptions that market participants would use in pricing the asset or liability | Paragraph 30 |

| Term | Definition | Paragraph |
|------|-----------|-----------|
| Market Participants | Buyers and sellers in the principal (or most advantageous) market for the asset or liability that are: independent of the reporting entity; knowledgeable; able to transact; and, willing to transact (not forced) | Paragraph 10 |
| Most Advantageous Market | The market in which the reporting entity would sell the asset or transfer the liability with the price that maximizes the amount that would be received for the asset or minimizes the amount that would be paid to transfer the liability, considering transactions costs in the respective market(s) | Paragraph 8 |
| Nonperformance Risk | The risk that the obligation will not be fulfilled | Summary |
| Observable Inputs | Inputs that reflect the assumptions market participants would use in pricing the asset or liability developed based on market data obtained from sources independent of the reporting entity | Paragraph 21 |
| Orderly Transaction | A transaction that assumes exposure to the market for a period prior to the measurement date to allow for marketing activities that are usual and customary for transactions involving such assets or liabilities; it is not a forced transaction | Paragraph 7 |
| Principal Market | The market in which the reporting entity would sell the asset or transfer the liability with the greatest volume and level or activity for the asset or liability | Paragraph 8 |
| Unobservable Inputs | Inputs that reflect the reporting entity's own assumptions about the assumptions market participants would use in pricing the asset or liability developed based on the best information available in the circumstances | Paragraph 21 |

# Chapter 2

# Intangible Assets And Goodwill

## SFAS NO. 141, BUSINESS COMBINATIONS

This chapter discusses the changes in regulatory requirements leading to the identification and measurement of intangibles. We discuss at length SFAS Nos. 141, 142, and 157 as well as the IPR&D Practice Aid. Chapter 3 will augment this discussion by providing a case study of a purchase price allocation, illustrated with the valuation of seven distinct identifiable intangible assets acquired in a business combination and a case study of both steps one and two of a goodwill impairment analysis.

## WHAT ARE INTANGIBLE ASSETS?

The Report of the Brookings Task Force on Intangibles (Brookings Task Force) defines intangibles as:

... nonphysical factors that contribute to or are used in producing goods or providing services, or that are expected to generate future productive benefits for the individuals or firms that control the use of those factors.[1]

The International Valuation Standards are, perhaps, a bit more precise in their definition of intangible assets:

... assets that manifest themselves by their economic properties; they do not have physical substance; they grant rights and privileges to their owner; and usually generate income for their owner. Intangible assets can be categorized as arising from: Rights; Relationships; Grouped Intangibles; or Intellectual Property.[2]

The International Valuation Standards Committee goes on to define each of those categories.

Probably the briefest definition was provided by the FASB:

... assets (not including financial assets) that lack physical substance.[3]

Per the FASB, intangible assets are distinguished from goodwill. The FASB provides specific guidance for the identification of intangible assets such that any asset not so identified would fall into the catch-all category of goodwill.

Each of these definitions is correct and, in its venue, appropriate, but the nature of intangible assets requires more explanation. Some intangible assets are a subset of human capital, which is a collection of education, experience, and skill of a company's employees. Structural capital is distinguished from human capital but also includes intangible assets such as process documentation and the organizational structure itself, which is the supportive infrastructure provided for human capital and encourages human capital to create and leverage its knowledge. Intangible assets are the codified physical descriptions of specific knowledge that can be owned and readily traded. Separability and transferability are fundamental prerequisites to the meaningful codification and measurement of intangible assets. Further, intangible assets receiving legal protection become intellectual property, which is generally categorized into five types: patents, copyrights, trade name (-marks and -dress), trade secrets, and know-how.

## WHY ARE INTANGIBLE ASSETS DIFFICULT TO MEASURE?

The Brookings Task Force succinctly described measurement difficulties when it said:

> Because one cannot see, or touch, or weigh intangibles, one cannot measure them directly but must instead rely on proxies, or indirect measures to say something about their impact on some other variable that can be measured.[4]

Over the years, the FASB has sought to change the historical cost focus of measurement. Apart from SFAS No. 157, there are approximately three dozen statements that require consideration of fair value.[5] Clearly, the identification and measurement of intangible assets is required. How is this done?

## THE NATURE OF INTANGIBLE ASSETS

Opportunity cost is a fundamental concept of finance and can be defined as the cost of something in terms of an opportunity foregone. Many finance courses focus on the opportunities available to utilize tangible assets, with the goal of applying those tangible assets to the opportunity with the highest return. Opportunities not selected can be viewed as returns foregone. The physical reality is that tangible assets can only be in one place at one time. Professor Lev looked at the physical, human, and financial assets (all considered tangible) as competing for the opportunity. In a sense, these assets are rival or scarce assets "... in which the scarcity is reflected by the cost of using the assets (the opportunity foregone)."[6]

Such assets distinguish themselves from intangible assets in that intangible assets do not rival each other for incremental returns. In fact, intangible assets can be applied to multiple uses for multiple returns. As Professor Lev says:

> The non-rivalry (or non-scarcity) attribute of intangibles – the ability to use such assets in simultaneous and repetitive applications without diminishing their usefulness – is a major value driver at the business enterprise level as well as at the national level. Whereas physical and financial assets can be leveraged to a limited degree by exploiting economies of scale or scope in production (a plant can be used for at most three shifts a day), the leveraging of intangibles to generate benefits – the scalability of these assets – is generally limited only by the size of the market. The usefulness of the ideas, knowledge, and research embedded in a new drug or a computer operating system is not limited by the diminishing returns to scale typical of physical assets (as production expands from two to three shifts, returns decrease due, for example, to the wage premium paid for the third shift and to employee fatigue). In fact, intangibles are often characterized by increasing returns to scale. An investment in the development of a drug or a financial instrument (a risk-hedging mechanism, for example), is often leveraged in the development of successor drugs and financial instruments. Information is cumulative, goes the saying.[7]

## IDENTIFICATION AND CLASSIFICATION

Identification of intangible assets is a broad endeavor. There are the well-accepted intangibles such as customer base, in-process research and development, and technology, and intellectual property intangibles such as patents, copyrights, trademarks, trade secrets, and know-how. The value of these assets typically account for most of an enterprise's total intangible value, depending on the industry. There are also unique intangible assets peculiar to an industry or enterprise, such as "the base membership in a cooperative that sells milk from a dairy herd."[8]

In an attempt to provide some structure to the recognition of identifiable intangible assets and to enhance the longevity of its financial model, the FASB classified intangibles into five categories:

1. Marketing-related intangible assets
2. Customer-related intangible assets
3. Artistic-related intangible assets
4. Contract-based intangible assets
5. Technology-based intangible assets[9]

The FASB provides an explanation and examples for each of the categories[10] (Exhibit 2.1). Notably, assembled workforce was excluded because it fails the separability and transferability test. An enterprise may have excellent employees who contribute mightily to the success of an organization, but they have no value if separated from the business. The FASB instead chose to categorize assembled workforce within the category of goodwill.[11] Exhibit 2.2 provides an expanded but unclassified list of intangibles.[12]

**Exhibit 2.1**   Examples of Intangible Assets that Meet the Criteria for Recognition Apart from Goodwill

The following are examples of intangible assets that meet the criteria for recognition as an asset apart from goodwill. The following illustrative list is not intended to be all-inclusive, thus, an acquired intangible asset might meet the recognition criteria of this Statement but not be included on that list. Assets designated by the symbol (∗) are those that would be recognized apart from goodwill because they meet the contractual-legal criterion. Assets designated by the symbol (◆) do not arise from contractual or other legal rights, but shall nonetheless be recognized apart from goodwill because they meet the separability criterion. The determination of whether a specific acquired intangible asset meets the criteria in this Statement for recognition apart from goodwill shall be based on the facts and circumstances of each individual business combination.

A. Marketing-related intangible assets

   1. Trademarks, trade names ∗
   2. Service marks, collective marks, certification marks ∗
   3. Trade dress (unique color, shape, or package design) ∗
   4. Newspaper mastheads ∗
   5. Noncompetition agreements ∗

B. Customer-related intangible assets

   1. Customer lists ◆
   2. Order or production backlog ∗
   3. Customer contracts and the related **customer relationships** ∗
   4. Noncontractual customer relationships ◆

C. Artistic-related intangible assets

   1. Plays, operas, and ballets ∗
   2. Books, magazines, newspapers, and other literary works ∗
   3. Musical works such as compositions, song lyrics, advertising jingles ∗
   4. Pictures and photographs ∗
   5. Video and audiovisual material, including motion pictures, music videos, and television programs ∗

D. Contract-based intangible assets

   1. Licensing, royalty, standstill agreements ∗
   2. Advertising, construction, management, service, or supply contracts ∗
   3. Lease agreements ∗
   4. Construction permits ∗
   5. Franchise agreements ∗
   6. Operating and broadcast rights ∗

7. Use rights such as landing, drilling, water, air, mineral, timber cutting, route authorities, and so forth *

8. Servicing contracts such as mortgage servicing contracts *

9. Employment contracts *

E. Technology-based intangible assets

1. Patented technology *

2. Computer software and mask works *

3. Internet domain names *

4. Unpatented technology ◆

5. Databases, including title plants ◆

6. Trade secrets including secret formulas, processes, recipes *

© Copyright by The Financial Accounting Standards Board. Used with permission.

**Exhibit 2.2** Illustrative Listing of Intangible Assets and Intellectual Properties Commonly Subject to Appraisal and Economic Analysis

| | |
|---|---|
| Advertising campaigns and programs | Licenses – professional, business, etc. |
| Agreements | Literary works |
| Airport gates and landing slots | Litigation awards and damage claims |
| Appraisal plants (files and records) | Loan portfolios |
| Awards and judgments (legal) | Locations value |
| Bank customers – deposit, loan, trust, credit card, etc. | Management contracts |
| | Manual (versus automated) databases |
| Blueprints and drawings | Manuscripts |
| Book and other publication libraries | Marketing and promotional materials |
| Brand names and logos | Masks and masters (for integrated circuits) |
| Broadcast licenses (ratio, television, etc.) | |
| Buy-sell agreements | Medical (and other professional) charts and records |
| Certificates of need for healthcare institutions | |
| | Mineral rights |
| Chemical formulations | Musical compositions |
| Claims (against insurers, etc.) | Natural resources |
| Computer software (both internally developed and externally purchased) | Newspaper morgue files |
| | Noncompete covenants |
| Computerized databases | Nondiversion agreements |
| Contracts | Open to ship customer orders |
| Cooperative agreements | Options, warrants, grants, rights – related to securities |
| Copyrights | |
| Credit information files | Ore deposits |
| Customer contracts | Patent applications |
| Customer lists | Patents – both product and process |
| Customer relationships | Permits |
| Designs, patterns, diagrams, schematics, technical drawings | Personality contracts |
| | Prescription drug files |

*(Continued)*

---

**Exhibit 2.2**   *(Continued)*

Development rights
Distribution networks
Distribution rights
Drilling rights
Easements
Employment contracts
Engineering drawings and related
  documentation
Environmental rights (and exemptions)
FCC licenses related to radio bands
  (cellular telephone, paging, etc.)
Favorable financing
Favorable leases
Film libraries
Food flavorings and recipes
Franchise agreements (commercial)
Franchise ordinances (governmental)
Going-concern value (and immediate
  use value)
Goodwill – institutional
Goodwill – personal
Goodwill – professional
Government contracts
Government programs
Governmental registrations
  (and exemptions)
Historical documents
HMO enrollment lists
Insurance expirations
Insurance in force
Joint ventures
Know-how and associated
  procedural documentation
Laboratory notebooks
Landing rights (for airlines)
Leasehold estates
Leasehold interests

Prizes and awards (related to professional
  recognition)
Procedural ("how we do things here")
  manuals and related
documentation
Production backlogs
Product designs
Property use rights
Proposals outstanding, related to contracts,
  customers, etc.
Proprietary processes – and related
  technical documentation
Proprietary products – and related technical
  documentation
Proprietary technology – and related
  technical documentation
Regulatory approvals (or exemptions
  from regulatory requirements)
Retail shelf space
Royalty agreements
Shareholder agreements
Solicitation rights
Subscription lists (for magazines, services,
  etc.)
Supplier contracts
Technical and specialty libraries (books,
  records, drawings, etc.)
Technical documentation
Technology sharing agreements
Title plants
Trade secrets
Trained and assembled workforce
Trademarks and trade names
Training manuals and related educational
  materials, courses, and programs
Use rights – air, water,
  land

## THE MEASUREMENT OF INTANGIBLE ASSETS

The International Valuation Standards (IVS) Guidance Note No. 6, *Business Valuation*, addresses factors to be considered in valuing intangible assets.[13] Further, in its delineation of applicable methodology, IVS Guidance Note No. 6 provides the basic economic approaches (the cost approach, the income approach, and the market approach) to valuing intangible assets.[14]

A key fundamental underlying the valuation of intangible assets is the concept of the tension between risk and return. As Professor Lev states:

> Assuredly, all investments and assets are risky in an uncertain business environment. Yet the riskiness of intangibles is, in general, substantially higher than that of physical and even financial assets. For one, the prospects of a total loss common to many innovative activities, such as a new drug development or an internet initiative, are very rare for physical or financial assets. Even highly risky physical projects, such as commercial property, rarely end up as a loss …. A comparative study of the uncertainty associated with R&D and that of property, plant, and equipment confirms the large risk differentials: the earnings volatility (a measurement of risk) associated with R&D is, on average, three times larger than the earnings volatility associated with physical investment.[15]

A fundamental tenet of economics holds that return requirements increase as risk increases, with many intangible assets being inherently more risky than tangible assets. It is reasonable to conclude that the returns expected on many intangible assets typically will be at or above the average rate of return (discount rate) for the company as a whole.[16] The relationship of the amount of return, the rate of return (including risk), and the value of the asset creates a mathematical formula used in analysis (see Exhibit 2.3).

---

**Exhibit 2.3**   Rate of Return Calculation

The income approach is heavily relied on when valuing intangibles. Typically, two of three elements are known or can be computed, thus leading to a solution for the third.

$$\text{If} \quad \frac{\$\,\text{Return}}{\text{Rate of Return}} \quad = \quad \text{Value for Intangible Asset}$$

$$\text{Then} \quad \frac{\$\,\text{Return}}{\text{Value}} \quad = \quad \text{Rate of Return}$$

$$\text{And} \quad \text{Rate of Return} \times \text{Value} \quad = \quad \$\,\text{Return}$$

---

The next sections discuss recent regulatory changes affecting intangible assets and goodwill.

## FAIR VALUE AND BUSINESS COMBINATIONS

The definition of fair value as stated in SFAS No. 141 is as follows:

> The fair value of an asset (or liability) is the amount at which that asset (or liability) could be bought (or incurred) or sold (or settled) in a current transaction between willing parties, that is, other than in a forced or liquidation sale.[17]

That definition is superseded by SFAS No. 157, which defines fair value as:

> Fair value is the price that would be received to sell an asset or paid to transfer a liability in an orderly transaction between market participants at the measurement date.[18]

In contrast to *fair value*, fair *market* value is defined in the Internal Revenue Code as:

> The price at which the property would change hands between a willing buyer and a willing seller when the former is not under any compulsion to buy and the latter is not under any compulsion to sell, both parties having reasonable knowledge of relevant facts.[19]

A principal difference between the FASB and IRS definitions is that fair value may consider certain (but not necessarily all) synergies and attributes of a specific buyer and a specific seller (*market participant* synergies, per the FASB), whereas fair market value may be viewed as a broader standard, contemplating a hypothetical willing buyer and a hypothetical willing seller.

A business combination occurs when an enterprise acquires net assets that constitute a business or equity interest of one or more enterprises and obtains control over that enterprise or enterprises.[20] Although there are certain exceptions, such as the acquisition of an equity interest held by minority shareholders and acquisitions of not-for-profit organizations, all business combinations as defined by the Statement are accounted for using the purchase method of accounting. With the issuance of SFAS No. 141, the use of the pooling of interests method was immediately prohibited. Application of the purchase method requires identification of all assets of the acquiring enterprise, both tangible and intangible. Any excess of the cost of an acquired entity over the net amounts assigned to the tangible and intangible assets acquired and liabilities assumed will be classified as goodwill.[21]

## RECOGNITION OF INTANGIBLE ASSETS

As stated earlier, the definition of intangible assets includes current and noncurrent assets (not including financial instruments) that lack physical substance.[22] An acquired intangible asset shall be recognized apart from goodwill if that asset arises from contractual or other legal rights. If an intangible asset does not arise from contractual or other legal rights, it shall be recognized apart from goodwill only if it is separable. That is, it must be capable of being separated or divided from the acquired enterprise and sold, transferred, licensed, rented, or exchanged (regardless of whether there is an intent to do so). An intangible asset that cannot be sold, transferred, licensed, rented, or exchanged individually is still considered separable if it can be paired with a related contract, asset, or liability and be sold, transferred, licensed, rented, or exchanged.

An important exception to the individual recognition of intangible assets is the value of an assembled workforce of "at-will" employees. Thus, a group of employees acquired in a business combination who are not bound by an employment agreement will be recorded as goodwill regardless of whether the asset meets the criteria for recognition apart from goodwill.[23] However, the assembled workforce still needs to be valued as a contributory asset (discussed in Chapter 3).

The foregoing discussion begs an obvious question: "customer relationships (at least those that are non-contractual) are not separable; why are they not lumped into goodwill?" In the real world, companies move in and out of non-contractual customer relationships as business dictates, with matters of supply, demand, quality and competition, to name just a few, dictating whether the customer relationship will continue in the future. Influenced by the SEC, which was concerned that treating non-contractual customer relationships as not being separable would result in ever-larger proportions of non-amortizable goodwill, and the FASB's Emerging Issues Task Force 02–17, which clarified the issue for practitioners, practice has evolved to the point where most customer relationships are treated as identifiable intangible assets apart from goodwill.[24]

Residual value should factor into determining the amount of a finite-lived intangible asset to be amortized and is defined as the estimated fair value of an intangible asset at the end of its useful life less any disposal costs. A recognized intangible asset with an indefinite useful life may not be amortized until its life is determined to be no longer indefinite. If no legal, regulatory, contractual, competitive, economic, or other factors limit the useful life of an intangible asset, the useful life of that asset should be considered indefinite. The term *indefinite* does not mean infinite. A recognized intangible asset that is not amortized must be tested for impairment annually and on an interim basis if an event or circumstance occurring between annual tests indicates that the asset might be impaired.[25]

## TAX EFFECTS

Intangible assets are generally valued after tax. Tax effects include providing for income taxes in any forecast of cash flow, providing for tax amortization of intangible assets over a 15-year period per Internal Revenue Code Sec. 197,[26] and capturing in the fair value of an intangible asset the "amortization benefit," the incremental value attributable to an intangible by virtue of its tax deductibility. Including the tax effects in the valuation process is common in the income and cost approaches (although there is some controversy about this, with some practitioners choosing to apply this approach on a pre-tax basis), but not typical in the market approach, because any tax benefit is already factored into the quoted market price.

## CONTRIBUTORY CHARGES (RETURNS ON AND OF)

As will be illustrated in Chapter 3, the most important intangible assets are valued using the Income Approach-Multiperiod Excess Earnings Method. This method honors the concept that the fair value of an identifiable intangible asset is equal to the present value of the net cash flows attributable to that asset, and that the net cash flows attributable to the subject asset must recognize the support of many other assets, tangible and intangible, which contribute to the realization of the cash flows. The contributory asset charges (of cash flow) are based on the fair value of the contributing assets. After-tax cash flows for certain identifiable intangible assets are charged after-tax amounts representing a "return on" and a "return of" these contributory assets based on the fair value of these items. The return *on* the asset refers to a hypothetical assumption whereby the project pays the owner of the contributory assets a fair return on the fair value of the hypothetically rented assets (in other words, return on is the payment for using the asset). For self-developed assets (such as assembled workforce or customer base), the annual cost to replace such assets should be factored into cash flow projections as part of the operating cost structure (e.g., sales and marketing expenses would serve as a proxy for a return of customer relationships). Similarly, the return *of* fixed assets is included in the cost structure as depreciation, which effectively acts as a surrogate for a replacement charge. An illustrative (only) example of the relationship of intangible asset returns is shown in Exhibit 2.4.

## PRESENT VALUE CONSIDERATIONS FOR INTANGIBLES

The FASB concludes that fair value is the objective when using present value in measurements at the initial recognition and fresh start of assets. Two techniques are specifically recognized: the discount rate adjustment technique and the expected present value technique.[27] The expected present value technique focuses on the variations in the amount and timing of estimating cash flows and their relative probability of occurrence, whereas the discount rate adjustment technique attempts to capture those same factors by focusing on the selection of a return rate that is commensurate with the risk. SFAS No. 157 notes five elements of a present value measurement that, taken together, capture the economic differences among assets:

1. An estimate of the future cash flow, or in more complex cases, series of future cash flows at different times
2. Expectations about possible variations in the amount or timing of those cash flows
3. The time value of money, represented by the risk-free rate of interest
4. The price for bearing the uncertainty inherent in the asset or liability
5. Other sometimes unidentifiable factors, including illiquidity and market imperfections[28]

Estimates of future cash flows are subject to a variety of risks and uncertainties, especially related to new product launches, such as the following:

• The time to bring the product to market
• The market and customer acceptance
• The viability of the technology
• Regulatory approval
• Competitor response
• The price and performance characteristics of the product[29]

A company's tangible and intangible rates of return can be presented as:

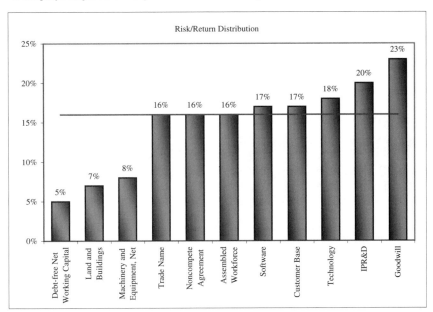

Where:
1. The midline of the distribution represents the *company's* discount rate (WACC of 16%)
2. Items below the midline represent returns on tangible assets (such as debt-free net working capital of 5% and land and building of 7%)
3. Items at or above the WACC of 16% represent returns on intangible assets (such as Trade Name of 16% and Technology of 18%)
4. The highest rate of return represents the riskiest asset, goodwill

Note: Rates are shown for illustrative purposes only and represent general relationships between assets. Actual rates must be selected based on a consideration of the facts and circumstances related to each entity and risk of underlying assests.

**Exhibit 2.4**  Risk/Return Distribution

The risk premium assessed in a discount rate should decrease as a project successfully proceeds through its continuum of development, because the uncertainty about accomplishing the necessary first step and each subsequent step diminishes.

## IN-PROCESS RESEARCH AND DEVELOPMENT

In this technological age, with research and development (R&D) activities constituting an enormous part of industrial activity, the financial reporting of assets to be used in R&D activities, especially specific in-process research and development (IPR&D)

projects, has become critically important. The FASB has addressed this issue by referencing "... the multiperiod excess earnings method, which is used to measure the fair value of certain intangible assets." This is referenced in SFAS No. 157, paragraph 18, which is then documented by footnote 10, which references the IPR&D Practice Aid. The IPR&D Practice Aid states, "This Practice Aid identifies what the Task Force members perceive as best practices related to defining and accounting for, disclosing, valuing, and auditing assets acquired to be used in R&D activities, including specific IPR&D projects."[30] All practitioners working in the area of fair value/intangible assets should be very familiar with the IPR&D Practice Aid.

In-process research and development can be generally defined as an R&D project that has not yet been completed. Acquired IPR&D is a subset of an intangible asset to be used in R&D activities. Costs to be allocated to assets acquired to be used in R&D activities should possess the characteristics of control and expected economic benefit, with fair value being estimable with reasonable reliability. If an asset to be used in R&D activities is a specific IPR&D project, that project should have both substance and be incomplete.[31]

SFAS No. 2, *Accounting for Research and Development Costs*, sets forth broad guidelines as to the activities that constitute R&D activities and defines R&D for GAAP purposes. Assets to be used in R&D activities subsequently are accounted for under FASB Interpretation No. 4, *Applicability of SFAS No. 2 to Business Combinations Accounted for by the Purchase Method*. GAAP generally requires that the fair value of acquired IPR&D be immediately charged to income, but may be amortized if an alternative future use exists for the asset. Separately identifiable assets include both tangible and intangible assets.

An acquiring company's interest in such assets is controllable by the combined enterprise such that it can obtain benefit from the asset and control others' access to the asset. Acquired IPR&D has economic benefit when the acquiring company can demonstrate that each such asset, either singly or in combination with other assets, will be used in post-combination R&D activities.[32]

At this writing, the FASB has issued an Exposure Draft, SFAS No. 141 Revised, which will modify SFAS No. 141 in some important areas. For example, SFAS No. 141R calls for acquired IPR&D to be *capitalized* rather than *expensed*, as currently called for by SFAS No. 141. A summary of the most significant changes embodied in SFAS No. 141R is included in Appendix 2.2.

FASB Statement of Financial Accounting Concepts 6, *Elements of Financial Statements*, states:

> Assets are probable future economic benefits obtained or controlled by a particular entity as a result of past transactions or events.... An asset has three essential characteristics: (a) it embodies a probable future economic benefit that involves a capacity, singly or in combination with other assets, to contribute directly or indirectly to future net cash flows, (b) a particular entity can obtain the benefit and control others' access to it, and (c) the transaction or other event giving rise to the entity's right to or control of the benefit has already occurred.[33]

Examples of control include:

- The combined enterprise has the ability to sell, lease, license, franchise, or use its rights to the R&D asset acquired.
- The combined enterprise has proprietary intellectual property rights, which it believes could be successfully defended if its ownership were challenged.[34]

The fair value of acquired IPR&D must be measurable; that is, it must be able to be estimated with reasonable reliability. The economic benefit of the product, service, or process that is expected from the IPR&D effort must be sufficiently determinable such that a reasonably reliable estimate of the future expected net cash flows can be made based on assumptions that are verifiable. For example, a reasonably reliable estimate of fair value may be determinable if the following seven components of IPR&D can be estimated with confidence:

1. A market for the product
2. Time needed to commercialize and market the product
3. Potential customers and market penetration
4. The effects of competitors' existing or potential products
5. The combined enterprise's share of the market
6. The selling price
7. Production and related costs for the product[35]

The basic form of an IPR&D life cycle will at some point lead to the acquiring company likely being able to estimate fair value with reasonable reliability. This basic form includes:

- *Conceptualization*, which is an idea, thought, or plan for a new product and includes an initial assessment of the potential market, cost, and technical issues for such concepts
- *Applied research*, which is the planned search or critical investigation aimed at the discovery of new knowledge, including assessing the feasibility of successfully completing the project
- *Development*, which translates the research into a detailed plan or design for a new product, service, or process
- *Preproduction*, which represents the business activities necessary to commercialize the asset[36]

To be recognized as an asset, specific IPR&D projects must have substance, which is the recognition of sufficient cost and effort that would enable the project's fair value to be estimated with reasonable reliability.[37] Further, the IPR&D must be incomplete in that there are remaining technological, engineering, or regulatory risks.[38]

Recommended financial statement disclosure includes but is not limited to the identification of the following by the acquiring company:

- A description of the projects to which value was ascribed, including the status of the project
- The values assigned to each of the assets acquired, including the amount of the in-process R&D charge
- The techniques used in each acquisition to value assets acquired to be used in R&D activities
- The key assumptions used in valuing the assets acquired to be used in R&D activities, such as:
  - The time frame for cash flows expected to be realized
  - The weighted average discount rates used in determining present values[39]

Cost should be assigned to all identifiable tangible and intangible assets, including any resulting from R&D activities of the acquired company or to be used in R&D activities of the combined enterprise. The acquiring company should allocate a portion of the purchase price to each acquired identifiable intangible asset that possesses either of the following characteristics:

- Produces cash flows that are largely independent of cash flows generated by other assets
- Could realistically be licensed, sold, transferred, exchanged, or disposed of in a transaction in which it is the only asset[40]

For the purpose of valuation, cash flows should be allocated to each intangible asset on an as-if-separated basis, representing the typical cash flow carve-outs and returns on and of charges in the multiperiod excess earnings model. Importantly, synergistic value only to the buyer may not be attributed to an acquired identifiable asset. Thus, buyer-specific synergistic value falls into goodwill, which is calculated on a residual basis. As stated in the IPR&D Practice Aid:

> A willing buyer may factor into the amount that it would pay to acquire the seller's business a portion of the incremental cash flows that are expected to inure to the benefit of that buyer. The incremental cash flows may include those resulting from strategic or synergistic components. If the buyer pays the seller any significant consideration for strategic or synergistic benefits in excess of those expected to be realized by market participants, the valuation specialist would identify those excess benefits and remove them from the valuation of assets acquired. Thus, the cost of the acquired company may include an element of synergistic value (that is, investment value). However, for purposes of assigning cost to the assets acquired in accordance with FASB Statement No. 141, the amount of the purchase price allocated to an acquired asset would not include any entity-specific synergistic value. Fair value does not include strategic or synergistic value resulting from

expectations about future events that are specific to a particular buyer because the value associated with those components is unique to the buyer and seller and would not reflect market-based assumptions. Therefore, entity-specific value associated with strategic or synergistic components would be included in goodwill. Fair value would incorporate expectations about future events that affect market participants. If the acquiring company concludes that the discounted cash flow method best approximates the fair value of an acquired asset, the discounted cash flows would incorporate assumptions that market participants would use in their estimates of fair values, future revenues, future expenses, and discount rates (if applicable).[41]

Although the determination of fair value revolves around the three classic approaches to valuation—cost, market, and income—the relief from royalties method and the excess earnings method are particularly relied upon.

The analyst should review certain information in order to properly evaluate management's identification and classification of assets acquired (including IPR&D intangibles). At a minimum, this would include:

- Presentations to the board of directors
- Offering memoranda
- Due diligence reports
- Press releases (both of the acquiring and the acquired companies)
- Web site materials
- Analysts reports
- Industry reports[42]

Prospective Financial Information (PFI) is provided by management, but the sources, methodologies, procedures, adjustments, and application must be tested by the valuer. The IPR&D Practice Aid states:

> ... PFI provided by management that is accepted by the valuation specialist without having been subjected to validating procedures by the valuation specialist would contradict the performance of best practices....[43]

Further, the IPR&D Practice Aid states:

> The valuation specialist does not simply accept PFI from management without investigating its suitability for use in the valuation analysis. The valuation specialist is responsible for evaluating the methodology and assumptions used by management in preparing the PFI and concluding whether the PFI is appropriate for use in valuing the assets acquired.[44]

As stated previously, the analyst should conclude and document that a particular R&D project is deemed to have substance. The basis for such documentation should include consideration of the following:

- Stage of completion of the project
- Treatment and emphasis given to the project in the company's product road map for the technology
- Acquired company's R&D budget
- Acquired company's R&D planning documents and related status reports
- R&D costs incurred by project and estimated costs to complete the project[45]

Further, the analyst must conclude that the R&D project is incomplete as of the acquisition date based on the following:

- Stage of development as indicated by the development milestones attained and yet to be reached
- Remaining technological, engineering, or regulatory risks to be overcome
- Remaining development costs to be incurred
- Remaining time to be spent to reach completion
- Probability of successful completion[46]

Finally, the valuation specialist should conclude and document whether the assets acquired to be used in R&D activities have an alternative future use. If so, the value of that asset would be capitalized and amortized pursuant to SFAS Nos. 141 and 142. If the assets acquired to be used in R&D activities do not have an alternative use, then those costs would be charged to expense as of the date of acquisition.[47]

## SFAS NO. 142, GOODWILL, AND OTHER INTANGIBLE ASSETS

SFAS No. 142 applies to all acquired intangible assets, whether acquired singly, as part of a group, or in a business combination. The Statement mandates that goodwill shall not be amortized over a defined period; rather, goodwill must be tested for impairment at least annually at the *reporting unit* level (see following paragraph). Although the FASB already had addressed asset impairment (originally SFAS No. 121, *Accounting for the Impairment of Long-Lived Assets and for Long-Lived Assets to be Disposed Of*, superseded by SFAS No. 144, *Accounting for the Impairment or Disposal of Long-Lived Assets*), goodwill and indefinite-lived intangible assets must be tested for impairment exclusively under the guidelines of SFAS No. 142.[48] Amortizable intangible assets are tested for impairment under SFAS No. 144 (see discussion under Case Study 2: Impairment Under SFAS No. 142).

All goodwill reported in the financial statements of a reporting unit should be tested for impairment as if the reporting unit were a stand-alone entity. A *reporting unit* is an operating segment (see SFAS No. 131, *Disclosures About Segments of an Enterprise and Related Information*) or one level below an operating segment (called a component). A component of an operating segment is a reporting unit if the component constitutes a business for which discrete financial information is available and segment management regularly reviews the operating results of that component. Goodwill must be defined and allocated at this component level. Entities that are not required to report segment information in accordance with SFAS No. 131 are nevertheless required to test goodwill for impairment at the reporting unit level.[49]

The nature of fair value of a reporting unit is that the synergies of operating in a combined entity, especially for shared overhead costs, are a fundamental part of the fair value of a reporting unit. SFAS No. 142 states:

> Substantial value may arise from the ability to take advantage of synergies and other benefits that flow from control over another entity. Consequently, measuring the fair value of a collection of assets and liabilities that operate together in a controlled entity is different from measuring the fair value of that entity's individual equity securities.[50]

Additionally, if you could not take into account the synergies of being part of a combined entity, there would be an immediate impairment, because such economy of scale synergies are a typical part of a control transaction. Thus, when employing a quoted market price in determining the fair value of a reporting unit, one must consider a control premium.[51]

All acquired goodwill must be assigned to reporting units. This will critically depend on the assignment of other acquired assets and assumed liabilities. These assets and liabilities will be assigned to reporting units based on the following criteria:

- The asset will be employed in or the liability relates to the operations of a reporting unit.
- The asset or liability will be considered in determining the fair value of the reporting unit.[52]

*Goodwill* is the excess of cost over the assets acquired and liabilities assumed, but this definition is deceptively simple. The amount of goodwill allocated to a reporting unit is contingent upon the expected benefits of the combination to the reporting unit.[53] This goodwill allocation is required even though other assets or liabilities of the acquired entity may not be assigned to that reporting unit (i.e., they may be assigned to other reporting units). A relative fair value allocation approach similar to that used when a portion of a reporting unit is disposed of (see SFAS No. 144) should be used to determine how goodwill should be allocated when an entity reorganizes its reporting structure in a manner that changes the composition of one or more of its reporting units. However, goodwill is ultimately tested for impairment pursuant to SFAS No. 142.[54]

The measurement of the fair value of intangibles and goodwill can be performed at any time during the fiscal year as long as the timing is consistent from year to year. Although different measurement dates can be used for different reporting units, whichever date is selected for a reporting unit must be consistent from year to year.

A detailed determination of the fair value of a reporting unit may be carried forward from one year to the next (i.e., no further impairment analysis is required) if all of the following criteria are met:

- The assets and liabilities that comprise the reporting unit have not changed significantly since the most recent fair value determination.
- The most recent fair value determination results in an amount that exceeds the carrying amount of the reporting unit by a substantial margin.
- Based on an analysis of events, it is determined that the possibility is remote that a fair value determination will be less than the current carrying amount of the reporting unit.[55]

However, the annual impairment test is to be accelerated, and goodwill of a reporting unit should be tested for impairment on an interim basis if an event occurs that would probably reduce the fair value of a reporting unit below its carrying value. Examples of such events are:

- A significant adverse change in legal factors or in the business climate
- An adverse action or assessment by a regulator
- Unanticipated competition
- A loss of key personnel
- A probable expectation that a reporting unit or a significant portion of a reporting unit will be sold or otherwise disposed of
- The testing for recoverability under SFAS No. 144 of a significant asset group within a reporting unit
- Recognition of a goodwill impairment loss in the financial statements of a subsidiary that is a component of a reporting unit[56]

## NATURE OF GOODWILL

The definition of goodwill warrants repeating: Goodwill is the excess of the cost of an acquired entity over the net of amounts assigned to assets acquired and liabilities assumed.[57] For GAAP purposes, goodwill includes all amounts that fail the criteria of an identified intangible asset. Importantly, the practitioner must understand that the nature of goodwill for financial reporting is different from that used in a legal setting. Such "legal goodwill" is generally considered to be all value above tangible asset value. For financial reporting, it helps to consider the elements of goodwill as follows:

- The excess of the fair values over the book values of the acquired entity's net assets at the date of acquisition.
- The fair values of other net assets that had not been recognized by the acquired entity at the date of acquisition.

- The fair value of the "going-concern" element of the acquired entity's existing business.

- The fair value of the expected synergies and other benefits from combining the acquiring entity's and acquired entity's net assets and businesses. Those synergies and other benefits are unique to each combination, and different combinations would produce different synergies and, hence, different values.

- Overvaluation of the consideration paid by the acquiring entity stemming from errors in valuing the consideration tendered.

- Overpayment or underpayment by the acquiring entity. Overpayment might occur, for example, if the price is driven up in the course of bidding for the acquired entity, while underpayment may occur in the case of a distress sale or fire sale.[58]

The FASB explained its rationale for including these elements this way:

- The Board continues to believe that the following analysis of those components is useful in understanding the nature of goodwill. The first two components, both of which relate to the acquired entity, conceptually are not part of goodwill. The first component is not an asset in and of itself but instead reflects gains that were not recognized by the acquired entity on its net assets. As such, that component is part of those assets rather than part of goodwill. The second component also is not part of goodwill conceptually; it primarily reflects intangible assets that might be recognized as individual assets.

- As the Board noted in both the 1999 Exposure Draft and the 2001 Exposure Draft, the third and fourth components are conceptually part of goodwill. The third component relates to the acquired entity and reflects the excess assembled value of the acquired entity's net assets. It represents the preexisting goodwill that was either internally generated by the acquired entity or acquired by it in prior business combinations. The fourth component relates to the acquired entity and acquiring entity jointly and reflects the excess assembled value that is created by the combination— the synergies that are expected from combining those businesses. The Board described the third and fourth components collectively as "core goodwill."

- The fifth and sixth components, both of which relate to the acquiring entity, also are not conceptually part of goodwill. The fifth component is not an asset in and of itself or even part of an asset but, rather, is a measurement error. The sixth component also is not an asset; conceptually it represents a loss (in the case of overpayment) or a gain (in the case of underpayment) to the acquiring entity. Thus, neither of those components is conceptually part of goodwill.[59]

## GOODWILL, INDEFINITE-LIVED INTANGIBLE ASSETS, AND THE IMPAIRMENT TEST

A recognized intangible asset shall be amortized over its useful life to the reporting entity unless that life is determined to be indefinite.[60] If no legal, regulatory, contractual, competitive, economic, or other factors limit the useful life of an intangible asset to the reporting entity, the useful life of the asset shall be considered to be indefinite. The term *indefinite* does not mean infinite.[61] An intangible asset that is not subject to amortization (an indefinite-life intangible) shall be tested for impairment in the same manner as goodwill. Such intangibles are tested annually and upon triggering events.[62]

Under SFAS No. 142, amortization of goodwill is not allowed; goodwill is tested annually for impairment. The impairment test is a two-step process. First, the fair value of the reporting unit is determined and compared with the carrying amount of the reporting unit, including goodwill.

The fair value of a reporting unit refers to the amount at which the unit as a whole could be bought or sold in a current transaction between willing parties. Quoted market prices in active markets are considered the best evidence of fair value and should be used as the basis for the measurement, if available. However, the market price of an individual share of stock (and thus the market capitalization of a reporting unit with publicly traded stock) may not be representative of the fair value of the reporting unit as a whole.[63] Certainly, stock prices rise and fall over time, and a stock price that is comparatively low at a certain date may not be indicative of impairment, which has a connotation of permanence. Further, a quoted price might be based on a thinly traded stock (i.e., inactive market), and thus unacceptable. Therefore, the quoted market price of an individual share of stock need not be the sole measurement basis of the fair value of a reporting unit. If a quoted market price of the shares of a reporting unit is not available, then the estimate of fair value should be based on the best information available, including prices for similar assets and liabilities and the results of other valuation techniques.[64]

A valuation technique based on multiples of earnings, revenue, or a similar performance measure may be used to estimate the fair value of a reporting unit if that technique is consistent with the objective of measuring fair value. Such measures may be appropriate, for example, when the fair value of an entity that has comparable operations and economic characteristics is observable and the relevant multiples of a comparable entity are known. Conversely, use of multiples would not be appropriate in situations in which the operations or activities of an entity for which the multiples are known are not of a comparable nature, scope, or size as the reporting unit for which fair value is being estimated.[65]

A present value technique is often the best available technique with which to estimate the fair value of a group of assets (such as a reporting unit). Two techniques are now allowed by SFAS No. 157: (1) the discount rate adjustment technique and (2) the expected present value technique. If an expected present value technique is used to measure fair value, estimates of future cash flows should be consistent with the objective of measuring fair value. Those cash flow estimates should incorporate assumptions that marketplace participants would use in their estimates of fair value whenever that information is available. Otherwise, an entity may use its own assumptions about market participant assumptions. Such cash flow estimates should be based on reasonable and supportable assumptions and should consider all available evidence. The weight given to the evidence should be commensurate with the extent to which the evidence can be verified objectively. If a range is estimated for the amounts or timing of possible cash flows, the likelihood of possible outcomes should be considered (see also SFAS No. 157, Appendix B [previously Statement of Financial Accounting Concepts No. 7, *Using Cash Flow Information and Present Value in Accounting Measurements*]).[66]

Goodwill impairment exists if the carrying amount of the reporting unit, including goodwill, exceeds the fair value of the reporting unit. In such a case, the second step of the goodwill impairment test is triggered. The second step of the goodwill impairment test requires performing what amounts to a new purchase price allocation as of the date of the impairment test—as if a business combination were consummated on the date of the impairment test, with the fair value of the reporting unit serving as a proxy for the purchase price. The new valuation work should include determining the new fair values of both the originally recognized assets and any new assets that may have been unrecognized at the valuation date but were developed between the acquisition date and the test date. The fair values of the assets at the test date are deducted from the fair value of the reporting unit to determine the *implied fair value of goodwill* at the test date. If the implied fair value of goodwill at the test date is lower than its carrying amount, goodwill impairment is indicated, and the carrying amount of goodwill is written down to its implied fair value.[67] Performing the new asset allocation answers the implied question, "What exactly is impaired: specifically identifiable tangible assets, specifically identifiable intangible assets, or goodwill?" This is where SFAS No. 144 controls.

As stated in SFAS No. 142:

> If goodwill and another asset (or asset group) of a reporting unit are tested for impairment at the same time, the other asset (or asset group) shall be tested for impairment before goodwill. For example, if a significant asset group is to be tested for impairment under Statement 144 (thus potentially requiring a goodwill impairment test), the impairment test for the significant asset group would be performed before the goodwill impairment test. If the asset group was impaired, the impairment loss would be recognized prior to goodwill being tested for impairment.[68]

This means that, in addition to impairment of goodwill, impairment of other assets must also be recognized. Thus, the asset values recognized on the balance sheet as of the date of the impairment test will be the lower of the carrying amount or fair value for each previously recognized tangible asset. For example, assume a company has a reporting unit whose assets have a fair value of $80,000,000, including goodwill of $35,000,000. For illustrative purposes, further assume that the relative fair values of the assets have been valued and recorded on the books of the acquirer as follows:

| | |
|---|---|
| Recognized Tangible Assets | $15,000,000 |
| Recognized Identifiable Intangible Assets | 30,000,000 |
| Goodwill | 35,000,000 |
| | |
| Fair Value of Reporting Unit Assets | $80,000,000 |

After one year, assume the carrying amounts of certain assets after amortization are:

| | |
|---|---|
| Recognized Tangible Assets | $12,000,000 |
| Recognized Identifiable Intangible Assets | 25,000,000 |

Now assume that an impairment test is performed at this time one year later, and the aggregate fair value of the assets of the reporting unit is $70,000,000. This decline in value indicates impairment (step one fails) but not necessarily a goodwill impairment charge of $10,000,000. A new asset allocation (step two) must be performed to determine the new goodwill amount. The assumptions of the fair values as of the date of the impairment test are:

| | |
|---|---|
| Recognized Tangible Assets | $13,000,000 |
| Unrecognized Tangible Assets* | 1,000,000 |
| Recognized Identifiable Intangible Assets | 20,000,000 |
| Unrecognized Identifiable Intangible Assets* | 7,000,000 |
| Goodwill | 29,000,000 |
| Fair Value of Reporting Unit | $70,000,000 |

*Assets acquired or developed after the acquisition date

The step two results are:

| | Net Carrying Amount | Fair Value | Impairment Amount | SFAS Citation |
|---|---|---|---|---|
| Recognized Tangible Assets | $12,000,000 | $13,000,000 | $0 | — |
| Unrecognized Tangible Assets | 0 | 1,000,000 | 0 | — |
| Recognized Identifiable Intangible Assets (with a defined life) | 25,000,000 | 20,000,000 | 5,000,000* | 144 |
| Unrecognized Identifiable Intangible Assets | 0 | 7,000,000 | 0 | — |
| Goodwill | 35,000,000 | 29,000,000 | 6,000,000 | 142 |
| Total | $72,000,000 | $70,000,000 | $11,000,000 | |

*Assumes the asset or asset group failed the recoverability test of SFAS No. 144 and impairment must be measured. If the asset or asset group does not fail the recoverability test the asset is deemed to be *not* impaired even though the carrying amount exceeds fair value.

In this example, step one would fail by $2,000,000 (total carrying amount of $72,000,000 less fair value of $70,000,000), but the step two analysis shows a required impairment expense of $11,000,000 ($5,000,000 under SFAS No. 144 and $6,000,000 under SFAS No. 142).

Of course, if the impairment test finds that the fair value of the reporting unit has not declined materially, no further analysis is required. *Increases* in goodwill value are never recognized.

# ENDNOTES

1. Margaret Blair and Steven Wallman, *Unseen Wealth: Report of the Brookings Task Force on Intangibles* (Washington, DC: Brookings Institution Press, 2001), p. 3.

2. International Valuation Guidance Note No. 4, *Intangible Assets* (2001), at 3.15.

3. Financial Accounting Standards Board, Statement of Financial Accounting Standards No. 141, *Business Combinations* (2001), p. 124.

4. Margaret Blair and Steven Wallman, *Unseen Wealth: Report of the Brookings Task Force on Intangibles* (Washington, DC: Brookings Institution Press, 2001), p. 15.

5. Michael Mard, Task Force Report to Business Valuation Subcommittee (2000).

6. Baruch Lev, *Intangibles: Management, Measurement and Reporting* (Washington, DC: Brookings Institution Press, 2001), p. 22.

7. Ibid., p. 23.

8. Estate of Tony Cordeiro, 51 TC 195 (1968).

9. Financial Accounting Standards Board, Statement of Financial Accounting Standards No. 141, *Business Combinations* (2001), at A14.

10. Ibid., at A14.

11. Ibid., at 39.

12. Robert F. Reilly and Robert P. Schweihs, *Valuing Intangible Assets*, (New York: McGraw-Hill, 1999), p. 65.

13. International Valuation Guidance Note No. 6, *Business Valuation* (2000, revised 2005), at 5.10.7.

14. Ibid., at 5.14.

15. Baruch Lev, *Intangibles: Management, Measurement and Reporting* (Washington, DC: Brookings Institution Press, 2001), p. 39.

16. Note, however, that the returns expected on some intangible assets may be below the company average for a service business that has mostly intangible assets.

17. Financial Accounting Standards Board, Statement of Financial Accounting Standards No. 141, *Business Combinations* (2001), Appendix F.

18. Financial Accounting Standards Board, Statement of Financial Accounting Standards No. 157, *Fair Value Measurements* (2006), at 5.

19. Internal Revenue Service, Revenue Ruling 59–60, § 2.02.

20. Financial Accounting Standards Board, Statement of Financial Accounting Standards No. 141, *Business Combinations* (2001), at 9.

21. Ibid., at 13–14.

22. Ibid., Appendix F.

23. Ibid., at 39.

24. The history behind the evolution of the treatment of customer relationships is more fully explored in *Fair Value for Financial Reporting, Meeting the New FASB Requirements*, by Alfred M. King (Hoboken, New Jersey: John Wiley & Sons, Inc.), pp. 143–144.

25. Financial Accounting Standards Board, Statement of Financial Accounting Standards No. 142, *Goodwill and Other Intangible Assets* (2001), at 11–14.

26. Certain intangible assets do not qualify for such treatment.

27. Financial Accounting Standards Board, Statement of Financial Accounting Standards No. 157, *Fair Value Measurements* (2006), Appendix B (formerly Statement of Financial Accounting Concepts No. 7, *Using Cash Flow Information and Present Value in Accounting Measurements*).

28. Ibid., at 39.

29. Randy J. Larson, et al., *Assets Acquired in a Business Combination to Be Used in Research and Development Activities: A Focus on Software, Electronic Devices, and Pharmaceutical Industries* (New York: AICPA, 2001), p. 91.

30. Ibid., Introduction, x.

31. Ibid., p. 20.

32. Ibid.

33. Financial Accounting Standards Board, Statement of Financial Accounting Concepts No. 6, *Elements of Financial Statements*, pp. 25–26.

34. Randy J. Larson, et al., *Assets Acquired in a Business Combination to Be Used in Research and Development Activities: A Focus on Software, Electronic Devices, and Pharmaceutical Industries* (New York: AICPA, 2001), p. 26.

35. Ibid., p. 29.

36. Ibid., p. 32.

37. Ibid., p. 33.

38. Ibid., p. 36.

39. Ibid., at 4.2.

40. Ibid., at 1.1.08.

41. Ibid., at 1.1.16.

42. Ibid., at 5.3.29.

43. Ibid., at 5.2.08.

44. Ibid., at 5.3.11.

45. Ibid., at 5.3.33.

46. Ibid.

47. Ibid.

48. Financial Accounting Standards Board, Statement of Financial Accounting Standards No. 142, *Goodwill and Other Intangible Assets* (2001), at 18.

49. Ibid., at 30.

50. Ibid., at 23, Footnote 16.

51. Ibid.

52. Ibid., at 32.

53. Ibid., at 34.

54. Ibid., at 39.

55. Ibid., at 27.

56. Ibid., at 28.

57. Ibid., Appendix F.

58. Financial Accounting Standards Board, Statement of Financial Accounting Standards No. 141, *Business Combinations* (2001), at B102.

59. Ibid., at B103–B105.

60. Financial Accounting Standards Board, Statement of Financial Accounting Standards No. 142, *Goodwill and Other Intangible Assets* (2001), at 12.

61. Ibid., at 11.

62. Ibid., at 17.

63. Ibid., at 23.

64. Ibid., at 23–24.

65. Ibid., at 25.

66. Ibid., at 24.

67. Ibid., at 20–21.

68. Ibid., at 29.

# Intellectual Property

One of the major difficulties in valuing intellectual property is determining the context of licensor/licensee negotiations. All too often this context is assumed or simplified, resulting in market royalty rates being applied out of context. Many valuation consultants traditionally develop royalty rates from any of three traditional sources: (1) from the client, if the client has negotiated its own licensing agreements; (2) from surveys performed by various professionals, generally in cooperation with trade associations; and (3) from judicial opinions, which vary greatly depending on individual fact patterns.

These traditional tools now should and can be augmented by databases of licensing agreements extracted from publicly available sources. Such market data is the most compelling evidence available to determine the appropriate royalty rate in a valuation.

The market comparison-transaction method initially has four steps to derive an overall value estimate: (1) *research* the appropriate market for guideline intellectual property transactions; (2) *verify* the information by confirming that the market data obtained is factually accurate and that the license exchange transactions reflect arm's-length market considerations; (3) *compare* the guideline license transactions' financial and operational aspects with the subject intellectual property; and (4) *reconcile* the various value indications into a single value indication or range of values.

## EMPIRICAL RESEARCH ON ROYALTY RATES

Proprietary research of intangible assets and intellectual properties is important in business valuation. The value the market perceives in intellectual property–intensive companies is associated with their intangible assets and intellectual properties. Valuation of such companies is more an exercise in intangible asset valuation methods than in traditional business valuation methods. Emphasis should be placed on proprietary studies (industry research, industry pricing metrics, and comparable intellectual property transactions). Research and verification of comparable data can be a very time-consuming process. Once an incredibly daunting endeavor, advances in information technology and the increasing availability of online public records have made research of intellectual property transactions a realistic undertaking.

There has been an explosion of intellectual property needs, especially coming from industries like pharmaceuticals, software, medical/surgical equipment, and telecommunications. Databases that gather and organize comparative intellectual property transactions are rapidly becoming the tool of the future to those valuers who specialize in intellectual property valuation. At the time of publication, there are three known Internet sites that have collated or will for a fee provide information specific to the valuer's needs. These services are offered by:

- RoyaltySource (www.royaltysource.com)
- Consor® (www.consor.com)
- The Financial Valuation Group (www.fvginternational.com)

The database developed by The Financial Valuation Group includes approximately 40 fields consisting of the names of the licensor and licensee, both the SIC and NAICS numbers for the licensor and the licensee, the type of agreement (i.e., trademark, patent, copyright), the industry name, the remuneration structure, royalty percentages (base rate, the low end and high end of variable rates), royalty dollars (base flat fee, annual, and variable fees), a description of the product or service, and more. The Financial Valuation Group's database now includes information in every two-digit SIC number, and consists of a compilation of intellectual property transactions from 1994 to 2001.

Each intellectual property transaction should be compared to the target company using the following guidelines:

- The specific legal rights of intellectual property ownership conveyed in the guideline transaction
- The existence of any special financing terms or other arrangements
- Whether the elements of arm's length existed for the sale or license conditions
- The economic conditions that existed in the appropriate secondary market at the time of the sale or license transaction
- The industry in which the guideline intellectual property was or will be used
- The financial and operational characteristics of the guideline properties, compared with the company's intellectual property

The last phase of the market approach valuation analysis is the reconciliation. The strengths and weaknesses of each guideline transaction are considered; the reliability and appropriateness of the market data are examined, including the analytical techniques applied. After considerable review, transactions selected should be reasonably similar to the company and then synthesized into a mean range and a median range.

## INTELLECTUAL PROPERTY TRANSACTIONS DATABASE

What are the royalty rates paid for licensing intellectual property? Today publicly available data will provide us with the best and most objective information about royalty rates being paid in the marketplace. Traditional surveys can have material weaknesses and can be unreliable for truly objective data.

In researching publicly available data to date, we have identified and collected data from approximately 3,000 transactions. The data was compiled in a proprietary database which reveals the following information.

### Transactions by Industry

As shown in Exhibit 2.5, industry groups as represented by the first two digits of the U.S. government SIC codes are represented in transactions in the database.

### Intellectual Property Typically Licensed

While there are approximately 90 distinctly different intangible assets, the majority of assets licensed are intellectual property assets, which can be grouped within categories (Exhibit 2.6). Patents tend to be the most-licensed intellectual property, with trademarks, products, and technology following respectively.

### Payment Structures of Intellectual Property Transactions

A comparison of the royalty payment structures disclosed in each transaction reveals that approximately half of the licensing agreements are based on a set percentage or set dollar amount. There are a surprising number of transactions that involve high/low

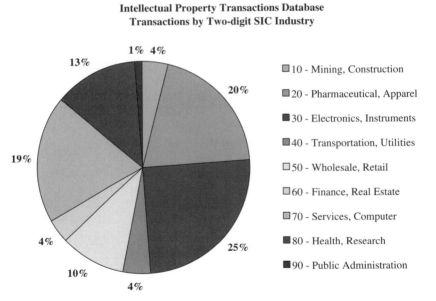

**Exhibit 2.5**   Transactions by Industry

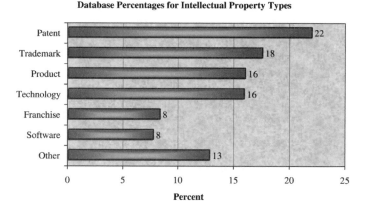

Database Percentages for Intellectual Property Types

**Exhibit 2.6**    Intellectual Property Typically Licensed

payments, which are usually based on performance and/or sales. Annual fee and monthly fee agreements tend to be set at a fixed amount paid on a regular basis throughout the life of the agreement. Shown in Exhibit 2.7 are various royalty rate payment structures by the reported transactions analyzed.

## Royalty Rates

Because royalty rates take so many economic structures, it can be difficult to interpret them in a manner that is useful for a particular need. Care should be used when applying summary information to support a particular fact situation.

As Exhibit 2.7 shows, 25% of the transactions researched have fixed royalty rate percentages. The range of royalty rates for this group are:

| | |
|---|---|
| Highest Percentage Royalty Rate: | 75.000% |
| Lowest Percentage Royalty Rate: | 0.003% |
| Average Percentage Royalty Rate: | 7.830% |

Analysis of licensing transactions similar to the particular fact situation would be necessary to determine a market royalty rate applicable to the situation. Assistance with interpreting royalty rate data from the information gathered is available from The Financial Valuation Group.

Payment Structures of Database Transactions

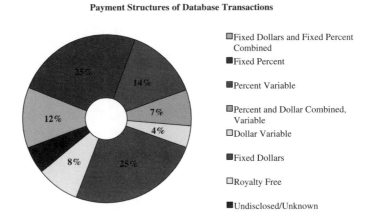

☐ Fixed Dollars and Fixed Percent Combined

■ Fixed Percent

■ Percent Variable

☐ Percent and Dollar Combined, Variable

☐ Dollar Variable

■ Fixed Dollars

☐ Royalty Free

■ Undisclosed/Unknown

**Exhibit 2.7**   Payment Structures of Intellectual Property Transactions

## Transaction Data Publicly Available

While analyzing the data, we discovered that it would require many individual data fields to capture the basic information required to economically interpret the various transactions.

Our research is based on publicly available data from such sources as company SEC filings over the period January 1, 1994 through 2001. One of our search techniques was to use a keyword search for terms like licensing agreement, royalty, trademark, patent, intellectual property, and copyright. Our professionals analyzed the information to add to our database consisting of various fields, including:

- Licensor Name and Demographics
- Licensee Name and Demographics
- Type of Agreement (i.e., Patent, Trademark, Copyright, etc.)
- Geographic Region of License
- Detailed Description of Licensed Intellectual Property
- Royalty Payment Structure
- Percentage Royalty Amount (Fixed, Low, High)
- Dollar Royalty Amount (Fixed, Low, High)

- Basis for Payment of Royalty (i.e., Net Sales, Annual Fee, Per Unit)
- Guaranteed Annual Royalties
- Maximum Lifetime Royalty
- Term of License Agreement
- Original or Amended
- Exclusivity
- Other Considerations of the Agreement

All of the information in The Financial Valuation Group's Intellectual Property Transactions Database is available to lawyers, intellectual property professionals, and valuation professionals. For more information about the costs and methods for obtaining the transactions data, visit www.fvginternational.com.

# Significant Changes in SFAS NO. 141R[1]

IX. The main changes between this proposed Statement and Statement 141 are described below:

## SCOPE

a. The requirements of this proposed Statement would be applicable to business combinations involving only mutual entities, business combinations achieved by contract alone, and the initial consolidation of variable interest entities that are businesses.

## DEFINITION OF A BUSINESS COMBINATION

b. This proposed Statement would amend the definition of a *business combination* provided in Statement 141. This proposed Statement defines a *business combination* as "a transaction or other event in which an acquirer obtains control of one or more businesses."

## DEFINITION OF A BUSINESS

c. This proposed Statement would provide a definition of a *business* and additional guidance for identifying when a group of assets constitutes a business. This proposed Statement would nullify the definitions provided in EITF Issue No. 98-3, "Determining Whether a Nonmonetary Transaction Involves Receipt of Productive Assets or of a Business," and FASB Interpretation No. 46 (revised December 2003), *Consolidation of Variable Interest Entities.*

---

[1] Financial Accounting Standards Board, Proposed Statement of Financial Accounting Standards No. 141R, Business Combinations, a replacement of FASB Statement No. 141 (Exposure Draft), (2005), at IX-XIII.

# MEASURING THE FAIR VALUE OF THE ACQUIREE

d.  This proposed Statement would require business combinations to be measured and recognized as of the acquisition date at the fair value of the acquiree, even if the business combination is achieved in stages or if less than 100 percent of the equity interests in the acquiree are owned at the acquisition date. Statement 141 required that a business combination be measured and recognized on the basis of the accumulated cost of the combination.

e.  This proposed Statement would require the costs the acquirer incurs in connection with the business combination to be accounted for separately from the business combination accounting. Statement 141 required direct costs of the business combination to be included in the cost of the acquiree.

f.  This proposed Statement would require all items of consideration transferred by the acquirer to be measured and recognized at fair value at the acquisition date. Therefore, this proposed Statement would require the acquirer to recognize contingent consideration arrangements at fair value as of the acquisition date. Subsequent changes in the fair value of contingent consideration classified as liabilities would be recognized in income, unless those liabilities are in the scope of, and therefore accounted for, in accordance with, FASB Statement No. 133, *Accounting for Derivative Instruments and Hedging Activities.*

g.  This proposed Statement would require the acquirer in a business combination in which the acquisition-date fair value of the acquirer's interest in the acquiree exceeds the fair value of the consideration transferred for that interest (referred to as a bargain purchase) to account for that excess by first reducing the goodwill related to that business combination to zero, and then by recognizing any excess in income. Statement 141 requires that excess to be allocated as a pro rata reduction of the amounts that would have been assigned to particular assets acquired.

# MEASURING AND RECOGNIZING THE ASSETS ACQUIRED AND THE LIABILITIES ASSUMED

h.  This proposed Statement would require the assets acquired and liabilities assumed to be measured and recognized at their fair values as of the acquisition date, with limited exceptions. Statement 141 required the cost of an acquisition to be allocated to the individual assets acquired and liabilities assumed based on their estimated fair values. However, Statement 141 also provided guidance for measuring some assets and liabilities that was inconsistent with fair value measurement objectives. Thus, those assets or liabilities may not have been recognized at fair value as of the acquisition date in accordance with Statement 141.

i.  This proposed Statement would amend FASB Statement No. 5, *Accounting for Contingencies,* to exclude from its scope assets or liabilities arising from contingencies acquired or assumed in a business combination. This proposed Statement would require assets and liabilities arising from contingencies that are acquired or assumed as part of a business combination to be measured and recognized at their fair value at the acquisition date if the contingency meets the definition of an asset or a liability in FASB Concepts Statement No. 6, *Elements of Financial Statements,* even if it does not meet the recognition criteria in Statement 5. After initial recognition, contingencies would be accounted for in accordance with applicable generally accepted accounting principles, except for those that would be accounted for in accordance with Statement 5 if they were acquired or incurred in an event other than a business combination. Those contingencies would continue to be measured at fair value with changes in fair value recognized in income in each reporting period. Statement 141 permitted deferral of the recognition of preacquisition contingencies until the Statement 5 recognition criteria were met and subsequent changes were recognized as adjustments to goodwill.

j.  This proposed Statement would prohibit costs associated with restructuring or exit activities that do not meet the recognition criteria in FASB Statement No. 146, *Accounting for Costs Associated with Exit or Disposal Activities,* as of the acquisition date from being recognized as liabilities assumed. Rather, they would be recognized as postcombination expenses of the combined entity when incurred. Previously, EITF Issue No. 95-3, "Recognition of Liabilities in Connection with a Purchase Business Combination," permitted costs that would result from a plan to exit an activity of an acquiree to be recognized as liabilities assumed at the acquisition date if specific criteria were met.

k.  This proposed Statement would require the acquirer in business combinations in which the acquirer holds less than 100 percent of the equity interests in the acquiree at the acquisition date, to recognize the identifiable assets and liabilities at the full amount of their fair values, with limited exceptions, and goodwill as the difference between the fair value of the acquiree, as a whole, and the fair value of the identifiable assets acquired and liabilities assumed. Statement 141 did not change the accounting for a step acquisition described in AICPA Accounting Interpretation 2, "Goodwill in a Step Acquisition," of APB Opinion No. 17, *Intangible Assets.* That Interpretation stated that when an entity acquires another entity in a series of purchases, the entity should identify the cost of each investment, the fair value of the underlying assets acquired, and the goodwill for each step acquisition. Statement 141 did not provide guidance for measuring the noncontrolling interests' share of the consolidated subsidiary's assets and liabilities at the acquisition date.

l.  Acquisitions of additional noncontrolling equity interests after the business combination would not be permitted to be accounted for using the acquisition method. In accordance with Proposed Statement, *Consolidated Financial Statements, Including Accounting and Reporting of Noncontrolling Interests in Subsidiaries,* acquisitions (or dispositions) of noncontrolling equity interests after the business combination would be accounted for as equity transactions.

m. The acquirer would be required to recognize separately from goodwill the acquisition-date fair value of research and development assets acquired in a business combination. This Statement supersedes Interpretation 4, which required research and development assets acquired in a business combination that have no alternative future use to be measured at their fair value and expensed at the acquisition date.

n. The acquirer would be required to account for any changes in the amount of its deferred tax benefits that are recognizable (through the increase or reduction of the acquirer's valuation allowance on its previously existing deferred tax assets) as a result of a business combination separately from that business combination. This Statement would amend Statement 109 to require such changes in the amount of the deferred tax benefits to be recognized either in income from continuing operations in the period of the combination or directly to contributed capital, depending on the circumstances. Statement 109 had required that a reduction of the acquirer's valuation allowance as a result of a business combination be recognized through a corresponding reduction to goodwill or certain noncurrent assets or an increase in negative goodwill.

# BENEFITS AND COSTS

X. The Boards have striven to issue a proposed Statement with common requirements that will fill a significant need and for which the costs imposed to apply it, as compared with other alternatives, are justified in relation to the overall benefits of the resulting information. The Boards concluded that this proposed Statement would, for the reasons previously noted, make several improvements to financial reporting that would benefit investors, creditors, and other users of financial statements.

XI. The Boards sought to reduce the costs of applying this proposed Statement. This proposed Statement would (a) require particular assets and liabilities (for example, those related to deferred taxes, assets held for sale, and employee benefits) to continue to be measured and recognized in accordance with existing generally accepted accounting principles rather than at fair value and (b) require its provisions to be applied prospectively rather than retrospectively. The Boards acknowledged that those two steps may diminish some benefits of improved reporting provided by this proposed Statement. However, the Boards concluded that the complexities and related costs that would result from imposing a fair value measurement requirement at this time to all assets acquired and liabilities assumed in a business combination and requiring retrospective application of the provisions of this proposed Statement are not justified.

XII. In addition, improving the consistency of the procedures used in accounting for business combinations, including international consistency, should help alleviate concerns that an entity's competitive position as a potential bidder is affected by differences in accounting for business combinations. Consistency in the accounting procedures also can reduce the costs to prepare financial statements, especially for entities with global operations. Moreover, such consistency also will enhance comparability of information among entities, which can lead to a better understanding of the resulting financial information and reduce the costs to users of analyzing that information.

## ISSUANCE

At the date of this writing, the FASB projects issuing. Statement of Financial Accounting Standards No. 141R, *Business Combinations, a Replacement of FASB Statement No. 141*, in the second half of 2007.

# Chapter 3

# Case Studies

## CASE STUDY 1: DETERMINING THE VALUE OF GOODWILL AND OTHER INTANGIBLE ASSETS IN A BUSINESS COMBINATION

Under GAAP, an acquiring company must record the fair value of the assets acquired in a business combination. As we've discussed, SFAS No. 141 mandates such purchase accounting for all acquisitions.[1] On its face, purchase accounting is a simple process—determine the total purchase price paid for an entity and allocate that purchase price to the various assets acquired. But, as we will see, the valuation of intangibles is more complex than that. This section presents an example of a purchase price allocation.

There are numerous complexities in a purchase price allocation, and there are various challenges to be met along the way. These challenges include but are not limited to:

- Determine the purchase price.[2] The purchase price is more than just the cash and/or publicly traded stock paid for an acquisition; notes issued and/or liabilities assumed increase the purchase price. Contingent considerations (see SFAS Nos. 141R and 157) muddy the waters (e.g., contingent events, earn-outs, restricted or nonmarketable securities tendered).

- Perform a valuation of the acquirer to determine the value of its stock if the purchase price includes the payment of stock of a privately held acquirer.

- Identify all acquired assets, tangible and intangible.

- Identify if the sum of the fair values of the assets may exceed the purchase price.

- Deal with situations where data for valuing or estimating the useful life of certain assets may be limited or not available.

The example presented in the following pages is of an acquisition of the *assets* of a privately held corporation, and may differ in the treatment of certain issues compared with an acquisition of stock or public company acquisition. While the numerous steps and processes are presented sequentially, in the real world the various activities are performed simultaneously over a period of weeks, often by a staff of several analysts.

SFAS No. 141 states that the cost of an acquired entity should be measured with reference to cash payments, fair values, or the assets distributed as consideration, and the fair values of liabilities incurred by an acquiring entity.[3] This adjusted purchase price may be alternately defined as the sum of all cash and stock paid, debt incurred, and liabilities assumed. In this example, the enterprise purchase price is assumed to be $209,000,000 based on the following assumptions:

| | |
|---|---:|
| Cash Paid[*] | $150,000,000 |
| Liabilities Assumed[**] | |
| Current Liabilities[***] | 25,000,000 |
| Current Maturities of Long-Term Debt | 4,000,000 |
| Long-Term Debt | 30,000,000 |
| Adjusted Purchase Price | $209,000,000 |

*Including capitalized acquisition costs [will change under SFAS No. 141R]
**Amounts stated at fair value
***Excluding externally funded debt

As used here, the term *adjusted purchase price* equates to the total paid for all of the acquired company's assets, and includes all payments and liabilities assumed. It is important to distinguish this measurement from the *invested capital* concept, which is defined as the sum of debt and equity in an enterprise on a long-term basis,[4] shown here as $184,000,000 ($209,000,000 − $25,000,000).

At this point, it is useful for the analyst to understand the overall magnitude of the intangible assets. This can be easily achieved by subtracting from the adjusted purchase price (or total asset value) the estimated fair value of the current and tangible assets. An analysis of the company's balance sheet and asset records as of the valuation date reveals the recorded or carrying value of the assets is $67,500,000, which consists of:

| | |
|---|---:|
| Cash | $1,500,000 |
| Marketable Securities | 4,000,000 |
| Accounts Receivable | 17,000,000 |
| Inventory | 12,000,000 |
| Prepaid Expenses | 3,000,000 |
| Land and Building | 10,000,000 |
| Machinery and Equipment | 15,000,000 |
| Organization Costs and Other Intangibles | 5,000,000 |
| Total Current and Tangible Assets | $67,500,000 |

The next step is to adjust recorded values to fair values, including final audited amounts, if available. In reality, separate valuations may be undertaken of material tangible assets. For example, a machinery and equipment analyst may be brought in to independently value the fixed assets if it is determined that (1) the fixed assets are material, and (2) the book values do not represent fair value. Similarly, the fair values of receivables and other current assets may not be reflected by their carrying value and may require adjustment to fair value. For purposes of this analysis, it is assumed that adjustments are required to certain asset accounts and that the fair values of cash, accounts receivable, inventory, and prepaid expenses are equal to their carrying values. After the adjustments, the fair values of the tangible assets are:

|  | Carrying Value | Fair Value |
|---|---|---|
| Cash | $1,500,000 | $1,500,000 |
| Marketable Securities | 4,000,000 | 8,000,000 (a) |
| Accounts Receivable | 17,000,000 | 17,000,000 |
| Inventory | 12,000,000 | 12,000,000 |
| Prepaid Expenses | 3,000,000 | 3,000,000 |
| Land and Buildings | 10,000,000 | 22,000,000 (b) |
| Machinery and Equipment | 15,000,000 | 19,000,000 (c) |
| Organization Costs and Other Intangibles | 5,000,000 | 0 (d) |
| Total Tangible Assets | $67,500,000 | $82,500,000 |

(a) Fair value of marketable securities, as marked to market
(b) Fair value per real estate appraisal
(c) Fair value per machinery and equipment appraisal
(d) Written off (see "Valuation of Current Assets" section later in this chapter)

The fair value of the tangible assets is $82,500,000, so the "gap" available for the aggregate fair value of all intangible assets is $126,500,000 ($209,000,000 − $82,500,000). The foregoing relationship is illustrated by a schematic presented in the form of a box (the box). Exhibits 3.1 and 3.2 set forth the general allocation formula according to the box, where the left side of the exhibit represents the asset side of the balance sheet, and the right represents the liabilities and equity section of the balance sheet.

The assumed values of the various categories of assets, liabilities, and equity are shown in Exhibit.3.2

While simple, the box analysis can be quite useful, especially when presented with complex purchase arrangements. Note that while current maturities of long-term debt are usually classified as current liabilities, this debt is included with the long-term portion in our valuation analysis because it represents part of the total invested capital in the business.

In our example, we established that the adjusted purchase price (cash paid plus liabilities assumed) is $209,000,000. By referring to Exhibit 3.2, it should be easily seen that this equates to a total asset value of $209,000,000 and that the total of intangible assets and goodwill is $126,500,000.

Data gathering and management interviews are important. Assume that an investigation of the target and its operations has been conducted, and it has been determined that there are seven intangible assets that are identifiable and are subject to being valued. At this point, the methodologies to be used to value the intangibles are fairly clear, although the valuation and allocation process is fluid, and changes in methods and approach may be made as the engagement proceeds. The intangibles and the approach or method to be used are set forth in the following table.

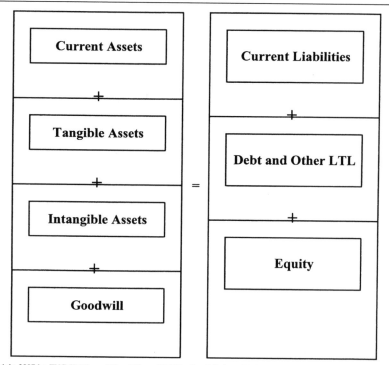

**Exhibit 3.1**   General Allocation Formula

| Asset | Type | Valuation Approach (Method) |
| --- | --- | --- |
| Software | Technology-based | Cost Approach (Cost to Re-create) |
| Assembled Workforce[5] | Goodwill | Cost Approach (Cost to Re-create) |
| Trade Name | Marketing-related | Income Approach (Relief from Royalties) |
| Noncompete Agreements | Contract-based | Income Approach (Before and After DCF) |
| Technology | Technology-based | Income Approach (Multiperiod Excess Earnings) |
| In-process Research | Technology-based | Income Approach (Multiperiod Excess Earnings) |
| Customer Relationships | Customer-related | Income Approach (Multiperiod Excess Earnings) |
| Goodwill | N/A | Residual |

The valuation of the purchased assets of Target Company will be performed using a combination of the cost and income approaches, with an element of market approach in selecting the royalty rate used in the trade name valuation. Detailed explanations of the three approaches are beyond the scope of this book but may be found in various valuation texts including *Financial Valuation: Applications and Models, 2nd edition,*

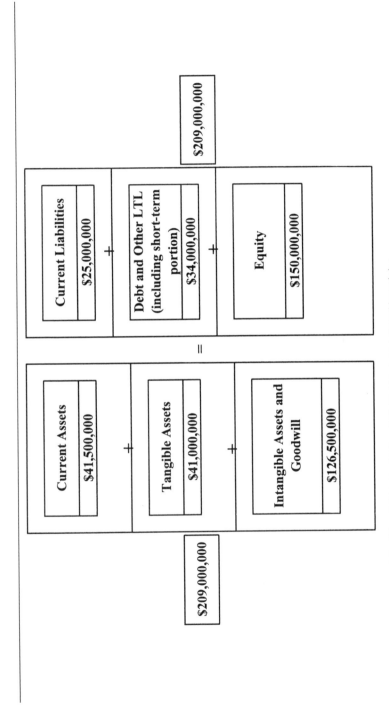

Current Assets $41,500,000 + Tangible Assets $41,000,000 + Intangible Assets and Goodwill $126,500,000 = $209,000,000

Current Liabilities $25,000,000 + Debt and Other LTL (including short-term portion) $34,000,000 + Equity $150,000,000 = $209,000,000

**Exhibit 3.2** Target Company Allocation Formula

by James Hitchner (Hoboken, New Jersey: John Wiley & Sons, Inc., 2006). The multiperiod excess earnings method of the income approach will be used to value technology, in-process research and development, and the customer base. However, the other assets must be valued first (aside from goodwill, which is valued using a residual method, where the value of all identified assets is subtracted from the total adjusted purchase price). This is because in the multiperiod excess earnings method, there is a deduction representing returns or contributory charges on the fair values of the other assets employed in the business.

## REMAINING USEFUL LIFE ANALYSIS

Identifiable assets must be analyzed to determine whether the asset has a finite or indefinite useful life. This subject is addressed in SFAS No. 142:

> The accounting for a recognized intangible asset is based on its useful life to the reporting entity. An intangible asset with a finite useful life is amortized; an intangible asset with an indefinite useful life is not amortized. The useful life of an intangible asset to an entity is the period over which the asset is expected to contribute directly or indirectly to the future cash flows of that entity.[6]

SFAS No. 142 mentions several pertinent factors that should be taken into account:

- Expected use of the asset
- Expected use of similar assets
- Legal, regulatory, and contractual provisions that may limit the useful life or enable renewal or extension
- The effects of obsolescence, demand, competition, and other economic factors
- Required future maintenance expenditures[7]

Analysts often rely on management's estimates of lives, decay rates, survivorship, etc. Analysts also rely on statistically based predictions of future behavior by developing *survivor curves* sometimes using tools such as Iowa-type Curves and the Weibull Distribution. The subject of "lifing" is very complex and beyond the scope of this book. There is no shortage of writings on the subject; for a start, try Chapter 1 of *Valuing Intangible Assets* by Robert F. Reilly and Robert P. Schweihs (New York: McGraw-Hill, 1999).

In the following example, it is assumed that various analyses and techniques have been performed to determine the remaining useful lives of the amortizable intangible, but those complexities will not be described.

## BUSINESS ENTERPRISE ANALYSIS

Our analysis will proceed with the development of a business enterprise analysis (BEA) using a discounted cash flow (DCF) methodology. Performing a BEA using a DCF requires several assumptions, including sales and operating expense projections, working capital, and capital expenditure requirements. The nature and underlying rationale for these assumptions are discussed throughout the chapter.

In this example, the adjusted purchase price is the total fair value of assets acquired and comprises invested capital (as previously defined), plus current liabilities. The adjusted purchase price is equivalent to current assets, plus tangible assets, intangible assets, and goodwill. The value of a business enterprise is equivalent to the value of the total invested capital of that business. This can be demonstrated by simply deducting the amount of current liabilities from current assets to calculate the value of the net working capital of the business. Again, the box analysis is helpful (see Exhibit 3.3).

Performing a BEA using a DCF is important in three major respects. First, it requires an in-depth review of the industry and of the Target Company's operations and results, both historical and projected. Second, it allows the analyst to ascertain the reasonableness of a purchase price by determining whether the expected future cash flows of an enterprise will support that purchase price. Third, in performing a BEA, revenue, earnings, and cash flow streams are forecast, which serve as the basis for valuing assets by the income approach.

## DISCOUNTED CASH FLOW METHOD

In the DCF method of the income approach, a pro forma analysis is made of the subject company to estimate future available cash flows. Available cash flow is the amount that could be paid out to providers of capital without impairment of business operations.

The annual projected available cash flows are then discounted to indicate a present value. The sum of the annual present values, including the present value of any estimated residual, equals the capitalized earnings of the business. When performed on a debt-free basis, the business's capitalized earnings equates to invested capital, defined as the sum of equity value plus the value of all interest-bearing debt.

Assumptions should generally be prepared by the client. The analyst might guide a client to produce meaningful projections and/or forecasts (projections), but, just as historical financial statements are the responsibility of management, not the auditor, the company must take responsibility for projections. It should be noted that the projections prepared by the acquirer may include results of synergies between the acquirer and the acquired. While it is an axiom that buyers do not like to pay for their own synergies, in fact it happens all the time. Also, many acquisitions fail to earn a return equal to the acquirer's cost of capital.

Nevertheless, while the projections used by a buyer most likely include synergies and thus help explain a purchase price, *buyer-specific* synergies are specifically excluded from the cash flows used to value intangibles. Only *market-participant* synergies should be included to comport with the definition of fair value. Thus, an appraiser may have to request from the client a second set of projections with buyer-specific synergies removed, thus representing an estimate of market participant projections. The removal of buyer-specific synergies will reduce the value of certain identifiable intangible assets and increase goodwill compared to what the fair value of

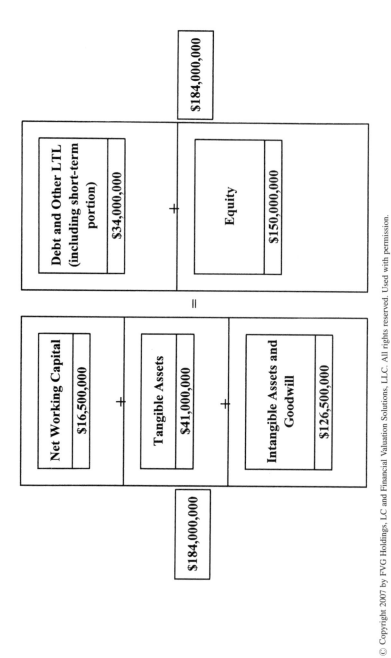

Net Working Capital
$16,500,000

+

Tangible Assets
$41,000,000

+

Intangible Assets and Goodwill
$126,500,000

$184,000,000

=

Debt and Other LTL (including short-term portion)
$34,000,000

+

Equity
$150,000,000

$184,000,000

**Exhibit 3.3** Target Company Invested Capital Allocation

those asset groups would have been using projections that include buyer-specific synergies.

Assumptions were made on the basis of internal company projections as presented to us. Also forecast are sales growth, product cost, operating expenses, and depreciation. As shown in Exhibit 3.4, principal assumptions utilized in developing the estimates of cash flow are:

- Sales are projected to increase from $60,000,000 in 2006 to $69,000,000 in 2007, growth of 15%, due to conversions, upgrades, new customers, and price increases. This increase is based largely on estimated growth in one of its key markets of 20%. However, the growth rate of the key market is expected to decline after 2008. The 10-year compound annual growth rate is 9.96%.

- Cost of sales (40% in 2007, improving to 39% thereafter) and operating expenses (30% in 2007, improving to 29% thereafter) excluding depreciation (tax basis—separately forecast using IRS MACRS tables) and amortization are also forecast. The prospective financial information is in line with Target Company's historical averages and with management's expectations at the time of the acquisition, and were felt to represent the best estimate of these costs. These assumptions are also in line with growth rates and margins expected by similar products from similar companies in the marketplace.

- Working capital requirements (debt free) were forecast at 15% of sales, based on the Company's historical working capital position, expected needs, and industry benchmarks.

- Capital expenditures are projected at 1% of net sales. This level of capital expenditures is considered adequate to support future levels of sales.

- Tax amortization of total intangible asset value is based on Sec. 197 of the Internal Revenue Code, which provides for such amortization over a 15-year period.[8] The amortization acts as a tax shield and is added back to cash flow. Annual amortization is $8,433,000 ($126,500,000 ÷ 15). The reader should note that this example is an asset purchase. In a stock purchase, the intangible assets generally are not amortizable for tax purposes absent a Sec. 338 election. However, a market participant in a business combination, namely the buyer for purposes of this discussion, is generally assumed to be an enterprise qualifying for Sec. 197 tax treatment and therefore an amortization benefit typically applies.

- Other Assumptions:
  - Required Rate of Return (discount rate)[*]      16.00%
  - Residual Growth Rate      5.00%
  - Tax Rate      40.00%

  [*] Discussed more fully in the next section, entitled "Discount Rate"

Assumptions are summarized in Exhibit 3.4, which presents the prospective financial information for a period of ten years.

**Exhibit 3.4** Target Company Business Enterprise Analysis — Assumptions as of December 31, 2006 ($000s)

| | Actual | | | | | | | | | | |
| | 2006 | 2007 | 2008 | 2009 | 2010 | 2011 | 2012 | 2013 | 2014 | 2015 | 2016 |
| | | | | | | | Forecast | | | | |
|---|---|---|---|---|---|---|---|---|---|---|---|
| **1. SALES** | | | | | | | | | | | |
| *Sales Growth Percentage* | | *15.0%* | *15.0%* | *12.5%* | *10.0%* | *10.0%* | *7.5%* | *7.5%* | *7.5%* | *7.5%* | *7.5%* |
| Net Sales | $60,000 | $69,000 | $79,350 | $89,269 | $98,196 | $108,015 | $116,116 | $124,825 | $134,187 | $144,251 | $155,070 |
| **2. EXPENSES** | | | | | | | | | | | |
| Cost of Sales | $24,000 | $27,600 | $30,947 | $34,815 | $38,296 | $42,126 | $45,285 | $48,682 | $52,333 | $56,258 | $60,477 |
| *Cost of Sales Percentage* | *40.0%* | *40.0%* | *39.0%* | *39.0%* | *39.0%* | *39.0%* | *39.0%* | *39.0%* | *39.0%* | *39.0%* | *39.0%* |
| Operating Expenses | $18,000 | $20,700 | $23,012 | $25,888 | $28,477 | $31,324 | $33,674 | $36,199 | $38,914 | $41,833 | $44,970 |
| *Operating Expenses Percentage* | *30.0%* | *30.0%* | *29.0%* | *29.0%* | *29.0%* | *29.0%* | *29.0%* | *29.0%* | *29.0%* | *29.0%* | *29.0%* |
| Depreciation (MACRS) | $1,750 | $3,097 | $5,171 | $3,961 | $3,120 | $2,544 | $2,649 | $2,762 | $2,011 | $1,246 | $1,551 |
| *Other Income (Expense), Net Percentage* | *0.0%* | *0.0%* | *0.0%* | *0.0%* | *0.0%* | *0.0%* | *0.0%* | *0.0%* | *0.0%* | *0.0%* | *0.0%* |
| **3. CASH FLOW** | | | | | | | | | | | |
| Capital Expenditures | | $690 | $794 | $893 | $982 | $1,080 | $1,161 | $1,248 | $1,342 | $1,443 | $1,551 |
| *Capital Expenditures Percentage* | *1.0%* | *1.0%* | *1.0%* | *1.0%* | *1.0%* | *1.0%* | *1.0%* | *1.0%* | *1.0%* | *1.0%* | *1.0%* |
| Projected Working Capital as Percent of Sales | 15.0% | | | | | | | | | | |
| (1) Projected Working Capital Balance | $16,500 | $10,350 | $11,903 | $13,390 | $14,729 | $16,202 | $17,417 | $18,724 | $20,128 | $21,638 | $23,260 |
| Projected Working Capital Requirement | | (6,150) | 1,553 | 1,488 | 1,339 | 1,473 | 1,215 | 1,306 | 1,404 | 1,510 | 1,623 |
| **4. OTHER** | | | | | | | | | | | |
| Effective Tax Rate | 40.0% | | | | | | | | | | |
| Required Rate of Return | 16.0% | | | | | | | | | | |
| Residual Growth Rate | 5.0% | | | | | | | | | | |

## AMORTIZATION OF INTANGIBLES (TAX)

Assumption: Intangibles receive 15-year tax life per Sec. 197

| | |
|---|---|
| Purchase Price | $150,000 |
| Plus: Liabilities Assumed | 59,000 |
| Adjusted Purchase Price | 209,000 |
| Less: Current and Tangible Assets | 82,500 |
| Amortizable Intangible Assets | $126,500 |
| Divide: Sec. 197 Amortization Period (Years) | 15 |
| Annual Amortization of Intangibles, Rounded | $8,433 |

Footnote:

(1) Balance at December 31, 2006 stated at fair value
Note: Some amounts may not foot due to rounding.

Cash flows in year 11 are increased by the residual growth rate and then capitalized into perpetuity by dividing by the capitalization rate, defined as the difference between the discount rate and the residual growth rate. This residual value is then discounted to present value to provide the net present value of the residual cash flow. The residual cash flow represents the expected cash flow for years 11 to perpetuity.

Because the Section 197 amortization has a finite amortization period of 15 years, the residual calculation must be adjusted so the amortization is not capitalized into perpetuity. First, the annual amortization of $8,433,000 is added back to year 10 cash flow. Thus, cash flow to be capitalized ignores any amortization benefit after year 10. After accounting for taxes at 40%, the present value of the remaining five years of tax amortization is added to the residual calculation. This amount is $2,697,000. After the adjustment, the amortization of intangibles reflects a benefit period of 15 years. The present value of the net cash flows, plus the present value of the residual, provides the total capitalized cash flow. The BEA is presented in Exhibit 3.5.

## DISCOUNT RATE

The appropriate rate of return for valuing the enterprise is the weighted average cost of capital (WACC). This rate is typically the weighted average of the return on equity capital and the return on debt capital. The weights are determined by the anticipated long-term industry average leverage position (i.e., average amount of debt capital to equity capital). The rate of return on debt capital is adjusted to reflect the fact that interest payments are tax deductible to the corporation.

The WACC is expressed in the following formula:

$$\text{WACC} = (k_e \times W_e) + (k_p \times W_p) + (k_{d(pt)}[1 - t] \times W_d)$$

Where:

$\text{WACC} = $ Weighted average cost of capital

$k_e = $ Cost of common equity capital

$W_e = $ Percentage of common equity in the capital structure, at market value

$k_p = $ Cost of preferred equity

$W_p = $ Percentage of preferred equity in the capital structure, at market value

$k_{d(pt)} = $ Cost of debt (pretax)

$t = $ Tax rate

$W_d = $ Percentage of debt in the capital structure, at market value[9]

The WACC represents the average rate of earnings investors require to induce them to supply all forms of long-term capital (debt and equity) to a company.

It is beyond the scope of this book to provide a detailed explanation of rates of return, and the reader is encouraged to refer to books or other sources that provide such

**Exhibit 3.5** Target Company Business Enterprise Analysis (BEA) - Cash Flow Forecast as of December 31, 2006 ($000s)

| | Actual | | | | | Forecast | | | | | |
|---|---|---|---|---|---|---|---|---|---|---|---|
| | 2006 | 2007 | 2008 | 2009 | 2010 | 2011 | 2012 | 2013 | 2014 | 2015 | 2016 |
| Sales Growth Percentage | | 15.0% | 15.0% | 12.5% | 10.0% | 10.0% | 7.5% | 7.5% | 7.5% | 7.5% | 7.5% |
| Net Sales | $60,000 | $69,000 | $79,350 | $89,269 | $98,196 | $108,015 | $116,116 | $124,825 | $134,187 | $144,251 | $155,070 |
| Cost of Sales | 24,000 | 27,600 | 30,947 | 34,815 | 38,296 | 42,126 | 45,285 | 48,682 | 52,333 | 56,258 | 60,477 |
| Gross Profit | 36,000 | 41,400 | 48,404 | 54,454 | 59,899 | 65,889 | 70,831 | 76,143 | 81,854 | 87,993 | 94,593 |
| Operating Expenses | 18,000 | 20,700 | 23,012 | 25,888 | 28,477 | 31,324 | 33,674 | 36,199 | 38,914 | 41,833 | 44,970 |
| Depreciation (MACRS) | 1,750 | 3,097 | 5,171 | 3,961 | 3,120 | 2,544 | 2,649 | 2,762 | 2,011 | 1,246 | 1,551 |
| Amortization of Intangibles (Tax) | 0 | 8,433 | 8,433 | 8,433 | 8,433 | 8,433 | 8,433 | 8,433 | 8,433 | 8,433 | 8,433 |
| Total Operating Expenses | 19,750 | 32,230 | 36,615 | 38,282 | 40,030 | 42,302 | 44,756 | 47,395 | 49,358 | 51,512 | 54,955 |
| Taxable Income | 16,250 | 9,170 | 11,788 | 16,171 | 19,870 | 23,587 | 26,075 | 28,749 | 32,496 | 36,481 | 39,638 |
| Income Taxes            40.0% | 6,500 | 3,668 | 4,715 | 6,469 | 7,948 | 9,435 | 10,430 | 11,499 | 12,998 | 14,593 | 15,855 |
| Net Income | $9,750 | $5,502 | $7,073 | $9,703 | $11,922 | $14,152 | $15,645 | $17,249 | $19,497 | $21,889 | $23,783 |
| **Net Cash Flow** | | | | | | | | | | | |
| Net Income | | $5,502 | $7,073 | $9,703 | $11,922 | $14,152 | $15,645 | $17,249 | $19,497 | $21,889 | $23,783 |
| Capital Expenditures | | (690) | (794) | (893) | (982) | (1,080) | (1,161) | (1,248) | (1,342) | (1,443) | (1,551) |
| Change in Working Capital | | 6,150 | (1,553) | (1,488) | (1,339) | (1,473) | (1,215) | (1,306) | (1,404) | (1,510) | (1,623) |
| Depreciation | | 3,097 | 5,171 | 3,961 | 3,120 | 2,544 | 2,649 | 2,762 | 2,011 | 1,246 | 1,551 |
| Amortization of Intangibles (Tax) | | 8,433 | 8,433 | 8,433 | 8,433 | 8,433 | 8,433 | 8,433 | 8,433 | 8,433 | 8,433 |
| Net Cash Flow | | $22,492 | $18,331 | $19,717 | $21,154 | $22,577 | $24,351 | $25,890 | $27,195 | $28,616 | $30,594 |
| (1) Present Value Factor, where Discount Rate     16.0% | | 0.9285 | 0.8004 | 0.6900 | 0.5948 | 0.5128 | 0.4421 | 0.3811 | 0.3285 | 0.2832 | 0.2441 |
| Present Value of Net Cash Flow | | $20,884 | $14,672 | $13,605 | $12,582 | $11,577 | $10,765 | $9,867 | $8,934 | $8,104 | $7,468 |

| | | 2017 | 2018 | 2019 | 2020 | 2021 |
|---|---|---|---|---|---|---|
| 2016 Taxable Income | $39,638 | | | | | |
| Plus: Intangible Asset Amortization | 8,433 | | | | | |
| Amortization of Intangibles (Pretax) | | $8,433 | $8,433 | $8,433 | $8,433 | $8,433 |
| 2016 Adjusted Taxable Income | 48,071 | | | | | |
| Less: Income Taxes 40.0% | 19,228 | | | | | |
| Tax Benefit of Amortization 40.0% | | $3,373 | $3,373 | $3,373 | $3,373 | $3,373 |
| (1) Present Value Factor | | 0.2105 | 0.1814 | 0.1564 | 0.1348 | 0.1162 |
| 2016 Adjusted Net Income | $28,843 | | | | | |
| Present Value of Tax Benefit | | $710 | $612 | $528 | $455 | $392 |
| 2017 Adjusted Net Income, Growth 5.0% | $30,285 | | | | | |
| Less: 2017 Working Capital Provision | (1,163) | | | | | |
| Sum = Present Value of Tax Benefit | $2,697 | | | | | |
| 2017 Adjusted Cash Flow | $29,122 | | | | | |
| Residual Cap. Rate, Perpetual Growth 5.0% | 11.00% | | | | | |
| Residual Value, 2017 | $264,745 | | | | | |
| (1) Present Value Factor | 0.2441 | | | | | |
| Present Value of Residual Cash Flow | $64,624 | | | | | |
| Present Value of Net Cash Flow, 2007–2016 | $118,458 | | | | | |
| Present Value of Residual Cash Flow | 64,624 | | | | | |
| Present Value of Amortization Tax Benefit, 2017–2021 | 2,697 | | | | | |
| **Total Invested Capital, Rounded** | **$186,000** | | | | | |

Footnote:
(1) Based on mid-period assumption

Note: Some amounts may not foot due to rounding.

guidance.[10] For this case, assume an equity discount rate (which in a corporate acquisition is often calculated using the Capital Asset Pricing Model) of 22% and a pretax cost of debt of 9.25% (prime plus 100 basis points as of December 29, 2006). Further, assume a capital structure of 35% debt and 65% equity. Theoretically, an "optimal" capital structure based upon how the valuation specialist would expect market participants to behave should be used to estimate a company's WACC in the case of an acquisition. Analysts often, where appropriate, rely on the capital structures of public companies as a proxy for what market participants would do. A target capital structure of approximately 35% debt and 65% equity was estimated for Target Company, based on a review of comparable publicly traded companies. Target Company has no preferred equity. Substituting these values into the WACC formula described previously provides the following:

$$
\begin{aligned}
\text{WACC} &= (22.00\% \times 65.00\%) + (9.25\%[1 - 40.00\%] \times 35.00\%) \\
&= (14.30\%) + (5.55\% \times 35.00\%) \\
&= (14.30\%) + (1.94\%) \\
&= 16.24\%
\end{aligned}
$$

Rounded to 16%

Applying the WACC to cash flows estimated earlier indicates the fair value of the invested capital of Target Company on the valuation date was \$186,000,000 (Exhibit 3.5). Actual invested capital is \$184,000,000 (Exhibit 3.3, cash paid plus the fair value of interest-bearing debt assumed, including current maturities), so we are confident that the DCF model reasonably reflects the value of the business. As noted earlier, in the real world the purchase price can exceed the BEA, especially if there has been competitive bidding among two or more potential buyers. For the purposes of this case study, we are assuming that the projections include market participant but not buyer-specific synergies, and that the deal was priced accordingly.

## VALUATION OF CURRENT, FINANCIAL AND PREVIOUSLY RECOGNIZED ASSETS

It is very important that the valuation analyst and the auditor have open lines of communication. Certain financial and other current assets are the province of the auditor, and the purchase price allocation must rely in part on audit conclusions for certain assets, such as cash and receivables. Marketable securities must be marked to market, often by simply obtaining brokerage statements. Previously recognized intangibles that represent capitalized historic expenditures, such as organization costs, typically are written off. The actual cash flow associated with these assets occurred in the past, and these assets usually cannot be separated or sold apart from the acquired entity as required under SFAS No. 141. Any other previously recorded intangible value will be subsumed in the current purchase price allocation and is to be reallocated.

## VALUATION OF TANGIBLE ASSETS

Few valuation analysts have the experience and training to operate outside their discipline to render valuation opinions on fixed assets. If material and/or complicated, the real estate and personal property must be independently appraised. In this example, it is assumed that a real estate appraiser determined the fair value of the land and improvements to be $22,000,000, and a personal property appraiser determined the value of the machinery and equipment to be $19,000,000.

## VALUATION OF INTANGIBLE ASSETS

### Discount Rates

For each asset valued in the following sections, a discount rate must be selected. For assets valued using the income approach, the discount rate is used to reduce future benefit streams to present value. For those assets and for assets valued using the cost approach, the discount rate is an important input for calculating the amortization benefit (see "Discount Rate" section in this chapter). That rate was employed in approximating the purchase price in the BEA and also for those assets judged to be about as risky overall as the business (trade name and noncompete agreement). Discount rates for the other intangible assets were selected based on our judgment of relative risk and approximate the rates of returns investors in the subject assets might require. For example, the IPR&D is incomplete and commercially unproven. Competitors likely are developing their own competing technologies. Thus, the rate of return on this asset is substantially higher than the WACC.

The rates of return on the other intangibles are similarly selected with reference to the WACC. The rates for the intangible assets are:

| | |
|---|---|
| Software | 17% |
| Assembled Workforce | 16% |
| Trade Name | 16% |
| Noncompete Agreement | 16% |
| Technology | 18% |
| In-process Research and Development | 20% |
| Customer Base | 17% |

Note: The discount rates shown here are for example purposes only and represent general relationships between assets. Actual rates must be selecetd based on consideration of the facts and circumstances related to each entity and risk of underlying assets.

### Software

Target Company employs a sophisticated array of computer programs to manage its product and production processes (Exhibit 3.6). All product software was developed in-house and is not commercially available. A cost approach was applied to value the software, because this asset is a supporting or contributory asset with no directly attributable revenue or income streams. However, if a revenue or income stream could be attributed to this asset, and if the software had saleable commercial applications, an income approach would have been considered, as that approach is often used in the valuation of software.

The company's software system comprises 20 modules, each made up of several programs written in a very sophisticated programming language. To apply this form of the cost approach, it is necessary to obtain a reliable indication of the cost to re-create the program. A line count (a management report detailing the number of lines of code per program and/or module) was obtained.

Next, it is necessary to determine the productivity with which the hypothetical recreation effort would take place. Here, management assessed a productivity rating of 1 to 3, noting that software rated 1 could be programmed at four lines of code per hour; software rated at 2 could be programmed at three lines of code per hour; and software rated 3, the most complex and difficult, could be programmed at two lines of code per hour. The coding rates encompass completely debugged program statements, including requirements definition, systems design, debugging and documentation, testing, and so forth. In performing this purchase price allocation, it was fortunate that management had maintained detailed records of programmer productivity and supplied their metrics for such development activity.

By dividing the lines of code for each module by the coding rate, the number of hours to re-create was developed, totaling 112,507 hours for the entire system. The sum of hours was then multiplied by the blended hourly rate of $119 per hour. In estimating the hourly rate, it was hypothesized that if the software were to be re-created today, a project team of 10 individuals would have to be assembled. The team would include one project manager, two systems analysts, one technical writer, four programmers, and two support persons. Using their fully burdened rates, the weighted average rate was calculated for the team at $119 per hour. These rates include employee benefits and facilities and overhead charges and approximate the rates that would be charged by a software consulting firm.

Reproduction cost of the software system was determined by multiplying the total number of hours to re-create by the blended hourly rate. Reproduction cost is defined as:

> ...the estimated cost to construct, at current prices as of the date of the analysis, an exact duplicate or replica of the subject intangible asset, using the same materials, production standards, design, layout, and quality of workmanship as the subject intangible asset. The reproduction intangible asset will include the same inadequacies, superadequacies, and obsolescence as the subject intangible asset.[11]

In this example, reproduction cost totals $13,388,333. Because reproduction cost equates to brand-new software, an obsolescence factor is applied to recognize the fact that the acquired software is not brand new. Rather, it may have redundant or extraneous code and likely has been patched over the years and contains other inefficiencies that brand-new software presumably would not have. For this application, after discussing the capabilities of the software with management, it was estimated that an obsolescence factor of 25% was warranted, reducing the reproduction cost to its replacement cost of $10,041,250.

Replacement cost is defined as:

> ...the estimated cost to construct, at current prices as of the date of the analysis, an intangible asset with equivalent utility to the subject intangible, using modern materials, production standards, design, layout, and quality of workmanship. The replacement intangible asset will exclude all curable inadequacies, superadequacies, and obsolescence that are present in the subject intangible asset.[12]

Replacement cost is then adjusted for taxes to recognize the deductibility of such expenses. As noted earlier this book, there is a diversity of practice and some practitioners do not tax-affect assets valued using the cost approach. The after-tax value is $6,024,750.

## Amortization Benefit

Added to the after-tax value is an amortization benefit, which reflects the additional value accruing to the asset brought about by the ability to deduct the amortization of the asset over its 15-year tax life. The amortization benefit is an element of the fair value of all intangible assets that are deductible for tax purposes.

The amortization benefit is essentially the present value of the tax savings resulting from amortizing the asset. A spreadsheet presentation of the calculation of the amortization benefit is presented in the IPR&D Practice Aid's Sample Valuation Report, Exhibit 5.2F. The calculation may be expressed in the following formula:

$$AB = PVCF \, {}^{*}(n/(n - ((PV(Dr, n, -1)^{*}(1 + Dr) \wedge 0.5) * T)) - 1)$$

Where:

$$AB = \text{Amortization benefit}$$
$$PVCF = \text{Present value of cash flows from the asset}$$
$$n = \text{15-year amortization period}$$
$$Dr = \text{Discount rate}$$
$$PV(Dr, n, -1)^{*}(1 + Dr) \wedge 0.5 = \text{Present value of an annuity of \$1 over 15 years,}$$
$$\text{at the discount rate}$$
$$T = \text{Tax rate}$$

Based on the cost approach, and after adjusting for taxes and amortization benefit, we concluded that the fair value of the software as of December 31, 2006 was $7,120,000 (rounded) (Exhibit 3.6). The remaining useful life is four years.

## Discount Rate for Amortization Benefit

The authors believe that the majority of practitioners use the same discount rate for calculating the amortization benefit as is used for the particular asset. The calculations in this book follow that protocol, which is also followed in the IPR&D Practice Aid. However, some practitioners argue that, since the amortization schedule under

**Exhibit 3.6**   Target Company Valuation of Acquired Software as of December 31, 2006
All software was developed internally by Target Company for its own use. Rights to the software
were transferred at acquisition.
The software is written in a very sophisticated programming language.
Valuation is based on cost to replace less obsolescence. Costs are based on internally developed
Company metrics for software development productivity.
Source: Leonard Riles, Director of Product Development

| In Place | Lines of Code | Productivity Assessment | (1) Rate | Hours to Recreate |
|---|---|---|---|---|
| Module 1 | 26,400 | 2 | 3.0 | 8,800 |
| Module 2 | 32,600 | 3 | 2.0 | 16,300 |
| Module 3 | 46,000 | 1 | 4.0 | 11,500 |
| Module 4 | 8,480 | 3 | 2.0 | 4,240 |
| Module 5 | 12,000 | 3 | 2.0 | 6,000 |
| Module 6 | 12,500 | 2 | 3.0 | 4,167 |
| Module 7 | 2,000 | 2 | 3.0 | 667 |
| Module 8 | 32,000 | 2 | 3.0 | 10,667 |
| Module 9 | 3,000 | 2 | 3.0 | 1,000 |
| Module 10 | 3,000 | 2 | 3.0 | 1,000 |
| Module 11 | 3,000 | 2 | 3.0 | 1,000 |
| Module 12 | 13,000 | 2 | 3.0 | 4,333 |
| Module 13 | 6,000 | 2 | 3.0 | 2,000 |
| Module 14 | 10,000 | 2 | 3.0 | 3,333 |
| Module 15 | 5,000 | 2 | 3.0 | 1,667 |
| Module 16 | 6,000 | 2 | 3.0 | 2,000 |
| Module 17 | 5,000 | 3 | 2.0 | 2,500 |
| Module 18 | 8,000 | 1 | 4.0 | 2,000 |
| Module 19 | 7,000 | 2 | 3.0 | 2,333 |
| Module 20 | 54,000 | 3 | 2.0 | 27,000 |
| Total Number of Lines | 294,980 | | | |

| | | | |
|---|---|---|---|
| Total Number of Hours to Recreate | | | 112,507 |
| Times: Blended Hourly Rate (see below) | | | $119 |
| Reproduction Cost | | | $13,388,333 |
| (2) Less: Obsolescence | | 25.0% | (3,347,083) |
| Replacement Cost | | | 10,041,250 |
| Less: Taxes | | 40.0% | (4,016,500) |
| After-tax Value Before Amortization Benefit | | | 6,024,750 |
| Amortization Benefit | | | |
| Discount Rate | | 17.0% | |
| Tax Rate | | 40.0% | |
| Tax Amortization Period (Years) | | 15 | |
| Amortization Benefit | | | 1,093,112 |

| | | |
|---|---|---|
| **Fair Value of Software, Rounded** | | **$7,120,000** |

## SOFTWARE DEVELOPMENT COSTS – ESTIMATED PROJECT TEAM

| Function | Number | Burdened Hourly rate |
|---|---|---|
| Project Manager | 1 | — $200.00 |
| Systems Analyst | 2 | 150.00 |
| Technical Writer | 1 | 125.00 |
| Programmer | 4 | 115.00 |
| Support | 2 | 50.00 |
| Blended Hourly Rate, Rounded | | $119.00 |

Footnotes:

(1) Lines of code per hour, based on productivity assessment for average module of programming
(2) Estimate based on number of lines of redundant/extraneous code, effective age, and remaining economic life of system. Remaining useful life of this asset is four years.
Note: Some amounts may not foot due to rounding.

Sec. 197 is set as of a moment in time (i.e., the acquisition date), the risk of the particular asset is of no relevance. These practitioners argue that the risk to the entity as a whole of enjoying the amortization benefits, contrasted with the risks of achieving the cash flows for individual assets is related to overall company risk as represented by the WACC. A few even argue that the rate should be a risk-free rate, inasmuch as the amortization is regulatory. As of this writing, the latter view is being presented by certain academics and has not found much traction among practitioners.

## ASSEMBLED WORKFORCE

The buyer of Target Company obtained an assembled and trained workforce. Considerable expenditures for recruiting, selecting, and training would be required to replace these employees with individuals of comparable skills and expertise. By acquiring fully trained personnel, the buyer avoided the expenditure required to hire and train equivalent personnel. The value of the assembled workforce is represented by the assemblage cost avoided. Therefore, the cost approach is the most appropriate valuation approach to value this asset. Using this method, the costs associated with employee recruitment, selection, and training provide the measurement of value.

**Exhibit 3.7** Target Company Valuation of Assembled Workforce as of December 31, 2006

| No. | Job Title | Salary | 20% Benefits | Total | (1) Train. Per. Cl. | Yrs. | 33.3% Cost | (2) 27.5% Recruit. | Interview & H.R. | Total |
|---|---|---|---|---|---|---|---|---|---|---|
| 1 | Member of Technical Staff | $90,000 | $18,000 | $108,000 | 1 | 0.125 | $4,496 | $24,750 | $375 | $29,621 |
| 2 | Member of Technical Staff | 80,250 | 16,050 | 96,300 | 2 | 0.375 | 12,025 | 22,069 | 750 | 34,844 |
| 3 | Member of Technical Staff | 60,000 | 12,000 | 72,000 | 2 | 0.375 | 8,991 | 16,500 | 750 | 26,241 |
| 4 | Member of Technical Staff | 44,953 | 8,991 | 53,944 | 1 | 0.125 | 2,245 | 12,362 | 375 | 14,982 |
| 5 | Member of Operations Staff | 71,641 | 14,328 | 85,969 | 1 | 0.125 | 3,578 | 19,701 | 375 | 23,654 |
| 6 | Account Executive | 91,170 | 18,234 | 109,404 | 1 | 0.125 | 4,554 | 25,072 | 375 | 30,001 |
| 7 | Member of Technical Staff | 107,888 | 21,578 | 129,466 | 2 | 0.375 | 16,167 | 29,669 | 750 | 46,586 |
| 8 | Member of Technical Staff | 33,244 | 6,649 | 39,893 | 1 | 0.125 | 1,661 | 9,142 | 375 | 11,178 |
| 9 | Vice President | 142,000 | 28,400 | 170,400 | 2 | 0.375 | 21,279 | 39,050 | 750 | 61,079 |
| 10 | Member of Technical Staff | 83,647 | 16,729 | 100,376 | 2 | 0.375 | 12,535 | 23,003 | 750 | 36,288 |
| 11 | Member of Operations Staff | 104,700 | 20,940 | 125,640 | 1 | 0.125 | 5,230 | 28,793 | 375 | 34,398 |
| 12 | Chief Architect | 155,500 | 31,100 | 186,600 | 3 | 0.750 | 46,603 | 42,763 | 1,500 | 90,866 |
| 13 | Director of Development | 135,000 | 27,000 | 162,000 | 2 | 0.375 | 20,230 | 37,125 | 750 | 58,105 |
| 14 | Member of Technical Staff | 77,772 | 15,554 | 93,326 | 2 | 0.375 | 11,654 | 21,387 | 750 | 33,791 |
| 15 | Account Executive | 94,950 | 18,990 | 113,940 | 1 | 0.125 | 4,743 | 26,111 | 375 | 31,229 |
| 16 | Member of Technical Staff | 81,300 | 16,260 | 97,560 | 1 | 0.125 | 4,061 | 22,358 | 375 | 26,794 |
| 17 | Chief Executive Officer | 250,000 | 50,000 | 300,000 | 1 | 0.125 | 12,488 | 68,750 | 375 | 81,613 |
| 18 | Member Marketing Staff | 99,000 | 19,800 | 118,800 | 1 | 0.125 | 4,945 | 27,225 | 375 | 32,545 |
| 19 | Member of Technical Staff | 82,000 | 16,400 | 98,400 | 2 | 0.375 | 12,288 | 22,550 | 750 | 35,588 |
| 20 | Member of Technical Staff | 57,460 | 11,492 | 68,952 | 1 | 0.125 | 2,870 | 15,802 | 375 | 19,047 |
| 21 | Account Executive | 106,400 | 21,280 | 127,680 | 2 | 0.375 | 15,944 | 29,260 | 750 | 45,954 |
| 22 | Member of Technical Staff | 107,867 | 21,573 | 129,440 | 2 | 0.375 | 16,164 | 29,663 | 750 | 46,577 |
| 23 | Member of Technical Staff | 110,000 | 22,000 | 132,000 | 3 | 0.750 | 32,967 | 30,250 | 1,500 | 64,717 |
| 24 | Vice President of American Sales | 135,000 | 27,000 | 162,000 | 2 | 0.375 | 20,230 | 37,125 | 750 | 58,105 |
| 25 | Member of Technical Staff | 71,892 | 14,378 | 86,270 | 2 | 0.375 | 10,773 | 19,770 | 750 | 31,293 |
| 26 | Member of Technical Staff | 96,343 | 19,269 | 115,612 | 2 | 0.375 | 14,437 | 26,494 | 750 | 41,681 |
| 27 | Member of Technical Staff | 114,500 | 22,900 | 137,400 | 1 | 0.125 | 5,719 | 31,488 | 375 | 37,582 |
| 28 | Member of Technical Staff | 47,028 | 9,406 | 56,434 | 1 | 0.125 | 2,349 | 12,933 | 375 | 15,657 |
| 29 | Account Executive | 90,660 | 18,132 | 108,792 | 1 | 0.125 | 4,528 | 24,932 | 375 | 29,835 |

| # | Title | | | | | | | | |
|---|---|---|---|---|---|---|---|---|---|
| 30 | Member of Technical Staff | 63,329 | 12,666 | 75,995 | 1 | 0.125 | 3,163 | 17,415 | 375 | 20,953 |
| 31 | Member of Operations Staff | 131,000 | 26,200 | 157,200 | 1 | 0.125 | 6,543 | 36,025 | 375 | 42,943 |
| 32 | Chief Financial Officer | 150,000 | 30,000 | 180,000 | 1 | 0.125 | 7,493 | 41,250 | 375 | 49,118 |
| 33 | Member of Technical Staff | 100,210 | 20,042 | 120,252 | 2 | 0.375 | 15,016 | 27,558 | 750 | 43,324 |
| 34 | Member of Technical Staff | 87,372 | 17,474 | 104,846 | 2 | 0.375 | 13,093 | 24,027 | 750 | 37,870 |
| 35 | Member of Technical Staff | 108,000 | 21,600 | 129,600 | 2 | 0.375 | 16,184 | 29,700 | 750 | 46,634 |
| 36 | Member of Technical Staff – Nonexempt | 22,326 | 4,465 | 26,791 | 1 | 0.125 | 1,115 | 6,140 | 375 | 7,630 |
| 37 | Member of Technical Staff | 70,000 | 14,000 | 84,000 | 1 | 0.125 | 3,497 | 19,250 | 375 | 23,122 |
| 38 | Director of Operations | 137,000 | 27,400 | 164,400 | 3 | 0.750 | 41,059 | 37,675 | 1,500 | 80,234 |
| 39 | Member of Technical Staff | 94,248 | 18,850 | 113,098 | 2 | 0.375 | 14,123 | 25,918 | 750 | 40,791 |
| 40 | Member of Operations Staff | 71,000 | 14,200 | 85,200 | 1 | 0.125 | 3,546 | 19,525 | 375 | 23,446 |
| 41 | Director of Marketing | 125,000 | 25,000 | 150,000 | 2 | 0.375 | 18,731 | 34,375 | 750 | 53,856 |
| 42 | Member of Technical Staff | 65,000 | 13,000 | 78,000 | 1 | 0.125 | 3,247 | 17,875 | 375 | 21,497 |
| 43 | Member of Technical Staff – Nonexempt | 42,950 | 8,590 | 51,540 | 1 | 0.125 | 2,145 | 11,811 | 375 | 14,331 |
| 44 | Member of Technical Staff | 90,000 | 18,000 | 108,000 | 1 | 0.125 | 4,496 | 24,750 | 375 | 29,621 |
| 45 | Member of Technical Staff | 109,000 | 21,800 | 130,800 | 2 | 0.375 | 16,334 | 29,975 | 750 | 47,059 |
| 46 | Member of Technical Staff | 84,200 | 16,840 | 101,040 | 1 | 0.125 | 4,206 | 23,155 | 375 | 27,736 |
| 47 | Member of Technical Staff | 128,500 | 25,700 | 154,200 | 3 | 0.750 | 38,511 | 35,338 | 1,500 | 75,349 |
| 48 | Member of Technical Staff | 80,900 | 16,180 | 97,080 | 1 | 0.125 | 4,041 | 22,248 | 375 | 26,664 |
| 49 | Member of Technical Staff | 60,300 | 12,060 | 72,360 | 1 | 0.125 | 3,012 | 16,583 | 375 | 19,970 |
| 50 | Member of Technical Staff | 58,500 | 11,700 | 70,200 | 1 | 0.125 | 2,922 | 16,088 | 375 | 19,385 |
| 51 | Director Release and Customer Support | 116,000 | 23,200 | 139,200 | 2 | 0.375 | 17,383 | 31,900 | 750 | 50,033 |
| 52 | Executive Assistant | 35,000 | 7,000 | 42,000 | 1 | 0.125 | 1,748 | 9,625 | 375 | 11,748 |
| 53 | Member of Technical Staff | 113,400 | 22,680 | 136,080 | 2 | 0.375 | 16,993 | 31,185 | 750 | 48,928 |
| 54 | Member of Technical Staff | 112,041 | 22,408 | 134,449 | 2 | 0.375 | 16,789 | 30,811 | 750 | 48,350 |
| 55 | Member of Operations Staff | 70,000 | 14,000 | 84,000 | 1 | 0.125 | 3,497 | 19,250 | 375 | 23,122 |
| 56 | Member of Technical Staff | 77,000 | 15,400 | 92,400 | 2 | 0.375 | 11,538 | 21,175 | 750 | 33,463 |
| 57 | Member of Technical Staff | 107,000 | 21,400 | 128,400 | 3 | 0.750 | 32,068 | 29,425 | 1,500 | 62,993 |
| 58 | Director of International Operations | 150,000 | 30,000 | 180,000 | 1 | 0.125 | 7,493 | 41,250 | 375 | 49,118 |
| 59 | Member of Technical Staff | 110,000 | 22,000 | 132,000 | 2 | 0.375 | 16,484 | 30,250 | 750 | 47,484 |
| 60 | Vice President and General Manager of EMEA | 145,000 | 29,000 | 174,000 | 2 | 0.375 | 21,728 | 39,875 | 750 | 62,353 |
| 61 | Account Executive | 82,500 | 16,500 | 99,000 | 1 | 0.125 | 4,121 | 22,688 | 375 | 27,184 |
| 62 | Account Executive | 75,261 | 15,052 | 90,313 | 2 | 0.375 | 11,278 | 20,697 | 750 | 32,725 |

*(continued)*

**Exhibit 3.7**  (Continued)

| No. | Job Title | Salary | 20% Benefits | Total | (1) Train. Per. Cl. | Yrs. | 33.3% Cost | (2) 27.5% Recruit. | Interview & H.R. | Total |
|---|---|---|---|---|---|---|---|---|---|---|
| 63 | Member of Technical Staff | 67,735 | 13,547 | 81,282 | 2 | 0.375 | 10,150 | 18,627 | 750 | 29,527 |
| 64 | Member of Technical Staff | 73,350 | 14,670 | 88,020 | 2 | 0.375 | 10,991 | 20,171 | 750 | 31,912 |
| 65 | Member of Technical Staff | 99,465 | 19,893 | 119,358 | 3 | 0.750 | 29,810 | 27,353 | 1,500 | 58,663 |
| Total 65 | | $6,134,752 | $1,226,950 | $7,361,702 | | | $770,302 | $1,687,060 | $41,625 | $2,498,987 |

| | |
|---|---|
| Replacement Cost of Assembled Workforce | $2,498,987 |
| Less: Taxes 40.0% | (999,595) |
| Costs Avoided, Net of Tax | 1,499,392 |
| Amortization Benefit | |
| Rate of Return 16.0% | |
| Tax Rate 40.0% | |
| Tax Amortization Period (Years) 15 | |
| Amortization Benefit | 285,879 |
| **Fair Value of Assembled Workforce, Rounded** | **$1,790,000** |

Footnotes:

(1) Qualified Replacement Training Months

| | Interview & H.R. | |
|---|---|---|
| | Hours | Rate |
| 1 = < 3 months | 5 | $75.00 |
| 2 = 3–6 months | 10 | $75.00 |
| 3 = 6–12 months | 20 | $75.00 |

(2) Source: Karl Malloney, Recruiter

Note: Some amounts may not foot due to rounding.

Recruiting costs are incurred to obtain a new employee, who may be either untrained or previously trained. The major components of recruiting costs are employment agencies, advertising, and other recruitment-related expense. In order to hire most professional-level employees with similar skill sets, an employment agency may be used, which would typically charge a fee based on the starting salary. For the level of employees employed by the Company, the average recruiting cost is 27.5% of starting salary.

Training costs are incurred to train employees and bring them to the level of performance normally expected from an individual in a given position. The training costs of an employee reflect the amount of time inefficiently used by a new employee (inefficiency training cost) and the time inefficiently used by a training supervisor (direct training cost) during the first few months on the job. Training and supervisory costs were estimated by multiplying the fully burdened weekly salary of the employee by the average amount of inefficiency incurred during the training period. The inefficiency estimate used here for training and supervisory costs is 33.3%, or one-third of the time. This can vary depending on the business. Interview costs are estimated based on average hours per employee class, as follows:

| Class | Hours |
|-------|-------|
| 1     | 5     |
| 2     | 10    |
| 3     | 20    |

The average fully burdened interview rate is $75.00 per hour.

The summation of the hiring and training costs results in the total cost to replace the assembled workforce, as shown in Exhibit 3.7. Based on the cost approach, and after adjusting for taxes at 40% and adding the amortization benefit, the fair value of the assembled workforce is estimated to be approximately $1,790,000 (rounded) as of December 31, 2006. No obsolescence is recognized for this asset in this example.

SFAS No. 141 specifically prohibits the recognition of assembled workforce as an intangible asset apart from goodwill.[13] However, in the application of the multi-period excess earnings method, which is used to value the Company's technology, in-process research and development, and customer base, contributory charges are taken on the fair values of all of the contributory assets acquired in the acquisition. The value of the assembled workforce is calculated so that a contributory charge on that asset may be taken. However, its fair value is included in goodwill in the final allocation of purchase price and is not separately represented.

## TRADEMARKS/TRADE NAME

In this example, Target Company has one valuable trade name. However, a company may have many trademarks/trade names, some with indefinite lives and some with finite lives. Depending on the purpose and scope of the valuation, each name or mark may be valued separately.[14]

All of the Company's products and services are sold under the "XXX" trade name, and each major product is identified by this trade name. Upon acquiring Target

**Exhibit 3.8** Target Company Valuation of Trade Name as of December 31, 2006 ($000s)

| | | 2007 | 2008 | 2009 | 2010 | 2011 | 2012 | 2013 | 2014 | 2015 | 2016 |
|---|---|---|---|---|---|---|---|---|---|---|---|
| (1) Net Sales from Business Enterprise Analysis | | $69,000 | $79,350 | $89,269 | $98,196 | $108,015 | $116,116 | $124,825 | $134,187 | $144,251 | $155,070 |
| Pretax Relief from Royalty | 2.0% | $1,380 | $1,587 | $1,785 | $1,964 | $2,160 | $2,322 | $2,497 | $2,684 | $2,885 | $3,101 |
| Income Tax Liability | 40.0% | 552 | 635 | 714 | 786 | 864 | 929 | 999 | 1,073 | 1,154 | 1,241 |
| After-tax Royalty | | $828 | $952 | $1,071 | $1,178 | $1,296 | $1,393 | $1,498 | $1,610 | $1,731 | $1,861 |
| (2) Present Value Income Factor | 16.0% | 0.9285 | 0.8004 | 0.6900 | 0.5948 | 0.5128 | 0.4421 | 0.3811 | 0.3285 | 0.2832 | 0.2441 |
| Present Value Relief from Royalty | | $769 | $762 | $739 | $701 | $665 | $616 | $571 | $529 | $490 | $454 |
| Sum of Present Value Relief from Royalty, 2007–2016 | | | $6,296 | | | | | | | | |
| Residual Calculation: | | | | | | | | | | | |
| 2016 After-tax Royalty | | $1,861 | | | | | | | | | |
| 2017 After-tax Royalty, Assuming Growth of | 5.0% | $1,954 | | | | | | | | | |
| Residual Capitalization Rate, Perpetual Growth | 5.0% | 11.0% | | | | | | | | | |
| Residual Value, 2017 | | $17,764 | | | | | | | | | |
| (2) Present Value Factor | | 0.2441 | | | | | | | | | |
| Fair Market Value of Residual | | | 4,336 | | | | | | | | |
| Present Value of Trade Name Royalty Flows | | | 10,632 | | | | | | | | |
| Amortization Benefit | | | | | | | | | | | |
| Discount Rate | 16.0% | | | | | | | | | | |
| Tax Rate | 40.0% | | | | | | | | | | |
| Tax Amortization Period (Years) | 15 | | | | | | | | | | |
| Amortization Benefit | | | 2,027 | | | | | | | | |
| **Fair Value of Trade Name, Rounded** | | | **$12,660** | | | | | | | | |

Footnotes:
(1)Figures shown from Business Enterprise Analysis (BEA)–Cash Flow Forecast (Exhibit 3.5)
(2)Based on mid-period assumption
Note: Some amounts may not foot due to rounding.

Company's assets, the buyer gained and paid for the right to use this trade name. The name valued in this section enjoys great recognition and prestige in Target Company's markets. The trade name "XXX" is recognized as representing the premier company in the industry. In most cases, the trade name identifies the top products available in the marketplace. The use of this trade name is considered critical to the continued success of the company and provides for a seamless and invisible ownership change by maintaining continuity in the minds of customers.

To value the trade name, the cost approach and the market approach were both considered and then rejected as not being feasible methods of valuation here. It can be difficult to accurately identify all of the costs related to recreating the trade name and building recognition, a factor required to use the cost approach. Trademarks and trade names rarely sell separately in the marketplace; thus, information required to perform a market approach is rarely available. A comprehensive method to value the name is a variant of the income approach known as the *relief from royalty method*. The premise of this valuation methodology is the assumption that an owner/operator of a company would be compelled to pay the rightful owner of the intangible asset (such as a trade name) if the owner/operator did not have the legal right to utilize the subject intellectual property. Because ownership of a trade name relieves a company from making such payments (royalties), the financial performance of the firm is enhanced to the extent that these royalty payments are avoided. The royalty is typically expressed as a pretax percentage of revenues.

The relief from royalty method equates the value of a trademark or trade name to the portion of the company's earnings which represents the pretax royalty that may have been paid for using the trade name. For the name valued, we have determined that a royalty rate of 2% is applicable, stated as a percentage of sales.

This pretax royalty rate was selected based on observed royalty rates in the market and on an analysis of the rate that the Company's margins could support. We observed market data in our own proprietary database documenting the range of royalty rates for trademarks to be 1% to 10%, with the median at 4%.

Thus, based largely on our review of publicly available data on trademark/trade name licensing transactions and a comparison of the name recognition between "XXX" and the guideline royalties, a 2% average royalty rate was selected to value the trade name. The BEA (shown in Exhibit 3.5) indicates that there are ample earnings to allow for this level of royalty payments and still earn a fair return on sales. That is, Target Company could easily pay these royalties if it did not own the right to use the trade name.

The rights to use the trade name transfer to the buyer in perpetuity, giving it an indefinite life. The fair value of the trade name is the present value of the royalties projected for the ten-year period 2007–2016, plus the present value of the residual at the end of the ten-year period, plus the amortization benefit. A 16% rate of return was chosen to reflect a risk assessment that the trade name was approximately as risky as the business overall.

Based on our analysis as presented in Exhibit 3.8, we concluded that the aggregate fair value of the trade name as of the valuation date was $12,660,000 (rounded).

## NONCOMPETE AGREEMENT

Article X, paragraph 10.1 of the purchase agreement identifies a separate agreement not to compete. The purchase agreement specifies that, for a period of three years commencing at the date of the purchase transaction, the Sellers will not engage in any activity that competes with Target Company. The valuation of noncompete agreements is typically performed by preparing two discounted cash flow models – one which is based on the BEA and assumes a noncompete agreement is in place and a second which assumes that the noncompete agreement is not in place. Presumably, in the absence of such an agreement, the Sellers would be free to compete and take business away from Target Company, and perhaps cause Target Company to spend more, thus reducing its margins. The value of having the noncompete agreement, then, is the difference in the present value of two cash flow projections, one whose underlying assumptions reflect competition from the covenantees, and one that assumes no competition, as shown in Exhibit 3.9a.

Compared with the cash flow scenario representing the status quo and which mirrors the BEA (i.e., with a noncompete agreement in place), the cash flow scenario under the assumption there is no agreement results in reduced cash flows due to the effects of competition. Under the assumption of competition, Sellers could negatively impact Target Company, affecting the growth of sales (i.e., the Seller, if not under a noncompete agreement, could theoretically go to work for a competitor or start a new company and cause Target Company to grow slower than otherwise projected) and incur more marketing and other expenses. Thus, the changed assumptions are:

| Revenues | With Noncompete Agreement in Place Exhibit 3.9b | Without Noncompete Agreement in Place Exhibit 3.9c |
|---|---|---|
| 2007 | $69,000 | $62,100 |
| 2008 | 79,350 | 63,480 |
| 2009 | 89,269 | 80,342 |
| 2010 | 98,196 | 98,196 |
| 2011 | 108,015 | 108,015 |

Variable expense percentages are assumed to be the same under both scenarios.

Net cash flows with and without the noncompete agreement in place are presented in Exhibit 3.9a. The present value of the cash flows including amortization benefit is $5,432,000. This amount is multiplied by a factor that takes into account the covenantee's perceived likelihood of competing, if the company hypothetically was not so constrained (it is rare that a seller would not be required to agree to a noncompete contract). Factors to consider in assessing this issue include age of covenantee, health, resources, ability, and desire to compete. Here, we estimate the factor at 50%. Thus, the fair value of the noncompete agreement is determined to be $2,720,000.

**Exhibit 3.9a**    Target Company Valuation of Noncompete Agreement as of December 31, 2006 ($000s)

| Comparison: Scenario I & Scenario II | For the Years Ended December 31, | | | | |
| --- | --- | --- | --- | --- | --- |
| | 2007 | 2008 | 2009 | 2010 | 2011 |
| Net Cash Flow | | | | | |
| (1) With Restrictive Covenant (Exhibit 3.9b) | $14,992 | $18,329 | $19,717 | $21,154 | $22,577 |
| (2) Without Restrictive Covenant (Exhibit 3.9c) | 14,733 | 16,370 | 16,881 | 19,815 | 22,577 |
| Reduction in Debt-free Net Cash Flow | $259 | $1,959 | $2,836 | $1,339 | $0 |
| Present Value Period | 1 | 2 | 3 | 4 | 5 |
| (3) Present Value Factor | 0.9285 | 0.8004 | 0.6900 | 0.5948 | 0.5128 |
| Present Value of Cash Flow | $241 | $1,568 | $1,957 | $796 | $0 |
| Sum, Present Value of Cash Flows | | | $4,562 | | |
| Amortization Benefit | | | | | |
| Discount Rate | 16.0% | | | | |
| Tax Rate | 40.0% | | | | |
| Tax Amortization Period (Years) | 15 | | | | |
| Amortization Benefit | | | 870 | | |
| Raw Value of Noncompete Agreement | | | $5,432 | | |
| (4) Probability of Competing | | | 50% | | |
| **Fair Value of Noncompete Agreement, Rounded** | | | **$2,720** | | |

Footnotes:

(1) See Projected Cash Flows Over Competitive Time Horizon, Scenario 1: With Noncompete Agreement With Seller In Place (Exhibit 3.9b).

(2) Year 4 cash flow reflects adjustment to working capital provision under the assumption of competition starting in Year 4. See Projected Cash Flows Over Competitive Time Horizon, Scenario 2: Without Noncompete Agreement With Seller In Place (Exhibit 3.9c).

(3) Based on mid-period assumption

(4) Based on discussions with management

Note: Some amounts may not foot due to rounding.

## TECHNOLOGY (EXISTING AND IN-PROCESS) AND CUSTOMER BASE

The company's technology, both existing and in-process, and its customer base are the critical value drivers, with the other assets playing a supporting role. The valuation method known as the multiperiod excess earnings method (MPEEM) is generally reserved for the "value drivers," the intangibles with the most direct relationship to the revenue and cash flow streams of an enterprise. But what is the analyst to do when it is not clear which of the value drivers are preeminent?

Here, the technology, both existing and in-process, can lay claim to being the assets with the most direct relationship to revenues and cash flows. However, an equally compelling argument can be made on behalf of the customer base—that group of loyal patrons who year after year (albeit with some annual attrition) purchase the Company's products and services and provide its lifeblood.

**Exhibit 3.9b**    Target Company Projected Cash Flows Over Competitive Time Horizon Scenario 1: With Noncompete Agreement with Seller in Place Discounted Cash Flow Analysis ($000s)

| Assumptions | 2007 | 2008 | 2009 | 2010 | 2011 |
|---|---|---|---|---|---|
| Cost of Goods Sold | 40.0% | 39.0% | 39.0% | 39.0% | 39.0% |
| Operating Expenses | 30.0% | 29.0% | 29.0% | 29.0% | 29.0% |
| Capital Expenditures Percent of Sales | 1.0% | 1.0% | 1.0% | 1.0% | 1.0% |
| Estimated Effective Tax Rate | 40.0% | 40.0% | 40.0% | 40.0% | 40.0% |
| Debt-free Net Working Capital Percent of Revenues | 15.0% | 15.0% | 15.0% | 15.0% | 15.0% |
| Base Year Revenues 2006 | $60,000 | | | | |

|  | For the Years Ended December 31, | | | | |
|---|---|---|---|---|---|
|  | 2007 | 2008 | 2009 | 2010 | 2011 |
| (1) Total Revenues | $69,000 | $79,350 | $89,269 | $98,196 | $108,015 |
| Cost of Goods Sold | 27,600 | 30,947 | 34,815 | 38,296 | 42,126 |
| Operating Expenses | 20,700 | 23,012 | 25,888 | 28,477 | 31,324 |
|  |  |  |  |  |  |
| EBITDA | $20,700 | $25,391 | $28,566 | $31,423 | $34,565 |
| *EBITDA Margin* | *30.0%* | *32.0%* | *32.0%* | *32.0%* | *32.0%* |
| Depreciation (MACRS) | $3,097 | $5,171 | $3,961 | $3,120 | $2,544 |
| Amortization | 8,433 | 8,433 | 8,433 | 8,433 | 8,433 |
|  |  |  |  |  |  |
| EBIT | $9,170 | $11,787 | $16,171 | $19,870 | $23,588 |
| *EBIT Margin* | *13.3%* | *14.9%* | *18.1%* | *20.2%* | *21.8%* |
| Income Taxes | $3,668 | $4,715 | $6,468 | $7,948 | $9,435 |
|  |  |  |  |  |  |
| Debt-free Net Income | $5,502 | $7,072 | $9,703 | $11,922 | $14,153 |
| *Debt-free Net Income Margin* | *8.0%* | *8.9%* | *10.9%* | *12.1%* | *13.1%* |
| Plus: Depreciation | $3,097 | $5,171 | $3,961 | $3,120 | $2,544 |
| Plus: Amortization | 8,433 | 8,433 | 8,433 | 8,433 | 8,433 |
| Less: Capital Expenditures | (690) | (794) | (893) | (982) | (1,080) |
| (2) Less: Incremental Working Capital | (1,350) | (1,553) | (1,488) | (1,339) | (1,473) |
|  |  |  |  |  |  |
| Debt-free Cash Flow | $14,992 | $18,329 | $19,717 | $21,154 | $22,577 |

Footnotes:

(1) Based on Business Enterprise Analysis (BEA) – Cash Flow Forecast (Exhibit 3.5)

(2) Incremental Working Capital in Year 1 reflects a lower provision than shown in the Business Enterprise Analysis (BEA) - Cash Flow Forecast (Exhibit 3.5) because the BEA provision normalizes from an actual balance, while the provision for the noncompete agreement only accounts for the incremental amount necessary based on the growth of revenues.

Note: Some amounts may not foot due to rounding.

As with so many appraisal issues, the analyst must make an informed judgment based on facts and circumstances. In this example, we have determined that the company's relationships with its customers are an important value driver, and therefore we will employ the MPEEM to value not only technology but also the customer base.

## The Multiperiod Excess Earnings Method

The MPEEM measures the present value of the future earnings to be generated during the remaining lives of the subject assets. Using the BEA as a starting point, pretax cash flows attributable to the acquired asset(s) as of the valuation date are calculated. As

**Exhibit 3.9c**   Target Company Projected Cash Flows Over Competitive Time Horizon Scenario 2: Without Noncompete Agreement with Seller in Place Discounted Cash Flow Analysis ($000s)

| Assumptions | 2007 | 2008 | 2009 | 2010 | 2011 |
|---|---|---|---|---|---|
| Cost of Goods Sold | 40.0% | 39.0% | 39.0% | 39.0% | 39.0% |
| Operating Expenses | 30.0% | 29.0% | 29.0% | 29.0% | 29.0% |
| Capital Expenditures Percent of Sales | 1.0% | 1.0% | 1.0% | 1.0% | 1.0% |
| Estimated Effective Tax Rate | 40.0% | 40.0% | 40.0% | 40.0% | 40.0% |
| Debt-free Net Working Capital Percent of Revenues | 15.0% | 15.0% | 15.0% | 15.0% | 15.0% |
| Base Year Revenues 2006 | $60,000 | | | | |

| | For the Years Ended December 31, | | | | |
|---|---|---|---|---|---|
| | 2007 | 2008 | 2009 | 2010 | 2011 |
| (1) Total Revenues | $69,000 | $79,350 | $89,269 | $98,196 | $108,015 |
| Decline in Revenues Caused by Competition of Seller | 10% | 20% | 10% | 0% | 0% |
| | | | | | |
| Decline in Revenues | $6,900 | $15,870 | $8,927 | $0 | $0 |
| | | | | | |
| Adjusted Base Revenues | 62,100 | 63,480 | 80,342 | 98,196 | 108,015 |
| Cost of Goods Sold | 24,840 | 24,757 | 31,333 | 38,296 | 42,126 |
| Operating Expenses | 18,630 | 18,409 | 23,299 | 28,477 | 31,324 |
| | | | | | |
| EBITDA | $18,630 | $20,314 | $25,710 | $31,423 | $34,565 |
| *EBITDA Margin* | *30.0%* | *32.0%* | *32.0%* | *32.0%* | *32.0%* |
| (2) Depreciation | $2,795 | $4,126 | $3,535 | $3,120 | $2,544 |
| Amortization | 8,433 | 8,433 | 8,433 | 8,433 | 8,433 |
| | | | | | |
| EBIT | $7,402 | $7,755 | $13,742 | $19,870 | $23,588 |
| *EBIT Margin* | *11.9%* | *12.2%* | *17.1%* | *20.2%* | *21.8%* |
| Income Taxes | $2,961 | $3,102 | $5,497 | $7,948 | $9,435 |
| | | | | | |
| Debt-free Net Income | $4,441 | $4,653 | $8,245 | $11,922 | $14,153 |
| *Debt-free Net Income Margin* | *7.2%* | *7.3%* | *10.3%* | *12.1%* | *13.1%* |
| Plus: Depreciation | $2,795 | $4,126 | $3,535 | $3,120 | $2,544 |
| Plus: Amortization | 8,433 | 8,433 | 8,433 | 8,433 | 8,433 |
| Less: Capital Expenditures | (621) | (635) | (803) | (982) | (1,080) |
| (3) Less: Incremental Working Capital | (315) | (207) | (2,529) | (2,678) | (1,473) |
| | | | | | |
| Debt-free Net Cash Flow | $14,733 | $16,370 | $16,881 | $19,815 | $22,577 |

Footnotes:

(1) Based on Business Enterprise Analysis (BEA) – Cash Flow Forecast (Exhibit 3.5)

(2) Depreciation in this exhibit give effect to an estimated reduction due to reduced net sales, which it is assumed would result in reduced capital expenditures.

(3) Incremental Working Capital in Year 1 reflects a lower provision than shown in the Business Enterprise Analysis (BEA) - Cash Flow Forecast (Exhibit 3.5) because the BEA provision normalizes from an actual balance, while the provision for the noncompete agreement only accounts for the incremental amount necessary based on the growth of revenues. Incremental Working Capital in other years reflect different amounts than shown in the BEA (Exhibit 3.5) in order to fund working capital balances based on different revenue projections.

Note: Some amounts may not foot due to rounding.

with the BEA, deductions are made for cost of goods sold and operating expenses. Contributory charges on the other identified assets are then taken.

As already noted in Chapter 2, *returns on and of* or *contributory charges* represent charges for the use of contributory assets employed to support the subject assets and help generate revenue. The cash flows from the subject assets must support charges for replacement of assets employed and provide a fair return to the owners of capital. The respective rates of return, while subjective, are directly related to the analyst's assessment of the risk inherent in each asset.

The following table from the IPR&D Practice Aid[15] provides examples of assets typically treated as contributory assets, and suggested bases for determining the fair return. Generally, it is presumed that the return *of* the asset is reflected in the operating costs when applicable (e.g., depreciation expense). The contributory asset charge is "the product of the asset's fair value and the required rate of return on the asset."[16]

| Asset | Basis of Charge |
| --- | --- |
| Working capital | Short-term lending rates for market participants (e.g., working capital lines or short-term revolver rates) |
| Fixed assets (e.g., property, plant, and equipment) | Financing rate for similar assets for market participants (e.g., terms offered by vendor financing), or rates implied by operating leases, capital leases, or both, typically segregated between returns of (i.e., recapture of investment) and returns on |
| Workforce (which is not recognized separately from goodwill), customer lists, trademarks, and trade names | Weighted average cost of capital (WACC) for young, single-product companies (may be lower than discount rate applicable to a particular project) |
| Patents | WACC for young, single-product companies (may be lower than discount rate applicable to a particular project). In cases where risk of realizing economic value of patent is close to or the same as risk of realizing a project, rates would be equivalent to that of the project. |
| Other intangibles, including base (or core) technology | Rates appropriate to the risk of the subject intangible. When market evidence is available, it should be used. In other cases, rates should be consistent with the relative risk of other assets in the analysis and should be higher for riskier assets. |

It is important to note that the assumed fair value of the contributory asset is not necessarily static over time. Working capital and tangible assets may fluctuate throughout the forecast period, and returns are typically taken on estimated average balances in each year. Average balances of tangible assets subject to accelerated depreciation (as is the case here) may decline as the depreciation outstrips capital expenditures in the early years of the forecast. While the carrying value of amortizable intangible assets declines over time, there is a presumption that such assets are replenished each year, so the contributory charge usually takes the form of a fixed charge each year. An exception to this rule is a noncompete agreement, which is not replenished and does not function as a supporting asset past its expiration period.

The return requirements used here are after-tax and are:

| Contributory Asset Charges | |
|---|---|
| Return On: | Rate |
| Net Working Capital | 5.0% |
| Land and Building | 7.0% |
| Machinery and Equipment | 8.0% |
| Software | 17.0% |
| Trade Name | 16.0% |
| Noncompete Agreement | 16.0% |
| Assembled Workforce | 16.0% |
| Technology | 18.0% |
| In-process Research and Development | 20.0% |
| Customer Base | 17.0% |

Note: The discount rates shown here are for example purposes only and represent general relationships between assets. Actual rates must be selected based on consideration of the facts and circumstances related to each entity and risk of underlying assets.

Those guidelines are generally followed here, although it should be noted that some practitioners use a specific "mini-WACC" for fixed assets (the weights reflecting the percentage financed [debt] and the percentage down [equity]). Lease rates are also sometimes used.

Required returns were deducted from the cash flows. *Returns on* working capital and fixed assets are taken on the average book balances for each year in the projection period, as determined in the development of the BEA. The *return of* is satisfied through the replenishment of the asset through ongoing expenditures. Contributory charges on the intangible assets are taken on the fair value at acquisition. The returns of these assets are satisfied by that portion of operating expenses that relate to the replenishment of the various intangibles. Total returns are allocated among the intangibles valued using the multiperiod excess earnings method (here, developed technology, in-process research and development, and customer base), usually on the basis of relative revenues, as presented in Exhibit 3.10.

To apply the MPEEM to both asset groups, technology and customer base, we have replicated the valuation model, with the important exception that for technology (both existing and in-process) we recognize a contributory asset charge on the customer base (the charge is then allocated between existing and in-process technology) and for the customer base we deduct a contributory asset charge on the technology. Assuming the analyst is working in Excel, a circular reference is avoided by, in a series of trial and error iterations, hard-entering the customer base value in the contributory asset schedule used for the technology returns and repeating the iterations until equilibrium is achieved. This is some times referred to as a "cross-charge" method.

**Exhibit 3.10** Target Company Calculation of Contributory Asset Charges as of December 31, 2006 ($000s)

Contributory Asset

| A. Asset Balances | 2007 | 2008 | 2009 | 2010 | 2011 | 2012 | 2013 |
|---|---|---|---|---|---|---|---|
| Net Working Capital | $13,425 | $11,126 | $12,646 | $14,060 | $15,466 | $16,810 | $18,071 |
| Land and Building | 21,934 | 21,815 | 21,718 | 21,640 | 21,580 | 21,536 | 21,503 |
| Machinery and Equipment, net | 17,849 | 14,551 | 10,900 | 8,348 | 6,582 | 5,125 | 3,631 |
| Software | 7,120 | 7,120 | 7,120 | 7,120 | 7,120 | 7,120 | 7,120 |
| Trade Name | 12,660 | 12,660 | 12,660 | 12,660 | 12,660 | 12,660 | 12,660 |
| Noncompete Agreement | 2,720 | 2,720 | 2,720 | 0 | 0 | 0 | 0 |
| Assembled Workforce | 1,790 | 1,790 | 1,790 | 1,790 | 1,790 | 1,790 | 1,790 |
| Technology | 16,560 | 16,560 | 16,560 | 16,560 | 16,560 | 16,560 | 16,560 |
| IPR&D | 4,530 | 4,530 | 4,530 | 4,530 | 4,530 | 4,530 | 4,530 |
| Customer Base | 7,090 | 7,090 | 7,090 | 7,090 | 7,090 | 7,090 | 7,090 |

| (1) B. Total Returns | Rate | 2007 | 2008 | 2009 | 2010 | 2011 | 2012 | 2013 |
|---|---|---|---|---|---|---|---|---|
| Net Working Capital | 5.0% | $671 | $556 | $632 | $703 | $773 | $840 | $904 |
| Land and Building | 7.0% | 1,535 | 1,527 | 1,520 | 1,515 | 1,511 | 1,507 | 1,505 |
| Machinery and Equipment, net | 8.0% | 1,428 | 1,164 | 872 | 668 | 527 | 410 | 290 |
| Software | 17.0% | 1,210 | 1,210 | 1,210 | 1,210 | 1,210 | 1,210 | 1,210 |
| Trade Name | 16.0% | 2,026 | 2,026 | 2,026 | 2,026 | 2,026 | 2,026 | 2,026 |
| Noncompete Agreement | 16.0% | 435 | 435 | 435 | 0 | 0 | 0 | 0 |
| Assembled Workforce | 16.0% | 286 | 286 | 286 | 286 | 286 | 286 | 286 |
| Technology | 18.0% | 2,981 | 2,981 | 2,981 | 2,981 | 2,981 | 2,981 | 2,981 |
| IPR&D | 20.0% | 906 | 906 | 906 | 906 | 906 | 906 | 906 |
| Customer Base | 17.0% | 1,205 | 1,205 | 1,205 | 1,205 | 1,205 | 1,205 | 1,205 |

| C. Distribution of Revenues | 2007 | 2008 | 2009 | 2010 | 2011 | 2012 |
|---|---|---|---|---|---|---|
| (2) Net Sales-Technology | $61,800 | $38,192 | $32,782 | $23,636 | $13,911 | |
| (3) Projected Sales per BEA | 69,000 | 79,350 | 89,269 | 98,196 | 108,015 | |
| Technology Percent of BEA | 89.57% | 48.13% | 36.72% | 24.07% | 12.88% | |
| (4) Net Sales-IPR&D | $7,200 | $12,557 | $11,853 | $10,733 | $7,692 | $4,447 |
| (3) Projected Sales per BEA | 69,000 | 79,350 | 89,269 | 98,196 | 108,015 | 116,116 |
| IPR&D Percent of BEA | 10.43% | 15.82% | 13.28% | 10.93% | 7.12% | 3.83% |

| D. Allocated Returns-Technology | 2007 | 2008 | 2009 | 2010 | 2011 |
|---|---|---|---|---|---|
| Net Working Capital | $601 | $268 | $232 | $169 | $100 |
| Land and Building | 1,375 | 735 | 558 | 365 | 195 |
| Machinery and Equipment, net | 1,279 | 560 | 320 | 161 | 68 |
| Software | 1,084 | 583 | 444 | 291 | 156 |
| Trade Name | 1,814 | 975 | 744 | 488 | 261 |
| Noncompete Agreement | 390 | 209 | 160 | 0 | 0 |
| Assembled Workforce | 257 | 138 | 105 | 69 | 37 |
| Customer Base | 1,080 | 580 | 443 | 290 | 155 |
| Total | $7,880 | $4,048 | $3,006 | $1,833 | $972 |

| E. Allocated Returns-IPR&D | 2007 | 2008 | 2009 | 2010 | 2011 | 2012 |
|---|---|---|---|---|---|---|
| Net Working Capital | $70 | $88 | $84 | $77 | $55 | $32 |
| Land and Building | 160 | 242 | 202 | 166 | 108 | 58 |
| Machinery and Equipment, net | 149 | 184 | 116 | 73 | 37 | 16 |
| Software | 126 | 192 | 161 | 132 | 86 | 46 |
| Trade Name | 211 | 321 | 269 | 221 | 144 | 78 |
| Noncompete Agreement | 45 | 69 | 58 | 0 | 0 | 0 |
| Assembled Workforce | 30 | 45 | 38 | 31 | 20 | 11 |
| Customer Base | 126 | 191 | 160 | 132 | 86 | 46 |
| Total | $917 | $1,332 | $1,088 | $832 | $536 | $287 |

Footnotes:
(1) Used for Customer Base (Exhibit 3.13), except no return is taken on Customer Base asset.
(2) Based on Valuation of Technology (Exhibit 3.11)
(3) Based on Business Enterprise Analysis (BEA) - Cash Flow Forecast (Exhibit 3.5)
(4) Based on Valuation of In-Process Research and Development (Exhibit 3.12)
Note: Some amounts may not foot due to rounding.

As an alternative to the cross-charge method, some analysts employ an analysis where projected cash flows are segmented into four areas:

1. Current customers buying new technology (value falls to customer relationships)
2. New customers buying existing technology (technology)
3. Current customers buying existing technology (% to customer relationships, % to technology)
4. New customers buying new technology (goodwill)

The advantage of this method is that discrete cash flows are developed for each asset, but at the cost of additional subjectivity.

## Technology

In applying the MPEEM to the valuation of the company's developed technology, we employed the BEA as a starting point, and pretax cash flows attributable to the technology that existed at the valuation date were calculated. This was accomplished by utilizing management's forecast of sales attributable to the existing technology, which are projected to decline over time as the technology becomes obsolete and competiturs increasingly impact sales. As with the BEA, deductions are made for cost of goods sold (40% of sales attributable to existing technology in 2007, and 39% after 2007) and operating expenses (20% of sales in 2007, then 19%, after deducting estimated development expenses of 10% from the operating expense base to reflect the fact that the developed technology should not be burdened by expenses of developing new technology). Contributory charges on the other identified assets, including the customer base, were taken. The discount rate of 18% reflects the higher relative risk of this asset compared with the business overall and the other intangibles.

Based on our analysis, we concluded that the fair value of the acquired technology on the valuation dates was $16,560,000 (rounded), as shown in Exhibit 3.11. As with the other intangible assets, the value is determined after deducting an income tax charge and adding an amortization benefit. The asset's remaining useful life is five years, but the survivor curve provides a means to record future amortization consistent with the contribution to cash flows in each year, rather than by the straight-line method.

## In-Process Research and Development

The value of in-process research and development was also estimated using the MPEEM. Similarly to our methodology for valuing the technology, a DCF model was constructed, starting with expected sales based on the technology that was in-process at the valuation date. For simplicity, we are assuming that the IPR&D will be completed in early 2007 and is projected to produce sales of $7,200,000. Sales are further projected to increase in 2008, then decline over time. Similar to the technology valuation, cost of sales was deducted at 40% of sales in 2007, 39% thereafter and operating expenses (20% of sales in 2007, then 19% thereafter [excluding any synergies] and net of development costs, which will no longer occur

**Exhibit 3.11**    Target Company Valuation of Technology as of December 31, 2006 ($000s)

|  | | Actual | | | Forecast | | |
|---|---|---|---|---|---|---|---|
|  | | 2006 | 2007 | 2008 | 2009 | 2010 | 2011 |
| (1) Net Sales-Existing Technology | | $60,000 | $61,800 | $38,192 | $32,782 | $23,636 | $13,911 |
| Cost of Sales | | 24,000 | 24,720 | 14,895 | 12,785 | 9,218 | 5,425 |
| Gross Profit | | 36,000 | 37,080 | 23,297 | 19,997 | 14,418 | 8,486 |
| (2) Operating Expenses | | 12,000 | 12,360 | 7,256 | 6,229 | 4,491 | 2,643 |
| (3) Depreciation | | 1,750 | 2,774 | 2,489 | 1,455 | 751 | 328 |
| Total Operating Expenses | | 13,750 | 15,134 | 9,745 | 7,684 | 5,242 | 2,971 |
| Taxable Income | | 22,250 | 21,946 | 13,552 | 12,313 | 9,176 | 5,515 |
| Income Taxes | 40.0% | 8,900 | 8,778 | 5,421 | 4,925 | 3,670 | 2,206 |
| Net Income | | $13,350 | 13,168 | 8,131 | 7,388 | 5,506 | 3,309 |
| (4) Residual Cash Flow Attributable to Technology | | | | | | | |
| Less: Returns on | | | | | | | |
| Net Working Capital | 5.0% | | 601 | 268 | 232 | 169 | 100 |
| Land and Building | 7.0% | | 1,375 | 735 | 558 | 365 | 195 |
| Machinery and Equipment, net | 8.0% | | 1,279 | 560 | 320 | 161 | 68 |
| Software | 17.0% | | 1,084 | 583 | 444 | 291 | 156 |
| Trade Name | 16.0% | | 1,814 | 975 | 744 | 488 | 261 |
| Noncompete Agreement | 16.0% | | 390 | 209 | 160 | 0 | 0 |
| Assembled Workforce | 16.0% | | 257 | 138 | 105 | 69 | 37 |
| Customer Base | 17.0% | | 1,080 | 580 | 443 | 290 | 155 |
| Sum of Returns | | | 7,880 | 4,048 | 3,006 | 1,833 | 972 |
| After-tax Residual Cash Flows | | | $5,288 | $4,083 | $4,382 | $3,673 | $2,337 |
| (5) 18.0% Present Value Factor for | | | 0.9206 | 0.7801 | 0.6611 | 0.5603 | 0.4748 |
| Residual Cash Flow | | | | | | | |
| Present Value of Residual Cash Flows | | | $4,868 | $3,185 | $2,897 | $2,058 | $1,110 |
| Sum of Present Values, 2007–2011 | | | $14,118 | | | | |
| Amortization Benefit | | | | | | | |
| Discount Rate | 18.0% | | | | | | |
| Tax Rate | 40.0% | | | | | | |
| Tax Amortization Period (Years) | 15 | | | | | | |
| Amortization Benefit | | | | 2,443 | | | |
| **Fair Value of Technology, Rounded** | | | | **$16,560** | | | |

Footnotes:
(1) Sales attributable to the existing technology, which are 100% of company sales in 2006, are projected to decline over time as the technology becomes obsolete and competitors increasingly impact sales.
(2) Excludes development expenses of 10% to reflect that developed technology should not be burdened by the expense of developing new technology.
(3) MACRS depreciation per Business Enterprise Analysis (BEA) - Cash Flow Forecast (Exhibit 3.5) allocated by relative net sales between Technology and IPR&D
(4) See Calculation of Contributory Asset Charges (Exhibit 3.10)
(5) Based on mid-period assumption

Note: Some amounts may not foot due to rounding.

relative to this technology). The useful life of the IPR&D was estimated to be six years. In addition, estimated contributory asset charges (see previous section) were taken, including charges on the customer base.

It is assumed for purposes of this example that the IPR&D is a brand-new, stand-alone technology not supported by the base or core technology, defined as technology that has value through its use or continued reuse within a product family.[17] If an IPR&D project is supported by a core or base technology, a contributory charge must be assessed. The sum of the present values is $3,911,000. We selected a discount rate of 20% to reflect the additional risk of the unproven technology. A six-year remaining useful life was estimated. After accounting for the amortization benefit, we concluded that the fair value of the IPR&D as of December 31, 2006 was $4,530,000 (Exhibit 3.12).[18]

## Customer Base

The customer base was also judged to be an important value driver, and the MPEEM was employed to value this asset. Because the value of the customer base is critically dependent on the company's technology, both existing and in-process (it's all they have to sell, after all), a contributory asset charge is taken on the technology assets when valuing the customer base. As part of the cash flow projection, a remaining useful life was estimated to be seven years, based on an analysis of sales statistics over a five-year historical period. The seven-year life produces a survivor curve whose survivorship is forecast to decline on a straight-line basis.

Using a discount rate of 17%, the sum of the present values of the cash flows is $6,004,000. After adding an amortization benefit, the fair value of this asset is determined to be $7,090,000 (rounded) (Exhibit 3.13).

## VALUATION OF GOODWILL

In the valuation of a successful business enterprise, there are often intangible assets that cannot be separately identified. These intangible assets are generally referred to as goodwill. The term *goodwill,* however, is sometimes used to describe the aggregate of all of the intangible assets of a business. In a more restricted sense, goodwill is the sum total of only the imponderable qualities that attract future new customers to the business.

In the final analysis, goodwill equates with a rate of return that is above normal returns in the industry, limited to the residual intangible asset that generates earnings in excess of a normal return on all of the other tangible and intangible assets. The present value of future cash flows contributing to goodwill at the time of acquisition can be calculated by summing the future excess earnings, then discounting to present value. Assuming all of the tangible and intangible assets have been identified and valued at the acquisition date, this process is simplified by use of the residual method. Under the residual method, the present value of the future excess earnings, or goodwill, is calculated by subtracting from the purchase price the fair value of all the identified

**Exhibit 3.12**   Target Company Valuation of In-Process Research and Development (IPR&D) as of December 31, 2006 ($000s)

|  |  | Forecast | | | | | |
| --- | --- | --- | --- | --- | --- | --- | --- |
|  |  | 2007 | 2008 | 2009 | 2010 | 2011 | 2012 |
| (1) Net Sales-IPR&D |  | $7,200 | $12,557 | $11,853 | $10,733 | $7,692 | $4,447 |
| Cost of Sales |  | 2,880 | 4,897 | 4,623 | 4,186 | 3,000 | 1,734 |
| Gross Profit |  | 4,320 | 7,660 | 7,230 | 6,547 | 4,692 | 2,713 |
| (2) Operating Expenses |  | 1,440 | 2,386 | 2,252 | 2,039 | 1,461 | 845 |
| (3) Cost to Complete |  | 750 | 0 | 0 | 0 | 0 | 0 |
| (4) Depreciation |  | 323 | 818 | 526 | 341 | 181 | 101 |
| Total Operating Expenses |  | 2,513 | 3,204 | 2,778 | 2,380 | 1,642 | 946 |
| Taxable Income |  | 1,807 | 4,456 | 4,452 | 4,167 | 3,050 | 1,767 |
| Income Taxes | 40.0% | 723 | 1,782 | 1,781 | 1,667 | 1,220 | 707 |
| Net Income |  | 1,084 | 2,674 | 2,671 | 2,500 | 1,830 | 1,060 |
| Residual Cash Flow Attributable to IPR&D |  |  |  |  |  |  |  |
| (5) Less: Returns on |  |  |  |  |  |  |  |
| Debt-free Net Working Capital | 5.0% | 70 | 88 | 84 | 77 | 55 | 32 |
| Land and Building | 7.0% | 160 | 242 | 202 | 166 | 108 | 58 |
| Machinery and Equipment, net | 8.0% | 149 | 184 | 116 | 73 | 37 | 16 |
| Software | 17.0% | 126 | 192 | 161 | 132 | 86 | 46 |
| Trade Name | 16.0% | 211 | 321 | 269 | 221 | 144 | 78 |
| Noncompete Agreement | 16.0% | 45 | 69 | 58 | 0 | 0 | 0 |
| Assembled Workforce | 16.0% | 30 | 45 | 38 | 31 | 20 | 11 |
| Customer Base | 17.0% | 126 | 191 | 160 | 132 | 86 | 46 |
| Sum of Returns |  | 917 | 1,332 | 1,088 | 832 | 536 | 287 |
| After-tax Residual Cash Flows |  | $167 | $1,342 | $1,583 | $1,668 | $1,294 | $773 |
| (6) 20.0% Present Value Factor for Residual Cash Flow |  | 0.9129 | 0.7607 | 0.6339 | 0.5283 | 0.4402 | 0.3669 |
| Present Value of Residual Cash Flows |  | $152 | $1,021 | $1,004 | $881 | $570 | $284 |
| Sum of Present Values, 2007–2012 |  | $3,911 |  |  |  |  |  |
| Amortization Benefit |  |  |  |  |  |  |  |
| Discount Rate | 20.0% |  |  |  |  |  |  |
| Tax Rate | 40.0% |  |  |  |  |  |  |
| Tax Amortization Period (Years) | 15 |  |  |  |  |  |  |
| Amortization Benefit |  | 619 |  |  |  |  |  |
| **Fair Value of IPR&D, Rounded** |  | **$4,530** |  |  |  |  |  |

Footnotes:

(1) Based on Management's forecast

(2) Excludes development expenses of 10% to reflect no future development costs relative to this technology.

(3) The cost to complete is typicaly known with certainty and cannot be avoided. With IPR&D, one often does not know if the project will be successful until the amounts are spent. Thus, some practitioners separately calculate the present value of inflows and the present value of outflows. We have elected to present the single calculation here, for simplicity and because the alternative treatment does not result in a materially different conclusion of value.

(4) MACRS depreciation per Business Enterprise Analysis (BEA) - Cash Flow Forecast (Exhibit 3.5) allocated by relative net sales between Technology and IPR&D

(5) See Calculation of Contributory Asset Charges (Exhibit 3.10)

(6) Based on mid-period assumption

Note: Some amounts may not foot due to rounding.

**Exhibit 3.13**   Target Company Valuation of Customer Base as of December 31, 2006 ($000s)

| Cash Flows | Actual | | | Projections | | | | |
|---|---|---|---|---|---|---|---|---|
| | 2006 | 2007 | 2008 | 2009 | 2010 | 2011 | 2012 | 2013 |
| (1) Net Sales-Existing Customers | $60,000 | $63,000 | $66,150 | $69,458 | $72,931 | $76,578 | $80,407 | $84,427 |
| Cost of Sales | 24,000 | 25,200 | 25,799 | 27,089 | 28,443 | 29,865 | 31,359 | 32,927 |
| Gross Profit | 36,000 | 37,800 | 40,352 | 42,369 | 44,488 | 46,713 | 49,048 | 51,500 |
| (2) Operating Expenses | 12,000 | 14,490 | 14,553 | 15,281 | 16,045 | 16,847 | 17,690 | 18,574 |
| Depreciation (MACRS) | 1,750 | 3,097 | 5,171 | 3,961 | 3,120 | 2,544 | 2,649 | 2,762 |
| Total Operating Expenses | 13,750 | 17,587 | 19,724 | 19,242 | 19,165 | 19,391 | 20,338 | 21,336 |
| Taxable Income | 22,250 | 20,213 | 20,628 | 23,127 | 25,323 | 27,321 | 28,710 | 30,164 |
| Income Taxes           40.0% | 8,900 | 8,085 | 8,251 | 9,251 | 10,129 | 10,929 | 11,484 | 12,066 |
| Net Income | $13,350 | 12,128 | 12,377 | 13,876 | 15,194 | 16,393 | 17,226 | 18,099 |

| Residual Cash Flow Attributable to Existing Customer Base | | | | | | | | |
|---|---|---|---|---|---|---|---|---|
| (3) Less: Returns on | | | | | | | | |
| Debt-free Net Working Capital | 5.0% | 671 | 556 | 632 | 703 | 773 | 840 | 904 |
| Land and Building | 7.0% | 1,535 | 1,527 | 1,520 | 1,515 | 1,511 | 1,507 | 1,505 |
| Machinery and Equipment, net | 8.0% | 1,428 | 1,164 | 872 | 668 | 527 | 410 | 290 |
| Software | 17.0% | 1,210 | 1,210 | 1,210 | 1,210 | 1,210 | 1,210 | 1,210 |
| Trade Name | 16.0% | 2,026 | 2,026 | 2,026 | 2,026 | 2,026 | 2,026 | 2,026 |
| Noncompete Agreement | 16.0% | 435 | 435 | 435 | 0 | 0 | 0 | 0 |
| Assembled Workforce | 16.0% | 286 | 286 | 286 | 286 | 286 | 286 | 286 |
| Technology | 18.0% | 2,981 | 2,981 | 2,981 | 2,981 | 2,981 | 2,981 | 2,981 |
| IPR&D | 20.0% | 906 | 906 | 906 | 906 | 906 | 906 | 906 |
| Sum of Returns | | 11,479 | 11,092 | 10,869 | 10,295 | 10,220 | 10,167 | 10,108 |
| After-tax Residual Cash Flows | | $649 | $1,285 | $3,008 | $4,899 | $6,173 | $7,059 | $7,990 |
| (4) Survivorship of Customer Base, Rounded | | 92.9% | 78.6% | 64.3% | 50.0% | 35.7% | 21.4% | 7.1% |
| Surviving Excess Cash Flows | | $603 | $1,010 | $1,934 | $2,450 | $2,204 | $1,511 | $567 |
| (5) 17.0% Present Value Factor for Residual Cash Flow | | 0.9245 | 0.7902 | 0.6754 | 0.5772 | 0.4934 | 0.4217 | 0.3604 |
| Present Value of Surviving Residual Cash Flows | | $557 | $798 | $1,306 | $1,414 | $1,087 | $637 | $204 |
| Sum of Present Values, 2007–2013 | | $6,004 | | | | | | |
| Amortization Benefit | | | | | | | | |
| Discount Rate | 17.0% | | | | | | | |
| Tax Rate | 40.0% | | | | | | | |
| Tax Amortization Period (Years) | 15 | | | | | | | |
| Amortization Benefit | | 1,089 | | | | | | |
| **Fair Value of Customer Base, Rounded** | | **$7,090** | | | | | | |

Footnotes:

(1) Assumes existing sales to existing customers will increase at a rate of 5% (to account for inflation and some real growth), before considering attrition.

(2) Excludes expenses of 7% for the solicitation of potential new customers to reflect that existing customers should not be burdened by the expense of developing new customers.

(3) See Calculation of Contributory Asset Charges (Exhibit 3.10)

(4) Assumes 7-year life, straight line (survivorship analysis per management)

(5) Based on mid-period assumption

Note: Some amounts may not foot due to rounding.

**Exhibit 3.14**  Target Company Valuation of Goodwill as of December 31, 2006 ($000s)

| | |
|---|---|
| Cash and Acquisition Costs | $150,000 |
| Debt-free Current Liabilities | 25,000 |
| Current Maturities of Long-term Debt | 4,000 |
| Long-term Debt | 30,000 |
| | |
| Adjusted Purchase Price | 209,000 |
| Less: Fair Value of Current Assets | (41,500) |
| Less: Fair Value of Tangible Assets | (41,000) |
| Less: Fair Value of Intangible Assets | |
|   Software | (7,120) |
|   Technology | (16,560) |
|   In-process Research and Development | (4,530) |
|   Trade Name | (12,660) |
|   Customer Base | (7,090) |
|   Noncompete Agreement | (2,720) |
| | |
| (1) **Residual Goodwill** | **$75,820** |

Footnote:
(1) Residual Goodwill includes the value of Assembled Workforce of $1.790 million.
Note: Some amounts may not foot due to rounding.

tangible and intangible assets. The remainder or residual amount equates with good-will. Keep in mind that under GAAP, goodwill includes assembled workforce, which must be separately valued to obtain a valid contributory charge for IPR&D, technology, and customer base. As a result and pursuant to SFAS No. 141, the indicated value of assembled workforce must be added to the indicated value of goodwill to arrive at the fair value of goodwill for financial statement reporting purposes.[19]

For financial reporting purposes, included in the goodwill value is the fair value of the assembled workforce of $1,790,000. Based on our analysis, we concluded that the fair value of goodwill on December 31, 2006, was $75,820,000 (see Exhibit 3.14).

## ALLOCATION OF PURCHASE PRICE

The summary of values is presented in Exhibit 3.15. In this exhibit, the valuation conclusions are separated into three groups: total current and tangible assets, total intangible assets, and goodwill. Individual asset valuations are presented within each group.

In addition to presenting the summary of values, this schedule provides a sanity check in the form of a weighted return calculation. The weighted return calculation employs the rate of return for each asset weighted according to its fair value relative to the whole. The weighted return must equal or approximate the overall WACC for the business.

**Exhibit 3.15**    Target Company Valuation Summary as of December 31, 2006 ($000s)

| | Fair Value | Return | Percent to Purchase Price | Weighted Return |
|---|---|---|---|---|
| **ASSET NAME** | | | | |
| Current Assets | $41,500 | | | |
| Debt-free Current Liabilities | 25,000 | | | |
| Net Working Capital | 16,500 | 5.00% | 9.0% | 0.45% |
| Land and Buildings | 22,000 | 7.00% | 12.0% | 0.84% |
| Machinery and Equipment, net | 19,000 | 8.00% | 10.3% | 0.83% |
| TOTAL NET WORKING CAPITAL AND TANGIBLE ASSETS | $57,500 | | | |
| Software | $7,120 | 17.00% | 3.9% | 0.66% |
| Technology | 16,560 | 18.00% | 9.0% | 1.62% |
| In-process Research and Development | 4,530 | 20.00% | 2.5% | 0.49% |
| Trade Name | 12,660 | 16.00% | 6.9% | 1.10% |
| Customer Base | 7,090 | 17.00% | 3.9% | 0.66% |
| Assembled Workforce | 1,790 | 16.00% | 1.0% | 0.16% |
| Noncompete Agreement | 2,720 | 16.00% | 1.5% | 0.24% |
| TOTAL INTANGIBLE ASSETS | $52,470 | | | |
| (1) GOODWILL (excluding assembled workforce) | $74,030 | 23.00% | 40.2% | 9.25% |
| TOTAL | $184,000 | | | 16.28% |

Footnote:
(1) For financial reporting purposes, the fair value of goodwill includes the fair value of assembled workforce for a total fair value of residual goodwill of $75.820 million.
Note: Some amounts may not foot due to rounding.

The returns for each asset are those actually used in the foregoing valuation methodology (i.e., for tangible assets and contributory intangible assets). For contributory intangible assets that were valued using a form of the income approach (trade name and noncompete agreement), the return is equal to the discount rate used to value that asset. Finally, the return for the assets valued under the excess earnings approach is also their discount rate.

It should be clear that the one asset that does not have a return is goodwill, and, admittedly, the return assigned is determined by trial and error. Essentially, the goodwill return is imputed based on determination of the overall weighted return needed to equal the WACC. By its nature, goodwill is the riskiest asset of the group, and therefore should require a return much higher than the overall business return. If a goodwill return of, say, 10% is required to achieve a weighted return of approximately 16%, this signals a problem, and the analyst will have to go back and review and revise his or her work—something is wrong! Thus, in this calculation, the goodwill return of 23% suggests that goodwill is substantially riskier than all of the other assets, but, at a return of 23%, it is still well within reason for a proven going concern. Thus, we are satisfied that the returns chosen for each asset are reasonable.

## CASE STUDY 2: IMPAIRMENT UNDER SFAS NO. 142

SFAS No. 142 requires goodwill (and other indefinitely lived intangibles) to be tested at least annually for impairment. The first step of the two-step impairment test, used to identify potential impairment, compares the fair value of the reporting unit with its carrying amount, including goodwill.[20] If the carrying value of the reporting unit exceeds its fair value, step two is triggered. The second step of the goodwill impairment test requires determining the amount of goodwill impairment associated with the impairment of the fair value of the reporting unit.[21] All long-lived assets must be tested for impairment before the goodwill impairment test. Step two involves preparing what amounts to a new purchase price allocation, and it is possible that, if the fair value of the reporting unit is impaired, some of the recorded asset fair values may also be impaired.

In this section an impairment test is presented, assumed to be one year later, of the entity valued in Case Study 1: Determining Goodwill and Other Intangible Assets in a Business Combination. In this example, the reporting unit and the business enterprise are the same; thus, the impairment test is done at the enterprise level. Larger companies will have multiple reporting units that must be separately analyzed. Our sample company is private, and we have determined that the best tool available is a DCF.

Obviously, the universe of acquired and acquirees is not limited to private companies. If the reporting entity is public, the first thing management is going to look at is the stock price. Certainly, a material decline in a company's stock price may indicate something is amiss and may be evidence enough to trigger step one of the impairment test—determining the total impairment of the reporting unit. Many public companies may observe a decline in their stock price between the two dates, but it is not sufficient to simply quantify the price decline of the stock and conclude that is the impairment amount. The reporting unit must be analyzed in detail to determine permanent impairment. A decline in the stock price may indicate something is wrong, but further analysis must be performed to determine how much, if any, of the impairment is permanent or temporary.

Chapter 2 discusses the types of events that might indicate impairment of the fair value of the reporting unit. This example is presented to acquaint the reader with the mechanics of SFAS No. 142 impairment testing. While the initial triggers indicating step two may differ depending on whether the company is public or private (a material decline in the stock price for the former and an analysis of business fundamentals for the latter), the mechanics of impairment testing will be similar, with the primary difference being that private companies, lacking a readily ascertainable stock price, will place greater reliance on DCF or perhaps guideline company analyses for step one testing. For step two, both public and private company valuations will rely primarily on traditional methodologies (SFAS No. 157 Level 3 Hierarchy) such as the DCF.

Returning to the example, one area of inquiry is to compare 2007 actual with the 2007 forecast performed last year in conjunction with the purchase price analysis. As can be seen, actual operating results for 2007 lag well behind the forecast performed a year ago.

|                    | 2006 Actual  | 2007 Forecast | 2007 Actual  |
|--------------------|--------------|---------------|--------------|
| Net Sales          | $60,000,000  | $69,000,000   | $56,000,000  |
| Cost of Sales      | 24,000,000   | 27,600,000    | 23,520,000   |
| Percent of Sales   | 40.0%        | 40.0%         | 42.0%        |
| Gross Profit       | $36,000,000  | $41,400,000   | $32,480,000  |
| Operating Expenses | 18,000,000   | 20,700,000    | 17,360,000   |
| EBITDA             | 18,000,000   | 20,700,000    | 15,120,000   |
| EBITDA Percent     | 30.0%        | 30.0%         | 27.0%        |

While still profitable, the reporting unit's earnings before interest, taxes, depreciation, and amortization (EBITDA) were $15,120,000, 16% below 2006 actual EBITDA and 27% below the 2007 forecast. This information certainly suggests that the reporting unit's value may be impaired, and we shall proceed with step one of the impairment study—determining the fair value of the reporting unit and comparing that value with its carrying amount.[22] If the carrying amount of a reporting unit exceeds its fair value, the second step of the goodwill impairment test is performed to measure the amount of goodwill impairment loss, if any.[23]

We suspect that impairment exists; now the challenge is to determine the fair value of the reporting unit as of the current date, December 31, 2007. Quoted market prices in active markets are considered the best evidence of fair value,[24] but the statement allows that present value techniques are often the best. In our example, the carrying value of the reporting unit exceeds its fair value, triggering step two.

If a reporting unit fails step one, the interrelationship between SFAS Nos. 142 and 144, *Accounting for the Impairment or Disposal of Long-Lived Assets,* can be a little confusing and warrants comment. SFAS No. 144 states:

> An impairment loss shall be recognized only if the carrying amount of a long-lived asset (asset group) is not recoverable and exceeds its fair value. The carrying amount of a long-lived asset (asset group) is not recoverable if it exceeds the sum of the undiscounted cash flows expected to result from the use and eventual disposition of the asset (asset group).[25]

SFAS No. 144 provides guidance as to when to test for recoverability:

> A long-lived asset (asset group) shall be tested for recoverability whenever events or changes in circumstances indicate that its carrying amount may not be recoverable.[26]

If goodwill and other assets are tested for impairment at the same time, the other assets are to be tested for impairment before goodwill.[27] The relatively poor financial performance described previously would probably be reason enough to test the recoverability of long-lived assets under paragraphs 7 and 8 of SFAS No. 144. As will be seen later, the noncompete and customer base assets would pass the recoverability test, which compares the assets' undiscounted cash flows with carrying values, but the technology asset would fail.

SFAS No. 144 contains similar language to SFAS No. 142 regarding the determination of fair value, stating a preference for quoted market prices but allowing other valuation techniques.[28] In our example, and surely most other situations, quoted market prices for intangibles will not be available (SFAS No. 157, Levels 1 and 2), requiring other techniques (SFAS No. 157, Level 3) as would be developed in an SFAS No. 142 step two analysis.

Additionally, impairment testing of intangible assets not subject to amortization is covered by SFAS No. 142, not SFAS No. 144. In reality, while SFAS No. 142 requires, "If goodwill and another asset . . . are tested for impairment at the same time, the other asset. . .shall be tested before goodwill,"[29] impairment testing under SFAS Nos. 142 and 144 will be performed simultaneously in most cases, but the final conclusion of goodwill will be determined subject to any revaluations of other assets.

As described in Case Study 1, a year ago the fair value of the assets of the reporting unit was determined to be $209,000,000. Now, after a year's depreciation, amortization (assuming MACRS-based depreciation for the depreciable tangible assets and straight-line amortization for the amortizable intangible assets), and the SFAS No. 2 charge for acquired in-process research and development, the carrying amount of the assets of the reporting unit is $188,713,000, as follows:

|  | December 31, 2006 Fair Value | December 31, 2007 Carrying Amount |
|---|---|---|
| Cash | $1,500,000 | $2,850,000 |
| Investments in Marketable Securities | 8,000,000 | 7,000,000 |
| Accounts Receivable | 17,000,000 | 13,000,000 |
| Inventory | 12,000,000 | 10,500,000 |
| Prepaid Expenses | 3,000,000 | 2,500,000 |
| Total Current Assets | 41,500,000 | 35,850,000 |
| Land and Building | 22,000,000 | 21,687,000 |
| Machinery and Equipment, net | 19,000,000 | 16,216,000 |
| Total Fixed Assets | 41,000,000 | 37,903,000 |
| Software | 7,120,000 | 5,340,000 |
| Technology | 16,560,000 | 13,250,000 |
| In-process Research and Development | 4,530,000 | 0 |
| Trade Name | 12,660,000 | 12,660,000 |
| Customer Base | 7,090,000 | 6,080,000 |

| | | |
|---|---|---|
| Noncompete Agreement | 2,720,000 | 1,810,000 |
| Total Identifiable Intangible Assets | 50,680,000 | 39,140,000 |
| Goodwill (Including Assembled Workforce) | 75,820,000 | 75,820,000 |
| Total Assets | $209,000,000 | $188,713,000 |

To recap, for the impairment study, step one is to determine the overall fair value of the reporting unit and compare that value with its carrying value. If the carrying value of the reporting unit exceeds the new (current) fair value, impairment is indicated, and we must then proceed to step two and determine the fair value of goodwill and other intangible assets (under SFAS Nos. 142 and 144).

## BUSINESS ENTERPRISE ANALYSIS

SFAS No. 142 requires that an analyst determine fair value first by looking at actual market prices of a company's stock. In this example, the company and reporting unit are the same. Because the company is privately held, no market prices or multiples are readily available. If the company were public, a material decline in the stock price would at least provide the rationale for performing further analysis in the step one test. But, as noted earlier, a decline in the stock price, while an indicator of the potential existence of impairment, may not by itself provide an accurate measure of permanent impairment, depending on the magnitude of the decline. So, for public or private companies, further analysis will be necessary.

The next phase of our analysis is the performance of a BEA as of December 31, 2007. The total fair value of the assets of the reporting unit comprises invested capital, which is the sum of the fair value of equity and interest-bearing debt, plus the fair values of current liabilities, and is equivalent to the fair values of current assets plus fixed and intangible assets. The purpose of the new BEA is to determine the new fair values of invested capital and total assets and to provide a framework for the revaluation of the other assets. SFAS No. 142 requires that the fair value of all of the assets of the reporting unit be determined as of December 31, 2007. However, the only impairment adjustments actually recognized in the financial records are the impairment of goodwill and other non-amortizable intangible assets under SFAS No. 142 and impairment of other long-lived assets under SFAS No. 144. *The excess fair value over the carrying value of recognized intangibles and the fair values of previously unrecognized intangibles, while employed in the calculation of goodwill impairment, are not recorded in the final year-end accounting adjustments.* We begin with a new DCF analysis as of December 31, 2007. The nature and underlying rationale for the DCF assumptions will be discussed throughout this chapter.

## DISCOUNTED CASH FLOW METHOD

In the DCF method using the discount rate adjustment technique, a pro forma analysis is made of the subject company to estimate future available cash flows. *Available cash flow* is the amount that could be paid out to providers of capital without impairment of business operations.

Principal assumptions utilized in developing the estimates of cash flow are:

- As of December 31, 2007, the outlook is less bullish than a year ago. Sales are now forecast to increase from $56,000,000 in 2007 to $58,800,000 in 2008, growth of 5%, based largely on a decline in the growth rate in one of its key markets and a delay in completing the IPR&D project that was in process as of December 31, 2006. A year ago the company was expecting double-digit growth for five years. The growth rate of the key market is still forecast to decline after 2008. The 10-year compound annual growth rate is 6.48%, down approximately 35% from the 10-year growth rate forecast a year ago.

- Operating margins before depreciation and amortization are forecast to decline to 27.5% in 2008, based on increased costs in 2007. Costs and expenses are expected to be brought back in line with the original forecast by 2011. In this forecast, cost of sales and operating expenses exclude depreciation (tax—separately forecast using MACRS tables) and amortization.

- Working capital requirements (debt-free) are still forecast at 15% of sales, based on the company's historical working capital position and projected needs.

- Capital expenditures are forecast at 1% of net sales. This level of capital expenditures is considered adequate to support future levels of sales.

- As discussed earlier, Section 197 of the Internal Revenue Code provides the tax amortization of total intangible asset value over a 15-year period. The amortization acts as a tax shield and is added back to cash flow. Annual amortization is $5,590,000 ($83,850,000 ÷ 15, rounded), as most practitioners believe that, under the fair value standard, the Section 197 amortization of intangible assets should be recalculated assuming an acquisition of the company occurred as of the date of the impairment test, resulting in a new amortization calculation and a new 15-year tax life.[30]

- Other Assumptions:
  - Required Rate of Return    16.00%
  - Residual Growth Rate       5.00%
  - Tax Rate                   40.00%

Assumptions are summarized in Exhibit 3.16, which presents the projected cash flows for a period of ten years.

Cash flows in 2017 were increased by the residual growth rate and then capitalized into perpetuity by the difference between the discount rate and the residual growth rate. This residual value was then discounted to present value to provide the net present value of the residual cash flow. The residual cash flow represents the expected cash flow for 2018 to perpetuity. The present value of the net cash flows, plus the present value of the residual, provides the total capitalized earnings. The BEA is presented in Exhibit 3.17.

**Exhibit 3.16** Target Company Business Enterprise Analysis—Assumptions as of December 31, 2007 ($000s)

|  | Actual | | | | | | Forecast | | | | |
|---|---|---|---|---|---|---|---|---|---|---|---|
|  | 2007 | 2008 | 2009 | 2010 | 2011 | 2012 | 2013 | 2014 | 2015 | 2016 | 2017 |
| **1. SALES** | | | | | | | | | | | |
| *Sales Growth Percentage* |  | *5.0%* | *10.0%* | *10.0%* | *8.0%* | *7.0%* | *5.0%* | *5.0%* | *5.0%* | *5.0%* | *5.0%* |
| Net Sales | $56,000 | $58,800 | $64,680 | $71,148 | $76,840 | $82,219 | $86,330 | $90,646 | $95,178 | $99,937 | $104,934 |
| **2. EXPENSES** | | | | | | | | | | | |
| Cost of Sales | $23,520 | $24,696 | $26,519 | $28,459 | $29,968 | $32,065 | $33,669 | $35,352 | $37,120 | $38,976 | $40,924 |
| *Cost of Sales Percentage* | *42.0%* | *42.0%* | *41.0%* | *40.0%* | *39.0%* | *39.0%* | *39.0%* | *39.0%* | *39.0%* | *39.0%* | *39.0%* |
| Operating Expenses | $17,360 | $17,934 | $19,404 | $21,344 | $22,284 | $23,843 | $25,036 | $26,287 | $27,602 | $28,982 | $30,431 |
| *Operating Expenses Percentage* | *31.0%* | *30.5%* | *30.0%* | *30.0%* | *29.0%* | *29.0%* | *29.0%* | *29.0%* | *29.0%* | *29.0%* | *29.0%* |
| Depreciation (MACRS) | $3,123 | $3,112 | $5,162 | $3,927 | $3,060 | $2,456 | $2,529 | $2,607 | $1,819 | $1,016 | $1,049 |
| *Other Income (Expense), Net Percentage* | *0.0%* | *0.0%* | *0.0%* | *0.0%* | *0.0%* | *0.0%* | *0.0%* | *0.0%* | *0.0%* | *0.0%* | *0.0%* |
| **3. CASH FLOW** | | | | | | | | | | | |
| Capital Expenditures |  | $588 | $647 | $711 | $768 | $822 | $863 | $906 | $952 | $999 | $1,049 |
| *Capital Expenditures Percentage* | *1.0%* | *1.0%* | *1.0%* | *1.0%* | *1.0%* | *1.0%* | *1.0%* | *1.0%* | *1.0%* | *1.0%* | *1.0%* |
| Projected Working Capital as Percent of Sales | 15.0% | | | | | | | | | | |
| (1) Projected Working Capital Balance | $16,150 | $8,820 | $9,702 | $10,672 | $11,526 | $12,333 | $12,949 | $13,597 | $14,277 | $14,991 | $15,740 |
| Projected Working Capital Requirement | | (7,330) | 882 | 970 | 854 | 807 | 617 | 647 | 680 | 714 | 750 |
| **4. OTHER** | | | | | | | | | | | |
| Effective Tax Rate | 40.0% | | | | | | | | | | |
| Required Rate of Return | 16.0% | | | | | | | | | | |
| Residual Growth Rate | 5.0% | | | | | | | | | | |

**AMORTIZATION OF INTANGIBLES**
Assumption: Intangibles receive 15-year tax life per Sec. 197

| Fair Value of Invested Capital | $137,000 |
|---|---|
| Plus: Current Liabilities | 25,000 |

*(continued)*

**Exhibit 3.16** (Continued)

| | |
|---|---|
| Total Fair Value of Assets | 162,000 |
| Less: Current and Tangible Assets | 78,150 |
| Fair Value of Amortizable Intangible Assets | $83,850 |
| Sec. 197 Amortization Period (Years) | 15 |
| (2) Annual Amortization of Intangibles (Pretax) | $5,590 |

Footnotes:

(1) Balance at December 31, 2007 stated at fair value.

(2) Calculated at impairment test date of December 31, 2007. Since we don't have a purchase price at this date, Sec. 197 tax amortization of intangibles is calculated based on the fair value of the enterprise determined here. The enterprise value depends in part on the amortization amount so, to avoid a circular reference in the calculation, the amount must be hard-entered in the BEA and that step repeated until the hard entered amortization amount and the amortization calculated based on the BEA achieve equilibrium.

Note: Some amounts may not foot due to rounding.

The impairment test presented in this example is assumed to be performed as of December 31, 2007.

**Exhibit 3.17** Target Company Business Enterprise Analysis (BEA) — Cash Flow Forecast as of December 31, 2007 ($000s)

| | Actual | | | | | | Forecast | | | | |
|---|---|---|---|---|---|---|---|---|---|---|---|
| | 2007 | 2008 | 2009 | 2010 | 2011 | 2012 | 2013 | 2014 | 2015 | 2016 | 2017 |
| Sales Growth Percentage | | 5.0% | 10.0% | 10.0% | 8.0% | 7.0% | 5.0% | 5.0% | 5.0% | 5.0% | 5.0% |
| Net Sales | $56,000 | $58,800 | $64,680 | $71,148 | $76,840 | $82,219 | $86,330 | $90,646 | $95,178 | $99,937 | $104,934 |
| Cost of Sales | 23,520 | 24,696 | 26,519 | 28,459 | 29,968 | 32,065 | 33,669 | 35,352 | 37,120 | 38,976 | 40,924 |
| Gross Profit | 32,480 | 34,104 | 38,161 | 42,689 | 46,872 | 50,153 | 52,661 | 55,294 | 58,059 | 60,962 | 64,010 |
| Operating Expenses | 17,360 | 17,934 | 19,404 | 21,344 | 22,284 | 23,843 | 25,036 | 26,287 | 27,602 | 28,982 | 30,431 |
| Depreciation (MACRS) | 3,123 | 3,112 | 5,162 | 3,927 | 3,060 | 2,456 | 2,529 | 2,607 | 1,819 | 1,016 | 1,049 |
| Amortization of Intangibles (Tax) | 5,590 | 5,590 | 5,590 | 5,590 | 5,590 | 5,590 | 5,590 | 5,590 | 5,590 | 5,590 | 5,590 |
| Total Operating Expenses | 26,073 | 26,636 | 30,156 | 30,861 | 30,933 | 31,889 | 33,154 | 34,484 | 35,010 | 35,588 | 37,070 |
| Taxable Income | 6,407 | 7,468 | 8,005 | 11,828 | 15,939 | 18,264 | 19,507 | 20,810 | 23,048 | 25,374 | 26,940 |
| Income Taxes | 2,563 | 2,987 | 3,202 | 4,731 | 6,376 | 7,306 | 7,803 | 8,324 | 9,219 | 10,150 | 10,776 |
| Net Income | $3,844 | $4,481 | $4,803 | $7,097 | $9,564 | $10,958 | $11,704 | $12,486 | $13,829 | $15,224 | $16,164 |
| Net Cash Flow | | | | | | | | | | | |
| Net Income | | $4,481 | $4,803 | $7,097 | $9,564 | $10,958 | $11,704 | $12,486 | $13,829 | $15,224 | $16,164 |
| Capital Expenditures | | (588) | (647) | (711) | (768) | (822) | (863) | (906) | (952) | (999) | (1,049) |
| Change in Working Capital | | 7,330 | (882) | (970) | (854) | (807) | (617) | (647) | (680) | (714) | (750) |
| Depreciation | | 3,112 | 5,162 | 3,927 | 3,060 | 2,456 | 2,529 | 2,607 | 1,819 | 1,016 | 1,049 |
| Amortization of Intangibles (Tax) | | 5,590 | 5,590 | 5,590 | 5,590 | 5,590 | 5,590 | 5,590 | 5,590 | 5,590 | 5,590 |
| Net Cash Flow | | $19,925 | $14,026 | $14,932 | $16,591 | $17,375 | $18,343 | $19,129 | $19,606 | $20,117 | $21,004 |
| (1) Present Value Factor, where Discount Rate | 16.0% | 0.9285 | 0.8004 | 0.6900 | 0.5948 | 0.5128 | 0.4421 | 0.3811 | 0.3285 | 0.2832 | 0.2441 |
| Present Value of Net Cash Flow | | $18,500 | $11,226 | $10,303 | $9,868 | $8,910 | $8,109 | $7,290 | $6,441 | $5,697 | $5,127 |

(continued)

**Exhibit 3.17** (Continued)

| | 2018 | 2019 | 2020 | 2021 | 2022 |
|---|---|---|---|---|---|
| Amortization of Intangibles (Pretax) | $5,590 | $5,590 | $5,590 | $5,590 | $5,590 |
| Tax Benefit of Amortization 40.0% | $2,236 | $2,236 | $2,236 | $2,236 | $2,236 |
| (1) Present Value Factor | 0.2105 | 0.1814 | 0.1564 | 0.1348 | 0.1162 |
| Present Value of Tax Benefit | $471 | $406 | $350 | $301 | $260 |
| Sum = Fair Value of Tax Benefit | $1,788 | | | | |

| | | |
|---|---|---|
| 2017 Taxable Income | | $26,940 |
| Plus: Intangible Asset Amortization | | 5,590 |
| 2017 Adjusted Taxable Income | | 32,530 |
| Less: Income Taxes | 40.0% | 13,012 |
| 2017 Adjusted Net Income | | $19,518 |
| 2018 Adjusted Net Income, Growth | 5.0% | $20,494 |
| Less: 2018 Working Capital Provision | | (787) |
| 2018 Adjusted Cash Flow | | $19,707 |
| Residual Cap. Rate, Perpetual Growth | 5.0% | 11.00% |
| Residual Value, 2018 | | $179,155 |
| (1) Present Value Factor | | 0.2441 |
| Present Value of Residual Cash Flow | | $43,732 |
| Present Value of Net Cash Flow, 2008–2017 | | $91,471 |
| Present Value of Residual Cash Flow | | 43,732 |
| Present Value of Amortization Tax Benefit, 2018–2022 | | 1,788 |
| **Total Invested Capital, Rounded** | | **$137,000** |

Footnote:
Based on mid-period assumption
Note: Some amounts may not foot due to rounding.
The impairment test presented in this example is assumed to be performed as of December 31, 2007.

## DISCOUNT RATE

The appropriate rate of return in valuing the enterprise (using the discount rate adjustment technique) is the WACC. This rate is typically the weighted average of the return on equity capital and the return on debt capital. The weights represent percentages of debt to total capital and equity to total capital. The rate of return on debt capital is adjusted to reflect the fact that interest payments are tax deductible to the corporation.

As of December 31, 2007, the equity discount rate is assumed to be 22.00%, (rounded), the same as last year (due to the rounding), and the pretax cost of debt 9.00% (borrowing rates generally have gone down). Substituting these values into the WACC formula described in Case Study 1 provides the following:

$$
\begin{aligned}
\text{WACC} &= (22.00\% \times 65.00\%) + (9.00\%[1 - 40.00\%] \times 35.00\%) \\
&= (14.30\%) + (5.40\% \times 35.00\%) \\
&= (14.30\%) + (1.89\%) \\
&= 16.19\%
\end{aligned}
$$

Rounded to, 16%

Applying the cost of capital to cash flows estimated earlier indicates the fair value of the invested capital of Target Company on the valuation date was $137,000,000 (Exhibit 3.17).

## VALUATION OF CURRENT AND TANGIBLE ASSETS

### Current Assets

As discussed in Case Study 1, the valuation of current assets requires cooperation between the analyst and auditor. Certain financial and other current assets are the province of the auditor, and the purchase price allocation should rely in part on audit conclusions for certain assets, such as cash and receivables. Marketable securities must be marked to market, often by simply obtaining brokerage statements. Previously recognized intangibles that represent capitalized historic expenditures, such as organization costs, are typically written off. The actual cash flow associated with these assets occurred in the past, and these assets typically cannot be separated or sold apart from the acquired entity as required under SFAS No. 141. Any other previously recorded intangible value is again subsumed in the current purchase price allocation.

The carrying amounts of the current assets as of December 31, 2007 are as follows:

### Fixed Assets

As has already been pointed out, very few business analysts have the experience and training to operate outside their disciplines to render valuation opinions on fixed assets. Usually, the real estate and personal property must be independently appraised.

| Asset | Carrying Amount |
|---|---|
| Cash | $2,850,000 |
| Marketable Securities | 7,300,000 |
| Accounts Receivable | 13,000,000 |
| Inventory | 10,500,000 |
| Prepaid Expenses | 2,500,000 |
| Total Current Asset Carrying Value | $36,150,000 |

In this example, it is assumed that the real estate appraiser who determined the fair value of the land and improvements to be $22,000,000 performed an update, and the fair value as of December 31, 2007 is $23,000,000. The fair value of the machinery and equipment is assumed to remain unchanged at $19,000,000.

## VALUATION OF INTANGIBLE ASSETS

### Computer Software

In reviewing the Company's software system, we found that two new modules were developed in 2007, and now there are 22 modules, each made up of several programs written in a very sophisticated programming language. The new line count is 332,980, up from 294,980 at December 31, 2006.

The next step is to determine the productivity with which the hypothetical re-creation effort would take place. Again, management assessed a productivity rating of 1 to 3, with the same rates: software rated 1 could be programmed at four lines of code per hour, software rated at 2 could be programmed at three lines of code per hour, and software rated 3, the most complex and difficult, could be programmed at two lines of code per hour.

Coding rates were assigned to the new modules and the calculation done as before. By dividing the lines of code by the coding rate, the number of hours to re-create totaled 126,840 hours for the entire system, up from 112,507 one year ago. The sum of hours was then multiplied by the blended hourly rate (fully burdened) of $125 per hour, an increase over the cost of $119 per hour calculated last year. *Reproduction cost* of the software system was determined by multiplying the total number of hours to re-create by the blended hourly rate. This amount totals $15,855,000.

If the software had been new as of the valuation date, the reproduction cost equates to brand-new software. As before, an obsolescence factor was applied to the reproduction cost to recognize the fact that the acquired software is not brand new. Rather, it may have redundant or extraneous code and likely has been patched over the years and contains other inefficiencies that brand-new software presumably would not have. This year the obsolescence factor is estimated at 25%, as the continued aging of the old modules more than offsets the addition of the new modules. The obsolescence factor brings the *replacement cost* to $11,891,250. This value is then adjusted for taxes to recognize the deductibility of such expenses. The after-tax value is $7,134,750. Added to this amount is an amortization benefit, which reflects the additional value of the ability to deduct the amortization of the asset over its 15-year tax life (for fair value it is assumed the asset is bought in a current transaction and amortized over a new 15-year period).[31] Based on the cost approach, and after adjusting for taxes and amortization benefit, it was concluded that the fair value of the software as of December 31, 2007 was $8,430,000 (rounded) (see Exhibit 3.18). One year later, the remaining useful life of the asset is three years.

As stated earlier, *SFAS No. 144* prohibits recognition of asset appreciation, which may be determined during the course of an impairment analysis. Fair value of the company's software is $8,430,000, which exceeds the carrying value of $5,340,000 ($7,120,000 less one year of straight-line amortization over a four-year life, rounded). Thus, no impairment is recognized. However, the current fair value will be used internally to represent the fair value of the asset for the purpose of assessing contributory asset charges and in the residual goodwill calculation.

## Assembled Workforce

The buyer of Target Company obtained an assembled and trained workforce of 65 employees. As of the date of the impairment test, headcount reductions had reduced the assembled workforce to 54 employees. As before, the cost approach (cost to recreate) was employed to value this asset. Using this method, the costs associated with employee recruitment, selection, and training provide the measurement of value.

Recruiting costs are incurred to obtain a new employee; as before, the average recruiting cost is 27.5% of starting salary. The training costs of an employee reflect the amount of time inefficiently used by a new employee (inefficiency training cost) and the time inefficiently used by a training supervisor (direct training cost) during the first few months on the job. Training costs were estimated by multiplying the fully burdened weekly salary of the employee or supervisor by the average amount of inefficiency incurred during the training period. The inefficiency estimate remains at 33.3%. Interview costs were estimated in the same manner as last year's analysis (shown in Case Study 1).

The summation of the hiring and training costs results in the total cost to replace the assembled workforce, shown in Exhibit 3.19. Based on the cost approach, and after adjusting for taxes at 40% and adding an amortization benefit, the fair value of the assembled workforce is estimated to be $1,510,000 (rounded) at December 31, 2007. No obsolescence is recognized for this asset (Exhibit 3.19).

SFAS No. 141 specifically prohibits the recognition of assembled workforce as an intangible asset apart from goodwill. However, in the application of the excess earnings method, which is used to value the Company's technology, in-process research and development, and customer base, "returns on" are taken on the fair values of all of the contributory assets acquired in the acquisition. The value of the assembled workforce is calculated so that such a return may be taken. However, its fair value is included in goodwill in the final allocation of purchase price.

**Exhibit 3.18**  Target Company Valuation of Acquired Software as of December 31, 2007
All software was developed internally by Target Company for its own use. Rights to the
software were transferred at acquisition.

The software is written in C++ programming language.

Valuation is based on cost to replace less obsolescence. Costs are based on internally developed
Company metrics for software development productivity.

Source: Leonard Riles, Director of Product Development

| In Place | Lines of Code | Productivity Assessment | (1) Rate | Hours to Recreate |
|---|---|---|---|---|
| Module 1 | 26,400 | 2 | 3.0 | 8,800 |
| Module 2 | 32,600 | 3 | 2.0 | 16,300 |
| Module 3 | 46,000 | 1 | 4.0 | 11,500 |
| Module 4 | 8,480 | 3 | 2.0 | 4,240 |
| Module 5 | 12,000 | 3 | 2.0 | 6,000 |
| Module 6 | 12,500 | 2 | 3.0 | 4,167 |
| Module 7 | 2,000 | 2 | 3.0 | 667 |
| Module 8 | 32,000 | 2 | 3.0 | 10,667 |
| Module 9 | 3,000 | 2 | 3.0 | 1,000 |
| Module 10 | 3,000 | 2 | 3.0 | 1,000 |
| Module 11 | 3,000 | 2 | 3.0 | 1,000 |
| Module 12 | 13,000 | 2 | 3.0 | 4,333 |
| Module 13 | 6,000 | 2 | 3.0 | 2,000 |
| Module 14 | 10,000 | 2 | 3.0 | 3,333 |
| Module 15 | 5,000 | 2 | 3.0 | 1,667 |
| Module 16 | 6,000 | 2 | 3.0 | 2,000 |
| Module 17 | 5,000 | 3 | 2.0 | 2,500 |
| Module 18 | 8,000 | 1 | 4.0 | 2,000 |
| Module 19 | 7,000 | 2 | 3.0 | 2,333 |
| Module 20 | 54,000 | 3 | 2.0 | 27,000 |
| Module 21 | 10,000 | 3 | 2.0 | 5,000 |
| Module 22 | 28,000 | 2 | 3.0 | 9,333 |

| | | | | |
|---|---|---|---|---|
| Total Number of Lines | 332,980 | | | |
| Total Number of Hours to Recreate | | | | 126,840 |
| Times: Blended Hourly Rate (see below) | | | | $125 |
| Reproduction Cost | | | | $15,855,000 |
| (2) Less: Obsolescence | | 25.0% | | (3,963,750) |
| Replacement Cost | | | | 11,891,250 |
| Less: Taxes | | 40.0% | | (4,756,500) |
| After-tax Value Before Amortization Benefit | | | | 7,134,750 |

Amortization Benefit

| | |
|---|---|
| Discount Rate | 17.0% |
| Tax Rate | 40.0% |
| Tax Amortization Period (Years) | 15 |

| | |
|---|---|
| Amortization Benefit | 1,294,507 |

| | |
|---|---|
| **Fair Value of Software, Rounded** | **$8,430,000** |

## SOFTWARE DEVELOPMENT COSTS—ESTIMATED PROJECT TEAM

| Function | Number | Burdened Hourly Rate |
|---|---|---|
| Project Manager | 1 | $210.00 |
| Systems Analyst | 2 | 160.00 |
| Technical Writer | 1 | 130.00 |
| Programmer | 4 | 120.00 |
| Support | 2 | 55.00 |
| Blended Hourly Rate, Rounded | | $125.00 |

Footnotes:

(1) Lines of code per hour, based on productivity assessment for average module of programming.

(2) Estimate based on number of lines of redundant/extraneous code, effective age, and remaining economic life of system. Remaining useful life is three years.

Note: Some amounts may not foot due to rounding.

The impairment test presented in this example is assumed to be performed as of December 31, 2007.

## Trademarks/Trade Name

As discussed earlier, Target Company has one valuable trade name. All of the Company's products and services are sold under the "XXX" trade name, and each major product is identified by this trade name.

The relief from royalty method was employed. A royalty rate of 2% is again applicable, stated as a percentage of sales. Applying this same rate to a lower sales forecast obviously results in a lower fair value as of December 31, 2007.

The rights to use the trade name transfer to the buyer in perpetuity, giving it an indefinite life. The fair value of the trade name is the present value of the royalties forecast for the ten-year period of 2008 to 2017, plus the present value of the residual at the end of the ten-year period, plus the amortization benefit. A 16% rate of return was again chosen to reflect a risk assessment that the trade name was about as risky as the business overall.

Based on our analysis as presented in Exhibit 3.20, we concluded that the aggregate fair value of the trade name as of the valuation date was $9,230,000. Because the carrying amount of this asset exceeds the fair value, the asset is

**Exhibit 3.19**  Target Company Valuation of Assembled Workforce as of December 31, 2007

| No. | Job Title | Salary | 20% Benefits | Total | (1) Train. Per. Cl. | (1) Train. Per. Yrs. | 33.3% Cost | (2) 27.5% Recruit. | Interview & H.R. | Total |
|---|---|---|---|---|---|---|---|---|---|---|
| 1 | Member of Technical Staff | $90,000 | $18,000 | $108,000 | 1 | 0.125 | $4,496 | $24,750 | $375 | $29,621 |
| 2 | Member of Technical Staff | 44,953 | 8,991 | 53,944 | 1 | 0.125 | 2,245 | 12,362 | 375 | 14,982 |
| 3 | Member of Operations Staff | 71,641 | 14,328 | 85,969 | 1 | 0.125 | 3,578 | 19,701 | 375 | 23,654 |
| 4 | Account Executive | 91,170 | 18,234 | 109,404 | 1 | 0.125 | 4,554 | 25,072 | 375 | 30,001 |
| 5 | Member of Technical Staff | 107,888 | 21,578 | 129,466 | 2 | 0.375 | 16,167 | 29,669 | 750 | 46,586 |
| 6 | Member of Technical Staff | 33,244 | 6,649 | 39,893 | 1 | 0.125 | 1,661 | 9,142 | 375 | 11,178 |
| 7 | Vice President | 142,000 | 28,400 | 170,400 | 2 | 0.375 | 21,279 | 39,050 | 750 | 61,079 |
| 8 | Member of Technical Staff | 83,647 | 16,729 | 100,376 | 2 | 0.375 | 12,535 | 23,003 | 750 | 36,288 |
| 9 | Member of Operations Staff | 104,700 | 20,940 | 125,640 | 1 | 0.125 | 5,230 | 28,793 | 375 | 34,398 |
| 10 | Chief Architect | 155,500 | 31,100 | 186,600 | 3 | 0.750 | 46,603 | 42,763 | 1,500 | 90,866 |
| 11 | Director of Development | 135,000 | 27,000 | 162,000 | 2 | 0.375 | 20,230 | 37,125 | 750 | 58,105 |
| 12 | Member of Technical Staff | 77,772 | 15,554 | 93,326 | 2 | 0.375 | 11,654 | 21,387 | 750 | 33,791 |
| 13 | Account Executive | 94,950 | 18,990 | 113,940 | 1 | 0.125 | 4,743 | 26,111 | 375 | 31,229 |
| 14 | Member of Technical Staff | 81,300 | 16,260 | 97,560 | 1 | 0.125 | 4,061 | 22,358 | 375 | 26,794 |
| 15 | Chief Executive Officer | 250,000 | 50,000 | 300,000 | 1 | 0.125 | 12,488 | 68,750 | 375 | 81,613 |
| 16 | Member of Technical Staff | 82,000 | 16,400 | 98,400 | 2 | 0.375 | 12,288 | 22,550 | 750 | 35,588 |
| 17 | Member of Technical Staff | 57,460 | 11,492 | 68,952 | 1 | 0.125 | 2,870 | 15,802 | 375 | 19,047 |
| 18 | Account Executive | 106,400 | 21,280 | 127,680 | 2 | 0.375 | 15,944 | 29,260 | 750 | 45,954 |
| 19 | Member of Technical Staff | 107,867 | 21,573 | 129,440 | 2 | 0.375 | 16,164 | 29,663 | 750 | 46,577 |
| 20 | Member of Technical Staff | 110,000 | 22,000 | 132,000 | 3 | 0.750 | 32,967 | 30,250 | 1,500 | 64,717 |
| 21 | Vice President of American Sales | 135,000 | 27,000 | 162,000 | 2 | 0.375 | 20,230 | 37,125 | 750 | 58,105 |
| 22 | Member of Technical Staff | 114,500 | 22,900 | 137,400 | 1 | 0.125 | 5,719 | 31,488 | 375 | 37,582 |
| 23 | Member of Technical Staff | 47,028 | 9,406 | 56,434 | 1 | 0.125 | 2,349 | 12,933 | 375 | 15,657 |
| 24 | Account Executive | 90,660 | 18,132 | 108,792 | 1 | 0.125 | 4,528 | 24,932 | 375 | 29,835 |

| # | Title | | | | | | | | |
|---|---|---|---|---|---|---|---|---|---|
| 25 | Member of Technical Staff | 63,329 | 12,666 | 75,995 | 1 | 0.125 | 3,163 | 17,415 | 375 | 20,953 |
| 26 | Member of Operations Staff | 131,000 | 26,200 | 157,200 | 1 | 0.125 | 6,543 | 36,025 | 375 | 42,943 |
| 27 | Chief Financial Officer | 150,000 | 30,000 | 180,000 | 1 | 0.125 | 7,493 | 41,250 | 375 | 49,118 |
| 28 | Member of Technical Staff | 100,210 | 20,042 | 120,252 | 2 | 0.375 | 15,016 | 27,558 | 750 | 43,324 |
| 29 | Member of Technical Staff | 87,372 | 17,474 | 104,846 | 2 | 0.375 | 13,093 | 24,027 | 750 | 37,870 |
| 30 | Director of Operations | 137,000 | 27,400 | 164,400 | 3 | 0.750 | 41,059 | 37,675 | 1,500 | 80,234 |
| 31 | Member of Technical Staff | 94,248 | 18,850 | 113,098 | 2 | 0.375 | 14,123 | 25,918 | 750 | 40,791 |
| 32 | Member of Operations Staff | 71,000 | 14,200 | 85,200 | 1 | 0.125 | 3,546 | 19,525 | 375 | 23,446 |
| 33 | Director of Marketing | 125,000 | 25,000 | 150,000 | 2 | 0.375 | 18,731 | 34,375 | 750 | 53,856 |
| 34 | Member of Technical Staff | 65,000 | 13,000 | 78,000 | 1 | 0.125 | 3,247 | 17,875 | 375 | 21,497 |
| 35 | Member of Technical Staff - Nonexempt | 42,950 | 8,590 | 51,540 | 1 | 0.125 | 2,145 | 11,811 | 375 | 14,331 |
| 36 | Member of Technical Staff | 90,000 | 18,000 | 108,000 | 1 | 0.125 | 4,496 | 24,750 | 375 | 29,621 |
| 37 | Member of Technical Staff | 109,000 | 21,800 | 130,800 | 2 | 0.375 | 16,334 | 29,975 | 750 | 47,059 |
| 38 | Member of Technical Staff | 84,200 | 16,840 | 101,040 | 1 | 0.125 | 4,206 | 23,155 | 375 | 27,736 |
| 39 | Member of Technical Staff | 60,300 | 12,060 | 72,360 | 1 | 0.125 | 3,012 | 16,583 | 375 | 19,970 |
| 40 | Member of Technical Staff | 58,500 | 11,700 | 70,200 | 1 | 0.125 | 2,922 | 16,088 | 375 | 19,385 |
| 41 | Director Release & Customer Support | 116,000 | 23,200 | 139,200 | 2 | 0.375 | 17,383 | 31,900 | 750 | 50,033 |
| 42 | Executive Assistant | 35,000 | 7,000 | 42,000 | 1 | 0.125 | 1,748 | 9,625 | 375 | 11,748 |
| 43 | Member of Technical Staff | 113,400 | 22,680 | 136,080 | 2 | 0.375 | 16,993 | 31,185 | 750 | 48,928 |
| 44 | Member of Technical Staff | 112,041 | 22,408 | 134,449 | 2 | 0.375 | 16,789 | 30,811 | 750 | 48,350 |
| 45 | Member of Operations Staff | 70,000 | 14,000 | 84,000 | 1 | 0.125 | 3,497 | 19,250 | 375 | 23,122 |
| 46 | Member of Technical Staff | 107,000 | 21,400 | 128,400 | 3 | 0.750 | 32,068 | 29,425 | 1,500 | 62,993 |
| 47 | Director of International Operations | 150,000 | 30,000 | 180,000 | 1 | 0.125 | 7,493 | 41,250 | 375 | 49,118 |
| 48 | Member of Technical Staff | 110,000 | 22,000 | 132,000 | 2 | 0.375 | 16,484 | 30,250 | 750 | 47,484 |
| 49 | Vice President and General Manager of EMEA | 145,000 | 29,000 | 174,000 | 2 | 0.375 | 21,728 | 39,875 | 750 | 62,353 |

*(continued)*

**Exhibit 3.19** (Continued)

| No. | Job Title | Salary | 20% Benefits | Total | (1) Train. Per. Cl. | Yrs. | 33.3% Cost | (2) 27.5% Recruit. | Interview & H.R. | Total |
|---|---|---|---|---|---|---|---|---|---|---|
| 50 | Account Executive | 82,500 | 16,500 | 99,000 | 1 | 0.125 | 4,121 | 22,688 | 375 | 27,184 |
| 51 | Account Executive | 75,261 | 15,052 | 90,313 | 2 | 0.375 | 11,278 | 20,697 | 750 | 32,725 |
| 52 | Member of Technical Staff | 67,735 | 13,547 | 81,282 | 2 | 0.375 | 10,150 | 18,627 | 750 | 29,527 |
| 53 | Member of Technical Staff | 73,350 | 14,670 | 88,020 | 2 | 0.375 | 10,991 | 20,171 | 750 | 31,912 |
| 54 | Member of Technical Staff | 99,465 | 19,893 | 119,358 | 3 | 0.750 | 29,810 | 27,353 | 1,500 | 58,663 |
| Total 54 | | $5,240,541 | $1,048,108 | $6,288,649 | | | $644,245 | $1,441,151 | $34,125 | $2,119,521 |

| | |
|---|---|
| Replacement Cost of Assembled Workforce | $2,119,521 |
| Less: Taxes  40.0% | (847,808) |
| Costs Avoided, Net of Tax | 1,271,713 |
| Amortization Benefit | |
| Rate of Return | 16.0% |
| Tax Rate | 40.0% |
| Tax Amortization Period (Years) | 15 |
| Amortization Benefit | 242,469 |
| **Fair Value of Assembled Workforce, Rounded** | **$1,510,000** |

Footnotes:
(1) Qualified Replacement Training Months

| | | Interview & H.R. | |
|---|---|---|---|
| | Hours | Rate | |
| 1 = < 3 months | 5 | $75.00 | |
| 2 = 3-6 months | 10 | $75.00 | |
| 3 = 6-12 months | 20 | $75.00 | |

(2) Source: Karl Malloney, Recruiter

Note: Some amounts may not foot due to rounding.

The impairment test presented in this example is assumed to be performed as of December 31, 2007.

**Exhibit 3.20** Target Company Valuation of Trade Name as of December 31, 2007 ($000s)

| | | 2008 | 2009 | 2010 | 2011 | 2012 | 2013 | 2014 | 2015 | 2016 | 2017 |
|---|---|---|---|---|---|---|---|---|---|---|---|
| (1) Net Sales from Business Enterprise Analysis | | $58,800 | $64,680 | $71,148 | $76,840 | $82,219 | $86,330 | $90,646 | $95,178 | $99,937 | $104,934 |
| Pretax Relief from Royalty | 2.0% | $1,176 | $1,294 | $1,423 | $1,537 | $1,644 | $1,727 | $1,813 | $1,904 | $1,999 | $2,099 |
| Income Tax Liability | 40.0% | 470 | 517 | 569 | 615 | 658 | 691 | 725 | 761 | 799 | 839 |
| After-tax Royalty | | $706 | $776 | $854 | $922 | $987 | $1,036 | $1,088 | $1,142 | $1,199 | $1,259 |
| (2) Present Value Income Factor | 16.0% | 0.9285 | 0.8004 | 0.6900 | 0.5948 | 0.5128 | 0.4421 | 0.3811 | 0.3285 | 0.2832 | 0.2441 |
| Present Value Relief from Royalty | | $655 | $621 | $589 | $548 | $506 | $458 | $415 | $375 | $340 | $307 |
| Sum of Present Value Relief from Royalty, 2008–2017 | | $4,814 | | | | | | | | | |
| Residual Calculation: | | | | | | | | | | | |
| 2017 After-tax Royalty | | $1,259 | | | | | | | | | |
| 2018 After-tax Royalty, Assuming Growth of | 5.0% | $1,322 | | | | | | | | | |
| Residual Capitalization Rate, Perpetual Growth of | 5.0% | 11.0% | | | | | | | | | |
| Residual Value, 2018 | | $12,018 | | | | | | | | | |
| (2) Present Value Factor | | 0.2441 | | | | | | | | | |
| Fair Market Value of Residual | | 2,934 | | | | | | | | | |
| Present Value of Trade Name Royalty Flows | | 7,748 | | | | | | | | | |
| Amortization Benefit | | | | | | | | | | | |
| Discount Rate | 16.0% | | | | | | | | | | |
| Tax Rate | 40.0% | | | | | | | | | | |
| Tax Amortization Period (Years) | 15 | | | | | | | | | | |
| Amortization Benefit | | 1,477 | | | | | | | | | |
| **Fair Value of Trade Name, Rounded** | | **$9,230** | | | | | | | | | |

Footnotes:

(1)Figures shown from Business Enterprise Analysis (BEA) - Cash Flow Forecast (Exhibit 3.17)
(2)Based on mid-period assumption
Note: Some amounts may not foot due to rounding.
The impairment test presented in this example is assumed to be performed as of December 31, 2007.

considered impaired, and the carrying amount will be written down to the new fair value per SFAS No. 142.

## Noncompetition Agreement

In the interest of brevity and because we already have a full noncompete analysis as an example in the previous section, assume that under the assumption of competition, sellers could negatively impact Target Company's sales for two years (i.e., the seller, if not under a noncompete agreement, could theoretically go to work for a competitor or start a new company and cause the target company to grow slower than otherwise forecast). Variable expense percentages are assumed to be the same for both scenarios.

The probability of the covenantor's competing and succeeding is still assessed at 50%. After reducing the gross value by the probability factor and adding an amortization benefit, the fair value of the noncompete agreement is determined to be $2,090,000.

The recoverability test of SFAS No. 144 indicates that the sum of the undiscounted cash flows (here, for five years, ignoring the residual) exceeds the carrying value. Thus, no impairment is recognized. The remaining useful life is now two years.

## Technology

As was done last year, the fair value of the Company's developed technology (as well as the fair values of in-process research and development and customer base) was determined using an income approach specifically, the multiperiod excess earnings method (MPEEM) (see discussion on pages 92–97), which measures the present value of the future earnings to be generated during the remaining lives of the assets. Using the BEA as a starting point, we calculated pretax cash flows attributable to the technology

| Contributory Asset Charges | |
|---|---|
| Return on: | Rate |
| Net Working Capital | 5.0% |
| Land and Building | 7.0% |
| Machinery and Equipment | 8.0% |
| Software | 17.0% |
| Trade Name | 16.0% |
| Noncompete Agreement | 16.0% |
| Assembled Workforce | 16.0% |
| Technology | 18.0% |
| IPR&D | 20.0% |
| Customer Base | 17.0% |

Note: The discount rates shown here are for example purposes only and represent general relationships between assets. Actual rates must be selected based on consideration of the facts and circumstances related to each entity and risk of underlying assets.

**Exhibit 3.21a**    Target Company Valuation of Noncompete Agreement as of December 31, 2007 ($000s)

| Comparison: Scenario I & Scenario II | For the Years Ended December 31, | | | | |
|---|---|---|---|---|---|
| | 2008 | 2009 | 2010 | 2011 | 2012 |
| Net Cash Flow | | | | | |
| (1) With Restrictive Covenant | $12,175 | $14,026 | $14,933 | $16,591 | $17,376 |
| (2) Without Restrictive Covenant | 11,869 | 11,673 | 12,986 | 16,596 | 17,381 |
| Reduction in Debt-free Net Cash Flow | $306 | $2,353 | $1,947 | ($5) | ($5) |
| Present Value Period | 1 | 2 | 3 | 4 | 5 |
| (3) Present Value Factor | 0.9285 | 0.8004 | 0.6900 | 0.5948 | 0.5128 |
| Present Value of Cash Flow | $284 | $1,883 | $1,343 | ($3) | ($3) |

**SFAS No. 144 Impairment Test**

| | | |
|---|---|---|
| (4) Sum of Undiscounted Cash Flows | | $2,298 |
| Sum, Present Value of Cash Flow | | $3,505 |
| Amortization Benefit | | |
| Discount Rate | 16.0% | |
| Tax Rate | 40.0% | |
| Tax Amortization Period (Years) | 15 | |
| Amortization Benefit | | 668 |
| Raw Value of Noncompete Agreement | | $4,174 |
| (5) Probability of Competing | | 50.0% |
| **Fair Value of Noncompete Agreement, Rounded** | | **$2,090** |

Footnotes:
(1) See Projected Cash Flows Over Competitive Time Horizon, Scenario 1: With Restrictive Covenant With Seller (Exhibit 3.21b)
(2) Year 3 cash flow reflects adjustment to working capital provision under the assumption of competition starting in Year 3. See Projected Cash Flows Over Competitive Time Horizon, Scenario 2: Without Restrictive Covenant With Seller (Exhibit 3.21c)
(3) Based on mid-period assumption
(4) The sum of the undiscounted cash flows of $2.298 million (after reducing the amount by the 50% probability factor) exceeds the carrying value of $1.810 million, indicating no impairment under SFAS No. 144.
(5) Based on discussions with management.
Note: Some amounts may not foot due to rounding.
The impairment test presented in this example is assumed to be performed as of December 31, 2007.

that existed at the valuation date. As with the BEA, deductions are made for cost of goods sold and operating expenses (adjusted to reflect the fact that the developed technology should not be burdened by expenses of developing new technology). We then adjusted for returns on the contributory assets, as presented in Exhibit 3.22.

**Exhibit 3.21b**    Target Company Projected Cash Flows Over Competitive Time Horizon
Scenario 1: With Noncompete Agreement with Seller as of December 31, 2007 ($000s)

| Assumptions | 2008 | 2009 | 2010 | 2011 | 2012 |
|---|---|---|---|---|---|
| Cost of Goods Sold | 42.0% | 41.0% | 40.0% | 39.0% | 39.0% |
| Operating Expenses | 30.5% | 30.0% | 30.0% | 29.0% | 29.0% |
| Capital Expenditures Percent of Sales | 1.0% | 1.0% | 1.0% | 1.0% | 1.0% |
| Estimated Effective Tax Rate | 40.0% | 40.0% | 40.0% | 40.0% | 40.0% |
| Debt-free Net Working Capital Percent of Revenues | 15.0% | 15.0% | 15.0% | 15.0% | 15.0% |
| Base Year Revenues 2007 | $56,000 | | | | |

|  | For the Years Ended December 31, | | | | |
|---|---|---|---|---|---|
|  | 2008 | 2009 | 2010 | 2011 | 2012 |
| (1) Total Revenues | $58,800 | $64,680 | $71,148 | $76,840 | $82,219 |
| Cost of Goods Sold | 24,696 | 26,519 | 28,459 | 29,968 | 32,065 |
| Operating Expenses | 17,934 | 19,404 | 21,344 | 22,284 | 23,843 |
| EBITDA | $16,170 | $18,757 | $21,344 | $24,588 | $26,311 |
| *EBITDA Margin* | *27.5%* | *29.0%* | *30.0%* | *32.0%* | *32.0%* |
| Depreciation (MACRS) | $3,112 | $5,162 | $3,927 | $3,060 | $2,456 |
| Amortization | 5,590 | 5,590 | 5,590 | 5,590 | 5,590 |
| EBIT | $7,468 | $8,005 | $11,828 | $15,938 | $18,265 |
| *EBIT Margin* | *12.7%* | *12.4%* | *16.6%* | *20.7%* | *22.2%* |
| Income Taxes | $2,987 | $3,202 | $4,731 | $6,375 | $7,306 |
| Debt-free Net Income | $4,481 | $4,803 | $7,097 | $9,563 | $10,959 |
| *Debt-free Net Income Margin* | *7.6%* | *7.4%* | *10.0%* | *12.4%* | *13.3%* |
| Plus: Depreciation | $3,112 | $5,162 | $3,927 | $3,060 | $2,456 |
| Plus: Amortization | 5,590 | 5,590 | 5,590 | 5,590 | 5,590 |
| Less: Capital Expenditures | (588) | (647) | (711) | (768) | (822) |
| (2) Less: Incremental Working Capital | (420) | (882) | (970) | (854) | (807) |
| Debt-free Cash Flow | $12,175 | $14,026 | $14,933 | $16,591 | $17,376 |

Footnotes:
(1) Based on Business Enterprise Analysis (BEA) - Cash Flow Forecast (Exhibit 3.17)
(2) Incremental Working Capital in Year 1 reflects a lower provision than shown in the Business Enterprise
    Analysis (BEA) - Cash Flow Forecast (Exhibit 3.17) because the BEA provision normalizes from an
    actual balance, while the provision for the noncompete agreement only accounts for the incremental
    amount necessary based on the growth of revenues.
Note: Some amounts may not foot due to rounding.
The impairment test presented in this example is assumed to be performed as of December 31, 2007.

**Exhibit 3.21c**    Target Company Projected Cash Flows Over Competitive Time Horizon

Scenario 2: Without Noncompete Agreement with Seller as of December 31, 2007 ($000s)

| Assumptions | 2008 | 2009 | 2010 | 2011 | 2012 |
|---|---|---|---|---|---|
| Cost of Goods Sold | 42.0% | 41.0% | 40.0% | 39.0% | 39.0% |
| Operating Expenses | 30.5% | 30.0% | 30.0% | 29.0% | 29.0% |
| Capital Expenditures Percent of Sales | 1.0% | 1.0% | 1.0% | 1.0% | 1.0% |
| Estimated Effective Tax Rate | 40.0% | 40.0% | 40.0% | 40.0% | 40.0% |
| Debt-free Net Working Capital Percent of Revenues | 15.0% | 15.0% | 15.0% | 15.0% | 15.0% |
| Base Year Revenues 2007 | $56,000 | | | | |

| | For the Years Ended December 31, | | | | |
|---|---|---|---|---|---|
| | 2008 | 2009 | 2010 | 2011 | 2012 |
| (1) Total Revenues | $58,800 | $64,680 | $71,148 | $76,840 | $82,219 |
| Decline in Revenues Caused by Competition of Seller | 20.0% | 20.0% | 0.0% | 0.0% | 0.0% |
| Decline in Revenues | $11,760 | $12,936 | $0 | $0 | $0 |
| Adjusted Base Revenues | 47,040 | 51,744 | 71,148 | 76,840 | 82,219 |
| Cost of Goods Sold | 19,757 | 21,215 | 28,459 | 29,968 | 32,065 |
| Operating Expenses | 14,347 | 15,523 | 21,344 | 22,284 | 23,843 |
| EBITDA | $12,936 | $15,006 | $21,345 | $24,588 | $26,311 |
| *EBITDA Margin* | *27.5%* | *29.0%* | *30.0%* | *32.0%* | *32.0%* |
| (2) Depreciation | $2,493 | $4,140 | $3,913 | $3,074 | $2,467 |
| Amortization | 5,590 | 5,590 | 5,590 | 5,590 | 5,590 |
| EBIT | $4,853 | $5,276 | $11,842 | $15,924 | $18,254 |
| *EBIT Margin* | *10.3%* | *10.2%* | *16.6%* | *20.7%* | *22.2%* |
| Income Taxes | $1,941 | $2,110 | $4,737 | $6,370 | $7,301 |
| Debt-free Net Income | $2,912 | $3,166 | $7,105 | $9,554 | $10,953 |
| *Debt-free Net Income Margin* | *6.2%* | *6.1%* | *10.0%* | *12.4%* | *13.3%* |
| Plus: Depreciation | $2,493 | $4,140 | $3,913 | $3,074 | $2,467 |
| Plus: Amortization | 5,590 | 5,590 | 5,590 | 5,590 | 5,590 |
| Less: Capital Expenditures | (470) | (517) | (711) | (768) | (822) |
| (3) Less: Incremental Working Capital | 1,344 | (706) | (2,911) | (854) | (807) |
| Debt-free Net Cash Flow | $11,869 | $11,673 | $12,986 | $16,596 | $17,381 |

Footnotes:

(1) Based on Business Enterprise Analysis (BEA) - Cash Flow Forecast (Exhibit 3.17)

(2) Depreciation in this exhibit gives effect to an estimated reduction due to reduced net sales, which it is assumed would result in reduced capital expenditures.

(3) Incremental Working Capital in Year 1 reflects a lower provision than shown in the Business Enterprise Analysis (BEA) - Cash Flow Forecast (Exhibit 3.17) because the BEA provision normalizes from an actual balance, while the provision for the noncompete agreement only accounts for the incremental amount necessary based on the growth of revenues. Incremental Working Capital in other years reflect different amounts than shown in the BEA (Exhibit 3.17) in order to fund working capital balances based on different revenue projections.

Note: Some amounts may not foot due to rounding.

The impairment test presented in this example is assumed to be performed as of December 31, 2007.

**Exhibit 3.22**  Target Company Calculation of Contributory Asset Charges as of December 31, 2007 ($000s)

Contributory Asset
A. Asset Balances

| | 2008 | 2009 | 2010 | 2011 | 2012 | 2013 | 2014 |
|---|---|---|---|---|---|---|---|
| Net Working Capital | $12,485 | $9,261 | $10,187 | $11,099 | $11,929 | $12,641 | $13,273 |
| Land and Building | 22,919 | 22,764 | 22,621 | 22,490 | 22,367 | 22,251 | 22,139 |
| Machinery and Equipment, net | 17,819 | 14,455 | 10,732 | 8,110 | 6,270 | 4,737 | 3,166 |
| Software | 8,430 | 8,430 | 8,430 | 8,430 | 8,430 | 8,430 | 8,430 |
| Trade Name | 9,230 | 9,230 | 9,230 | 9,230 | 9,230 | 9,230 | 9,230 |
| Noncompete Agreement | 2,090 | 2,090 | 0 | 0 | 0 | 0 | 0 |
| Assembled Workforce | 1,510 | 1,510 | 1,510 | 1,510 | 1,510 | 1,510 | 1,510 |
| Technology | 9,610 | 9,610 | 9,610 | 9,610 | 9,610 | 9,610 | 9,610 |
| IPR&D | 3,830 | 3,830 | 3,830 | 3,830 | 3,830 | 3,830 | 3,830 |
| Customer Base | 7,680 | 7,680 | 7,680 | 7,680 | 7,680 | 7,680 | 7,680 |

(1) B. Total Returns

| | Rate | 2008 | 2009 | 2010 | 2011 | 2012 | 2013 | 2014 |
|---|---|---|---|---|---|---|---|---|
| Net Working Capital | 5.0% | $624 | $463 | $509 | $555 | $596 | $632 | $664 |
| Land and Building | 7.0% | 1,604 | 1,593 | 1,583 | 1,574 | 1,566 | 1,558 | 1,550 |
| Machinery and Equipment, net | 8.0% | 1,426 | 1,156 | 859 | 649 | 502 | 379 | 253 |
| Software | 17.0% | 1,433 | 1,433 | 1,433 | 1,433 | 1,433 | 1,433 | 1,433 |
| Trade Name | 16.0% | 1,477 | 1,477 | 1,477 | 1,477 | 1,477 | 1,477 | 1,477 |
| Noncompete Agreement | 16.0% | 334 | 334 | 0 | 0 | 0 | 0 | 0 |
| Assembled Workforce | 16.0% | 242 | 242 | 242 | 242 | 242 | 242 | 242 |
| Technology | 18.0% | 1,730 | 1,730 | 1,730 | 1,730 | 1,730 | 1,730 | 1,730 |
| IPR&D | 20.0% | 766 | 766 | 766 | 766 | 766 | 766 | 766 |
| Customer Base | 17.0% | 1,306 | 1,306 | 1,306 | 1,306 | 1,306 | 1,306 | 1,306 |

C. Distribution of Revenues

| | 2008 | 2009 | 2010 | 2011 | 2012 |
|---|---|---|---|---|---|
| (2) Net Sales-Technology | $50,400 | $45,360 | $30,845 | $21,180 | |
| (3) Forecast Sales per BEA | 58,800 | 64,680 | 71,148 | 76,840 | |
| | | | | | |
| Technology Percent of BEA | 85.71% | 70.13% | 43.35% | 27.56% | |
| | | | | | |
| (4) Net Sales-IPR&D | $8,400 | $12,852 | $13,818 | $14,334 | |
| (3) Forecast Sales per BEA | 58,800 | 64,680 | 71,148 | 76,840 | |

| IPR&D Percent of BEA | 14.29% | 19.87% | 19.42% | 18.65% | 10.10% |
|---|---|---|---|---|---|

## D. Allocated Returns Technology

|  | 2008 | 2009 | 2010 | 2011 | 2012 |
|---|---|---|---|---|---|
| Net Working Capital | $535 | $325 | $221 | $153 | $60 |
| Land and Building | 1,375 | 1,117 | 686 | 434 | 158 |
| Machinery and Equipment, net | 1,222 | 811 | 372 | 179 | 51 |
| Software | 1,228 | 1,005 | 621 | 395 | 145 |
| Trade Name | 1,266 | 1,036 | 640 | 407 | 149 |
| Noncompete Agreement | 286 | 234 | 0 | 0 | 0 |
| Assembled Workforce | 207 | 170 | 105 | 67 | 24 |
| Customer Base | 1,119 | 916 | 566 | 360 | 132 |
| Total | $7,238 | $5,614 | $3,211 | $1,995 | $719 |

## E. Allocated Returns-IPR&D

|  | 2008 | 2009 | 2010 | 2011 | 2012 |
|---|---|---|---|---|---|
| Net Working Capital | $89 | $92 | $99 | $104 | $60 |
| Land and Building | 229 | 317 | 307 | 294 | 158 |
| Machinery and Equipment, net | 204 | 230 | 167 | 121 | 51 |
| Software | 205 | 285 | 278 | 267 | 145 |
| Trade Name | 211 | 293 | 287 | 276 | 149 |
| Noncompete Agreement | 48 | 66 | 0 | 0 | 0 |
| Assembled Workforce | 35 | 48 | 47 | 45 | 24 |
| Customer Base | 187 | 260 | 254 | 244 | 132 |
| Total | $1,208 | $1,591 | $1,439 | $1,351 | $719 |

Footnotes:
(1) Used for Customer Base (Exhibit 3.25), except no return is taken on Customer Base asset.
(2) Based on Valuation of Technology (Exhibit 3.23)
(3) Based on Business Enterprise Analysis (BEA) - Cash Flow Forecast (Exhibit 3.17)
(4) Based on Valuation of In-process Research and Development (Exhibit 3.24)
Note: Some amounts may not foot due to rounding. The impairment test presented in this example is assumed to be performed as of December 31, 2007.

Although the forecast survivorship roll-off of the technology spans a four-year period, a contributory asset charge on the noncompete agreement stops after two years, its remaining useful life (the contractual life at December 31, 2006 was three years). This is because, unlike the other assets, the noncompete agreement is not replenished or renewed through ongoing expenditures, and it has no value when its contractual life is over. This is generally true for nonrenewable contractual assets.

The discount rate of 18% reflects the higher risk of this asset compared with the business overall. Based on our analysis, we concluded that the fair value of the acquired technology on the valuation date was $9,610,000 (rounded), as shown in Exhibit 3.23.

The recoverability test of SFAS No. 144 indicates that the sum of the undiscounted cash flows of $11,338,000 is less than the carrying amount of $13,250,000. Thus, the asset is considered impaired under SFAS No. 144. The remaining useful life of the revalued asset is four years.

## In-Process Research and Development

The value of the IPR&D was also estimated using the income approach. Similar to our methodology for valuing technology, the DCF model was constructed, starting with expected sales based on the technology that was in-process at the valuation date. In this example, it is assumed that the IPR&D that was being developed as of the date of the impairment study was delayed, contributing to the company's decline in performance, and is now scheduled to be completed in early 2008 and is forecast to produce sales of $8,400,000.

Similar to the technology valuation, cost of sales and operating expenses (net of development costs, which will no longer occur relative to this technology) are deducted. We re-evaluated the expected survivorship pattern, and the useful life of the IPR&D is now estimated to be five years. In addition, estimated required returns were taken on the contributory assets (see previous section), except for existing technology (see discussion in Case Study 1).

The sum of the present values is $3,309,000. A discount rate of 20% was selected to reflect the additional risk of the unproven technology. After accounting for the amortization benefit, the fair value of the IPR&D (as shown in Exhibit 3.24) as of December 31, 2007 was $3,830,000.

The fair value of acquired IPR&D was written off in 2007 under SFAS No. 2. The fair value of IPR&D concluded herein will be used in the determination of goodwill impairment but will not be recognized: the carrying value of IPR&D will continue to be zero.

## Valuation of Customer Base

The fair value of the Company's customer base was also determined using the MPEEM. As before, returns were taken on contributory assets including technology and IPR&D.

We then re-evaluated a study related to the expected life of the customer base and concluded the same survivor curve based on a seven-year remaining useful life, which

**Exhibit 3.23**  Target Company Valuation of Technology as of December 31, 2007 ($000s)

| | Actual | | Forecast | | |
|---|---|---|---|---|---|
| | 2007 | 2008 | 2009 | 2010 | 2011 |
| (1) Net Sales-Existing Technology | $56,000 | $50,400 | $45,360 | $30,845 | $21,180 |
| Cost of Sales | 23,520 | 21,168 | 18,598 | 12,338 | 8,260 |
| Gross Profit | 32,480 | 29,232 | 26,762 | 18,507 | 12,920 |
| (2) Operating Expenses | 11,760 | 10,332 | 9,072 | 6,169 | 4,024 |
| (3) Depreciation | 3,123 | 2,667 | 3,620 | 1,702 | 843 |
| Total Operating Expenses | 14,883 | 12,999 | 12,692 | 7,871 | 4,867 |
| Taxable Income | 17,597 | 16,233 | 14,070 | 10,636 | 8,053 |
| Income Taxes           40.0% | 7,039 | 6,493 | 5,628 | 4,254 | 3,221 |
| Net Income | $10,558 | 9,740 | 8,442 | 6,382 | 4,832 |
| Residual Cash Flow Attributable to Technology | | | | | |
| (4) Less Returns on | | | | | |
| Net Working Capital | 5.0% | 535 | 325 | 221 | 153 |
| Land and Building | 7.0% | 1,375 | 1,117 | 686 | 434 |
| Machinery and Equipment, net | 8.0% | 1,222 | 811 | 372 | 179 |
| Software | 17.0% | 1,228 | 1,005 | 621 | 395 |
| Trade Name | 16.0% | 1,266 | 1,036 | 640 | 407 |
| Noncompete Agreement | 16.0% | 286 | 234 | 0 | 0 |
| Assembled Workforce | 16.0% | 207 | 170 | 105 | 67 |
| Customer Base | 17.0% | 1,119 | 916 | 566 | 360 |
| Sum of Returns | | 7,238 | 5,614 | 3,211 | 1,995 |

*(continued)*

**Exhibit 3.23**   (Continued)

| | | | | |
|---|---|---|---|---|
| (5) After-tax Residual Cash Flows | $2,502 | $2,828 | $3,171 | $2,837 |
| (6) 18.0%Present Value Factor for Residual Cash Flow | 0.9206 | 0.7801 | 0.6611 | 0.5603 |
| Present Value of Residual Cash Flows | $2,303 | $2,206 | $2,096 | $1,590 |

**SFAS No. 144 Impairment Test**

| | |
|---|---|
| Sum of Undiscounted Cash Flows | $11,338 |
| | |
| Sum of Present Values, 2008-2011 | $8,195 |
| Amortization Benefit | |
| Discount Rate | 18.0% |
| Tax Rate | 40.0% |
| Tax Amortization Period (Years) | 15 |
| | |
| Amortization Benefit | 1,418 |
| | |
| **Fair Value of Technology, Rounded** | **$9,610** |

Footnotes:

(1) Sales attributable to existing Technology, which are 100% of Company sales in 2007, are projected to decline over time as the technology becomes obsolete and competitors increasingly impact sales.

(2) Excludes development expenses of 10% to reflect that developed technology should not be burdened by expenses of developing new technology.

(3) MACRS depreciation per Business Enterprise Analysis (BEA) - Cash Flow Forecast (Exhibit 3.17) allocated by relative net sales between Technology and IPR&D

(4) See Calculation of Contributory Asset Charges (Exhibit 3.22)

(5) The sum of the undiscounted cash flows of $11.338 million is less than the carrying amount of $13.250 million, indicating impairment under SFAS No. 144.

(6) Based on mid-period assumption

Note: Some amounts may not foot due to rounding.

The impairment test presented in this example is assumed to be performed as of December 31, 2007

**Exhibit 3.24**   Target Company Valuation of In-Process Research and Development (IPR&D) as of December 31, 2007($000s)

| | | | | Forecast | | | |
|---|---|---|---|---|---|---|---|
| | | 2008 | 2009 | 2010 | 2011 | 2012 | |
| (1) Net Sales-IPR&D | | $8,400 | $12,852 | $13,818 | $14,334 | $8,304 | |
| Cost of Sales | | 3,528 | 5,269 | 5,527 | 5,590 | 3,239 | |
| Gross Profit | | $4,872 | $7,583 | $8,291 | $8,744 | $5,065 | |
| (2) Operating Expenses | | 1,722 | 2,570 | 2,764 | 2,723 | 1,578 | |
| (3) Cost to Complete | | 240 | 0 | 0 | 0 | 0 | |
| (4) Depreciation | | 445 | 1,026 | 763 | 571 | 248 | |
| Total Operating Expenses | | 2,407 | 3,596 | 3,527 | 3,294 | 1,826 | |
| Taxable Income | | 2,465 | 3,987 | 4,764 | 5,450 | 3,239 | |
| Income Taxes | 40.0% | 986 | 1,595 | 1,906 | 2,180 | 1,296 | |
| Net Income | | 1,479 | 2,392 | 2,858 | 3,270 | 1,943 | |
| Residual Cash Flow Attributable to IPR&D | | | | | | | |
| (5) Less Returns on | | | | | | | |
| Net Working Capital | 5.0% | 89 | 92 | 99 | 104 | 60 | |
| Land and Building | 7.0% | 229 | 317 | 307 | 294 | 158 | |
| Machinery and Equipment, Net | 8.0% | 204 | 230 | 167 | 121 | 51 | |
| Software | 17.0% | 205 | 285 | 278 | 267 | 145 | |
| Trade Name | 16.0% | 211 | 293 | 287 | 276 | 149 | |
| Noncompete Agreement | 16.0% | 48 | 66 | 0 | 0 | 0 | |
| Assembled Workforce | 16.0% | 35 | 48 | 47 | 45 | 24 | |
| Customer Base | 17.0% | 187 | 260 | 254 | 244 | 132 | |

*(continued)*

**Exhibit 3.24** (Continued)

| Sum of Returns | 1,208 | 1,591 | 1,439 | 1,351 | 719 |
|---|---|---|---|---|---|
| After-tax Residual Cash Flows | $271 | $801 | $1,419 | $1,919 | $1,224 |
| (6) 20.0% Present Value Factor for Residual Cash Flow | 0.9129 | 0.7607 | 0.6339 | 0.5283 | 0.4402 |
| | | | | | |
| Present Value of Residual Cash Flows | $247 | $609 | $900 | $1,014 | $539 |
| Sum of Present Values, 2008-2012 | $3,309 | | | | |
| Amortization Benefit | | | | | |
| Discount Rate | 20.0% | | | | |
| Tax Rate | 40.0% | | | | |
| Tax Amortization Period (Years) | 15 | | | | |
| | | | | | |
| Amortization Benefit | 523 | | | | |
| **Fair Value of IPR&D Rounded** | **$3,830** | | | | |

Footnotes:

(1) Based on management's forecast

(2) Excludes development expenses of 10% to reflect no future development costs relative to this technology.

(3) The cost to complete is typically known with certainty and cannot be avoided. With IPR&D, one often does not know if the project will be successful until the amounts are spent. Thus, some practitioners separately calculate the present value of inflows and the present value of outflows. We have elected to present the single calculation here, for simplicity and because the alternative treatment does not result in a materially different conclusion of value.

(4) MACRS depreciation per Business Enterprise Analysis (BEA) - Cash Flow Forecast (Exhibit 3.17) allocated by relative net sales between Technology and IPR&D

(5) See Calculation of Contributory Asset Charges (Exhibit 3.22)

(6) Based on mid-period assumption

Note: Some amounts may not foot due to rounding.

The impairment test presented in this example is assumed to be performed as of December 31, 2007.

was degraded straight-line. The surviving cash flows (the excess cash flows multiplied by the forecast survivorship of the customer base in each year), after providing for returns on the other assets, are attributable to the customer base. The discount rate of 18% reflects our judgment that the risk of this asset is about the same as the business overall.

Based on our analysis, we concluded that the fair value of the customer base on the valuation date was $7,680,000 (rounded), as shown in Exhibit 3.25. The recoverability test of SFAS No. 144 indicates the sum of the undiscounted cash flows of $11,258,000 exceeds the carrying amount of $6,080,000. Thus, the asset is not considered impaired.

## Valuation of Goodwill

Again, goodwill is calculated using the residual method, by subtracting from the purchase price the fair value of all the identified tangible and intangible assets. Remember, goodwill includes assembled workforce, which must be separately valued to obtain a valid return for IPR&D and technology. As a result, and pursuant to SFAS No. 141, the indicated value of assembled workforce of $1,510,000 must be added to the indicated value of goodwill to arrive at the fair value of goodwill for financial statement reporting purposes. Based on this analysis, the fair value of residual goodwill on December 31, 2007 was $37,980,000 (Exhibit 3.26).

## CONCLUSION

As the fair value of goodwill has declined from $75,820,000 to $37,980,000, an impairment loss is recognized in the amount of $37,840,000. Other assets indicating impairment are:

|  | Carrying Amount Before Impairment December 31, 2007 | Fair Value December 31, 2007 | Impairment Year End December 31, 2007 |
|---|---|---|---|
| Technology (SFAS No. 144) | $13,250,000 | $9,610,000 | $3,640,000 |
| Trade Name (SFAS No. 142) | 12,660,000 | 9,230,000 | 3,430,000 |
| **TOTAL** | $25,910,000 | $18,840,000 | $7,070,000 |

Assets other than long-lived assets are not subject to impairment review. In the case of software and IPR&D, the fair values as of December 31, 2007 exceed the carrying amounts, thus they are not impaired, while the non-amortizable trade name is impaired under SFAS No. 142 because the fair value is less than the carrying amount. Technology is impaired under SFAS No. 144 because the undiscounted cash flows are less than the carrying amount. No adjustments are made to reflect valuation differences. A summary of the impairment study is presented in Exhibit 3.27. Total impairment losses for 2007 are $44,910,000.

**Exhibit 3.25** Target Company Valuation of Customer Base as of December 31, 2007 ($000s)

| Cash Flows | | Actual | | | Projections | | | | |
|---|---|---|---|---|---|---|---|---|---|
| | | 2007 | 2008 | 2009 | 2010 | 2011 | 2012 | 2013 | 2014 |
| (1) Net SalesExisting Customers | | $56,000 | $58,800 | $61,740 | $64,827 | $68,068 | $71,471 | $75,045 | $78,797 |
| Cost of Sales | | 23,520 | 24,696 | 25,313 | 25,931 | 26,547 | 27,874 | 29,268 | 30,731 |
| Gross Profit | | 32,480 | 34,104 | 36,427 | 38,896 | 41,521 | 43,597 | 45,777 | 48,066 |
| (2) Operating Expenses | | 13,440 | 13,818 | 14,200 | 14,910 | 14,975 | 15,724 | 16,510 | 17,335 |
| Depreciation (MACRS) | | 3,123 | 3,112 | 5,162 | 3,927 | 3,060 | 2,456 | 2,529 | 2,607 |
| Total Operating Expenses | | 16,563 | 16,930 | 19,362 | 18,837 | 18,035 | 18,180 | 19,039 | 19,942 |
| Taxable Income | | 15,917 | 17,174 | 17,065 | 20,059 | 23,486 | 25,417 | 26,738 | 28,124 |
| Income Taxes | 40.0% | 6,367 | 6,870 | 6,826 | 8,024 | 9,395 | 10,167 | 10,695 | 11,250 |
| Net Income | | $9,550 | 10,304 | 10,239 | 12,035 | 14,091 | 15,250 | 16,043 | 16,874 |
| Residual Cash Flow Attributable to Existing Customer Base | | | | | | | | | |
| (3) Less: Returns on | | | | | | | | | |
|    Net Working Capital | 5.0% | | 624 | 463 | 509 | 555 | 596 | 632 | 664 |
|    Land and Building | 7.0% | | 1,604 | 1,593 | 1,583 | 1,574 | 1,566 | 1,558 | 1,550 |
|    Machinery and Equipment, net | 8.0% | | 1,426 | 1,156 | 859 | 649 | 502 | 379 | 253 |
|    Software | 17.0% | | 1,433 | 1,433 | 1,433 | 1,433 | 1,433 | 1,433 | 1,433 |
|    Trade Name | 16.0% | | 1,477 | 1,477 | 1,477 | 1,477 | 1,477 | 1,477 | 1,477 |
|    Noncompete Agreement | 16.0% | | 334 | 334 | 0 | 0 | 0 | 0 | 0 |
|    Assembled Workforce | 16.0% | | 242 | 242 | 242 | 242 | 242 | 242 | 242 |
|    Technology | 18.0% | | 1,730 | 1,730 | 1,730 | 1,730 | 1,730 | 1,730 | 1,730 |
|    IPR&D | 20.0% | | 766 | 766 | 766 | 766 | 766 | 766 | 766 |
| Sum of Returns | | | 9,636 | 9,194 | 8,599 | 8,426 | 8,312 | 8,217 | 8,115 |
|    After-tax Residual Cash Flows | | | $668 | $1,045 | $3,436 | $5,665 | $6,938 | $7,826 | $8,759 |
| (4) Survivorship of Customer Base, Rounded | | | 92.9% | 78.6% | 64.3% | 50.0% | 35.7% | 21.4% | 7.1% |
| Surviving Excess Cash Flows | | | $621 | $821 | $2,209 | $2,833 | $2,477 | $1,675 | $622 |
| (5) 17.00% Present Value Factor for Residual Cash Flow | | | 0.9245 | 0.7902 | 0.6754 | 0.5772 | 0.4934 | 0.4217 | 0.3604 |
| Present Value of Surviving Residual Cash Flows | | | $574 | $649 | $1,492 | $1,635 | $1,222 | $706 | $224 |
| (6) Sum of Undiscounted Cash Flows | | $11,258 | | | | | | | |
| Sum of Present Values, 2008–2014 | | $6,502 | | | | | | | |
| Amortization Benefit | | | | | | | | | |
|    Discount Rate | 17.0% | | | | | | | | |
|    Tax Rate | 40.0% | | | | | | | | |
|    Tax Amortization Period (Years) | 15 | | | | | | | | |
| Amortization Benefit | | 1,180 | | | | | | | |
| **Fair Value of Customer Base, Rounded** | | **$7,680** | | | | | | | |

Footnotes:

(1) Assumes existing sales to existing customers will increase at a rate of 5% (to account for inflation and some real growth), before considering attrition.

(2) Excludes expenses of 7% for the solicitation of potential new customers to reflect that existing customers should not be burdened by the expense of developing new customers.

(3) See Calculation of Contributory Asset Charges (Exhibit 3.22)

(4) Assumes 7-year life, straight-line (survivorship analysis per management)

(5) Based on mid-period assumption

(6) The sum of the undiscounted cash flows of $11.258 million exceeds the carrying amount of $6,080 million, indicating no impairment under SFAS No. 144.

Note: Some amounts may not foot due to rounding. The impairment test presented in this example is assumed to be performed as of December 31, 2007.

**Exhibit 3.26**   Target Company Valuation of Goodwill as of December 31, 2007 ($000s)

| | |
|---|---:|
| Total Value of Invested Capital | $137,000 |
| Debt-free Current Liabilities | 20,000 |
| Total Liabilities and Equity | 157,000 |
| Less: Fair Value of Current Assets | (36,150) |
| Less: Fair Value of Tangible Assets | (42,000) |
| Less: Fair Value of Intangible Assets | |
|   Software | (8,430) |
|   Technology | (9,610) |
|   In-process Research and Development | (3,830) |
|   Trade Name | (9,230) |
|   Customer Base | (7,680) |
|   Noncompete Agreement | (2,090) |
| **(1) Residual Goodwill** | **$37,980** |

Footnote:

(1) Residual Goodwill includes the value of Assembled Workforce of $1.51 million.

Note: Some amounts may not foot due to rounding.

The impairment test presented in this example is assumed to be performed as of December 31, 2007.

**Exhibit 3.27** Target Company Summary of Fair Values and Impairment Losses as of December 31, 2007 ($000s)

| | Fair Value 12/31/06 | Carrying Amount Before Impairment 12/31/07 | Fair Value 12/31/07 | Carrying Amount After Impairment 12/31/07 | Impairment Charge 12/31/07 |
|---|---|---|---|---|---|
| Cash | $1,500 | $2,850 | $2,850 | $2,850 | na |
| Investments in Marketable Securities | 8,000 | 7,000 | 7,300 | 7,000 | na |
| Accounts Receivable | 17,000 | 13,000 | 13,000 | 13,000 | na |
| Inventory | 12,000 | 10,500 | 10,500 | 10,500 | na |
| Prepaid Expenses | 3,000 | 2,500 | 2,500 | 2,500 | na |
| TOTAL CURRENT ASSETS | 41,500 | 35,850 | 36,150 | 35,850 | 0 |
| Land and Buildings | 22,000 | 21,687 | 23,000 | 21,687 | 0 |
| Machinery and Equipment, net | 19,000 | 16,216 | 19,000 | 16,216 | 0 |
| TOTAL LONG-LIVED TANGIBLE ASSETS | 41,000 | 37,903 | 42,000 | 37,903 | 0 |
| TOTAL CURRENT AND TANGIBLE ASSETS | 82,500 | 73,753 | 78,150 | 73,753 | 0 |
| Software | 7,120 | 5,340 | 8,430 | 5,340 | 0 |
| (1) Technology | 16,560 | 13,250 | 9,610 | 9,610 | (3,640) |
| (2) In-process Research and Development | 4,530 | 0 | 3,830 | 0 | 0 |
| (3) Trade Name | 12,660 | 12,660 | 9,230 | 9,230 | (3,430) |
| Customer Base | 7,090 | 6,080 | 7,680 | 6,080 | 0 |
| Noncompete Agreement | 2,720 | 1,810 | 2,090 | 1,810 | 0 |
| TOTAL IDENTIFIED INTANGIBLE ASSETS | 50,680 | 39,140 | 40,870 | 32,070 | (7,070) |
| GOODWILL (including assembled workforce) | 75,820 | 75,820 | 37,980 | 37,980 | (37,840) |
| TOTAL ASSETS | $209,000 | $188,713 | $157,000 | $143,803 | ($44,910) |

Footnotes:

(1) Impaired under SFAS No. 144

(2) The carrying value of the acquired in-process research and development was written off in 2007 under SFAS No. 2. The fair value is used in the determination of goodwill impairment, but the carrying value will continue to be zero.

(3) Impaired under SFAS No. 142

Note: Some amounts may not foot due to rounding.

The impairment test presented in this example is assumed to be performed as of December 31, 2007.

# ENDNOTES

1. Financial Accounting Standards Board, Statement of Financial Accounting Standards No. 141, *Business Combinations* (2001), at 13.

2. SFAS No. 141 requires allocation of the fair value of assets acquired to the cost of the acquired entity. As presented in Appendix 2.2, under forthcoming SFAS No. 141R, the cost of the acquired entity ceases to be an issue and the acquirer must measure the assets acquired and liabilities assumed at fair value regardless of cost.

3. Financial Accounting Standards Board, Statement of Financial Accounting Standards No. 141, *Business Combinations* (2001), at 20.

4. American Society of Appraisers, *Business Valuation Standards* (2005), p. 24.

5. SFAS No. 141 prohibits Assembled Workforce from recognition as an intangible asset apart from goodwill. However, the asset is valued here to provide a basis for a return in the multiperiod excess earnings methodology. Its value is included in Goodwill in the final analysis.

6. Financial Accounting Standards Board, Statement of Financial Accounting Standards No. 142, *Goodwill and Other Intangible Assets* (2001), at 11.

7. Ibid.

8. I.R.C. § 197(a) (July 1991).

9. James R. Hitchner, *Financial Valuation: Applications and Models, 2nd edition,* (Hoboken, New Jersey: John Wiley & Sons, Inc., 2006), pg 1182.

10. For example, see *Cost of Capital, Estimation and Applications*, by Shannon P. Pratt, (New York: John Wiley & Sons Inc., 1998), and *Financial Valuation: Applications and Models, 2nd edition*, by James R. Hitchner, (Hoboken, New Jersey: John Wiley & Sons Inc., 2006).

11. Robert F. Reilly and Robert P. Schweihs, *Valuing Intangible Assets* (New York: McGraw-Hill, 1999), p. 122.

12. Ibid.

13. Financial Accounting Standards Board, Statement of Financial Accounting Standards No. 141, *Business Combinations* (2001), at 39.

14. Trade names and trademarks must be considered individually to determine their remaining useful life. Trade names and trademarks that are associated with a company name or logo (e.g., McDonald's) typically have indefinite lives. Many product trade names and trademarks also will have an indefinite life if no reasonable estimate can be made of the end of the product life (e.g., Coca-Cola). However, the valuer must be careful to find out whether there is a planned phase-out of a product or ascertain whether it can be estimated with reasonable certainty that a name will lose value or be abandoned over time. In such a case, a finite life is suggested and, therefore, an amortization period is warranted. Remember, for tax purposes, generally all intangibles are amortizable over a 15-year life.

15. Randy J. Larson, et al., *Assets Acquired in a Business Combination to be Used in Research and Development Activities: A Focus on Software, Electronic Devices, and Pharmaceutical Industries* (New York: AICPA, 2001), at 5.3.64.

16. Ibid.

17. Randy J. Larson, et al., *Assets Acquired in a Business Combination to be Used in Research and Development Activities: A Focus on Software, Electronic Devices, and Pharmaceutical Industries* (New York: AICPA, 2001), at 5.3.47.

18. It should be noted that for accounting purposes, the fair value of IPR&D is written off immediately pursuant to SFAS No. 2, *Accounting for Research and Development Costs.*

19. Financial Accounting Standards Board, Statement of Financial Accounting Standards No. 141, *Business Combinations* (2001), at B169.

20. Financial Accounting Standards Board, Statement of Financial Accounting Standards No. 142, *Goodwill and Other Intangible Assets* (2001), at 19. The comparison can be performed at the equity, investment capital, or even total asset level. The valuation specialist must judge what is most appropriate in the circumstances.

21. Financial Accounting Standards Board, Statement of Financial Accounting Standards No. 142, *Goodwill and Other Intangible Assets* (2001), at 20.

22. SFAS No. 142 at paragraph 27 describes three conditions that, if all are present, allow a previous impairment analysis to be carried forward form one year to the next without further analysis. These criteria are (1) the assets and liabilities that make up the reporting unit have not changed significantly since the most recent fair value determination, (2) the most recent fair value determination resulting in an amount that exceeded the carrying amount of the reporting unit by a substantial margin, and (3) based on an analysis of events that have occurred and circumstances that have changed since the most recent fair value determination, the likelihood that a current fair value determination would be less than the current carrying amount of the reporting unit is remote.

23. Financial Accounting Standards Board, Statement of Financial Accounting Standards No. 142, *Goodwill and Other Intangible Assets* (2001), at 19.

24. Ibid., at 23.

25. Financial Accounting Standards Board, Statement of Financial Accounting Standards No. 144, *Accounting for the Impairment or Disposal of Long-Lived Assets* (2001), at 7.

26. Ibid., at 8.

27. Financial Accounting Standards Board, Statement of Financial Accounting Standards No. 142, *Goodwill and Other Intangible Assets* (2001), at 29.

28. Financial Accounting Standards Board, Statement of Financial Accounting Standards No. 144, *Accounting for the Impairment or Disposal of Long-Lived Assets* (2001), at 22.

29. Financial Accounting Standards Board, Statement of Financial Accounting Standards No. 142, *Goodwill and Other Intangible Assets* (2001), at 29.

30. Since we don't have a purchase price at this date, Sec. 197 tax amortization of intangibles is calculated based on the fair value of the enterprise determined here. The enterprise value depends in part on the amortization amount so, to avoid a circular reference in the calculation, the amount must be "hard-entered" in the BEA spreadsheet and that step repeated until the hard entered amortization amount and the amortization calculated base on the BEA achieve equilibrium.

31. Financial Accounting Standards Board, Statement of Financial Accounting Standards No. 142, *Goodwill and Other Intangible Assets* (2001), at 23.

# Chapter 4

# Reports and Reporting Standards

## BUSINESS VALUATION REPORTING STANDARDS[1]

### OVERVIEW

At the time of this writing, report writing in the valuation community is guided by standards in the United States promulgated by the American Society of Appraisers (ASA), the Institute of Business Appraisers (IBA), The Appraisal Foundation (TAF), and the National Association of Certified Valuation Analysts (NACVA). Originally authorized by Congress, TAF standards are often referred to as USPAP, the acronym of its standards known as the Uniform Standards of Professional Appraisal Practice. The ASA, by the way, requires its appraisers to adhere to USPAP. The other U.S. valuation associations do not have this requirement.

As of this writing, the American Institute of Certified Public Accountants (AICPA) released an exposure draft of the "Statement on Standards for Valuation Services—Valuation of a Business, Business Ownership Interest, or Intangible Assets." These proposed standards, which are far more detailed than the other valuation standards, outline 11 areas that should be included in a valuation report.

On July 27, 2006, the Internal Revenue Service (IRS) released its "IRM 4.48.4, Engineering Program, Business Valuation Guidelines" and "IRM 4.48.5, Intangible Property Valuation Guidelines." Where the proposed AICPA reporting standards are clearly specified, the IRS report writing standards (¶4.48.4.4 and 4.48.5.4) are quite general, with the underlying requirement being to clearly communicate the results, identify the information relied upon, communicate the methodology and reasoning, and identify supporting documentation. Accordingly, these IRS standards give the appraiser a great deal of latitude as to what to include or not include in a report depending on the needs in each case. However, like several other of the reporting standards, IRS reporting standards require a signed statement by the appraiser asserting truth, correctness, lack of bias, no present or prospective interests, assumptions and limiting conditions, and the absence of a fee contingency.

The reporting standards of NACVA, IBA, ASA, and TAF, seem generally to be between the degree of detail expressed by the AICPA and the IRS. The differences may be attributed to the style of each organization.

So what is common to these sets of valuation standards? First, these standards are considered by the organizations to be minimum standards or requirements. Second, the standards not only address what must be included in the valuation report, but also what areas the valuator should consider in developing an opinion. These considerations probably originated, in part, from the IRS's Revenue Ruling 59–60.[2] And third, all but the IRS standards address professional ethics. The common thread in the reporting standards of each organization is that certain elements must be communicated in a manner that is clear, accurate, and not misleading. These elements include the following:

- Engagement aspects
- Analysis of information and development of value
- Conclusion and signature
- Financial information used
- Limiting conditions and assumptions
- Appraiser representations

At first glance, the process of comparing the various business valuation reporting standards seems fairly straightforward. All that is needed is to check that all the standards require a signature, or a certificate, or report date, and so on. At second glance, such is not the case. Because each standard was written by different organizations, each with a unique style, the standards are, in fact, different in many respects. One could say, "They're pretty much the same," and this may be generally true, but the multiple writing styles do create technical differences. Therefore, it is the responsibility of every valuation specialist to be familiar with those reporting standards promulgated by their respective organization and not to rely on exclusively Exhibit 4.2, which incorporates our interpretation.

## TYPES OF REPORTS

In simple terms, AICPA, ASA, USPAP, and IBA valuation standards permit the valuation specialist to prepare reports that are considered by the authors to be less in detail or "verbiage" than comprehensive or full reports. In Exhibit 4.1, the names of the *full reports* as well as the *other reports* are summarized.

## NACVA

NACVA provides only one form of report, "A Written Report," when expressing a conclusion of value as an opinion of value and therefore a single number, or an estimate of value, which can be expressed as a single number or a range of values. Both the opinion and estimate must meet its "minimum reporting criteria." Other valuation services, such as litigation support or calculations, are not subject to the reporting standards as well as the development standards.

**Exhibit 4.1**  Permitted Valuation/Appraisal Reports

| Organization | Oral Report | Litigation Exception | Name of Full Report | Name of "Other Report(s)" |
|---|---|---|---|---|
| NACVA | No | Yes | A Written Report | None |
| USPAP | Yes | No | Appraisal Report | Restricted Use Appraisal Report |
| ASA | Yes | No (1) | Comprehensive Written Business Valuation Report | Expert Report |
| IBA | Yes | No | Formal Written Appraisal Report | Letter Form Written Appraisal Report |
| | | | | Preliminary Report (Identified as "Limited") |
| AICPA | Yes | Yes | Detailed Report | Summary Report |
| | | | | Calculation Report |

Footnote:
(1) ASA provides "Procedural Guidelines: PG-1 Litigation Support: Role of the Independent Financial Expert," which is non-authoritative.

© Copyright 2007 by Donald P. Wisehart, ASA, CPA/ABV, CVA, MST. Used with permission.

## TAF (USPAP)

USPAP permits the valuation specialist the choice of two written reports, the Appraisal Report, the contents of which are specified in Standards 10-2(a), or the Restricted Use Appraisal Report, the contents of which are specified in Standard 10-2(b). "The essential difference between these options (Appraisal Report vs. Restricted Use Appraisal Report) is in the content and level of information provided."[3] A Restricted Use Appraisal Report must "state a prominent use restriction that limits use of the report to the client and warns that the appraiser's opinion and conclusions set forth in the report may not be understood properly without additional information in the appraiser's work."[4] Also, many of the differences in the two written reports lie in the appraiser's written form of either "summarizing" the content of his or her report in the case of an Appraisal Report, or "stating" the content in the Restricted Use Appraisal Report. USPAP *Advisory Opinion 28,Scope of Work Decision, Performance, and Disclosure*, and *Advisory Opinion 29, An Acceptable Scope of Work*, give the appraiser further guidance as to USPAP's Scope of Work Section requirements.[5]

## ASA

For the most part, the ASA has but one written report, the Comprehensive Written Business Valuation Report, the reporting standards of which are at BSV-III. Of the five organizations—NACVA, ASA, IBA, AICPA, and IRS—the ASA is the only one that requires that all valuation engagements of its members also comply with USPAP,

**Exhibit 4.2** Report Standard Comparative Chart

| Standard | NACVA | ASA (Full) | AICPA (Full) | AICPA (Summary) | AICPA (Calculation) | IBA (Full) | IBA (Letter) | USPAP 10–20 (1) |
|---|---|---|---|---|---|---|---|---|
| **Engagement identification requirements** | | | | | | | | |
| Client | | USPAP | 52 | 71 | 76 (2) | 5.3 | 4.3 | (a) (i) |
| Subject being valued | 4.3.b.1 | p19 IV | 52 | 71 | 76 | 5.3 | 4.3 | (a) (iii) |
| Interest being valued | 4.3.b.2 | p19 IV | 52 | 71 | | 5.3 | 4.3 | (a) (iii) |
| Valuation (or Effective) or Calculation Date | 4.3.b.3 | p19 IV | 52 | 71 | 76 | 5.3 | 4.3 | (a) (vii) |
| Report Date | 4.3.b.4 | p19 IV | 52 | 71 | 76 | 5.3 | 4.3 | (a) (vii) |
| Type of report | | | 52 | 71 | | | | |
| Standard of value defined | 4.3.b.6 | p19 IV | 52 | 71 | | 5.3 | 4.3 | (a) (vi) (3) |
| Premise of value | 4.3.b.7 | p19 IV | 52 | 71 | | 5.3 | 4.3 | (a) (vi) (3) |
| Purpose and intended use of the valuation | 4.3.b.5 | p19 IV | 52 | 71 | | 5.3 | 4.3 | (a) (ii) |
| Sources of information disclosed | | | 53 | 71 | | 5.3 | | (a) (ix) |
| Interviewees | | | 53 | | | | | |
| Site visit disclosure or lack of | | | 53 (4) | | | 1.19 (5) | | |
| **Analysis and development of value requirements** | | (6) | | | | | | (7) |
| Nature and history of business | 3.4.a | p19 V (8) | 57 (9) | | | 5.3 (10) | | (a) (iii) |
| Economic conditions, present and outlook | 3.4.b | p19 V | 57 | | | 5.3 | | (a) (ix) |
| Past, current and future prospects of business/industry | 3.4.c/d/e | p19 VI | 58 | | | 5.3 | | (a) (ix) |
| Financial Analysis of earnings/dividend capacity | | | 58 | | | | | |
| Past sales of interest in the business being appraised | 3.4.g | p19 V | 61 | | | 5.3 | | (a) (ix) |
| Market prices of similar businesses publicly traded | 4.3.b.14 | p20 VII | 61 | | | | | (a) (ix) |
| Similar business/interest sales | | p20 VII | 61 | | | 5.3 | 4.3 | (a) (ix) |
| Ownership, Size, nature, restrictions and agreements | 4.3.b.13 | p20 VII | 61 | | | 5.3 | 4.3 | (a) (ix) |
| Extent the interest appraised contains ownership | Implied | p20 VII B | 52 | 71 | 76 | 5.3 | 4.3 | (a) (iv) |
| Extent interest has or lacks elements of marketability | Implied | p20 VII B | 52 | 71 | 76 | 5.3 | 4.3 | (a) (v) |

|  | | | | | | | | |
|---|---|---|---|---|---|---|---|---|
| Valuation approaches and methods used | 4.3.b.15 (6) | p20 VII A | 59–62 | 71 | 76 (2) | 5.3 | | (a) (ix) |
| Valuation approaches and methods considered | 4.3.b.15 | USPAP | 59–62 | | | 5.3 | | (a) (ix) |
| Valuation approaches and methods rejected | | | | | | | | |
| **Conclusion of value and signature** | 4.3.d | USPAP | 68 | 71 | 76 | 5.3 | 4.5 | (a) (ix) |
| Estimate or opinion disclosure | 4.3.d | p20 VIII | 68 | 71 | | 5.5 | | (a) (ix) |
| Signature of primary appraiser | 4.3.b.17 | p18 II(A) | 68 | 71 | 76 | 1.30 | 1.30 | (a) (xi) |
| Firm signature option | 1.2.k | p18 II(A) | 68 | 71 | 76 | 1.30 | 1.30 | (a) (ix) |
| **Financial information disclosure** | 4.3.b.9 | p19 VI | 54–56 | | | 5.5 | 4.5 | |
| Historical financial statement (F/S) summaries | 4.3.b.16 | p19 VI A | 58 | | | | | (a) (ix) |
| Adjustments to historical F/S summaries | 4.3.b.17 | p19 VI B | 63 | | | | | (a) (ix) |
| Adjusted F/S summaries | 4.3.b.18 | Implied | 58 | | | | | (a) (ix) |
| Projected/forecasted F/S including assumptions | 4.3.b.19 | p19 VI C | 58 | | | | | (a) (ix) |
| Tax return information | | | 53 | | | | | |
| If appropriate, financial comparison to industry | | p19 VI D | 58 | | | | | |
| **Limiting conditions and assumptions** | 4.3.b.8 | p18 III | 52 | 71 | | 5.3 | | (a) (x) |
| The scope of work of the appraisal | 4.3.b.8 | USPAP | 52 | 71 | | | 4.3 | (a) (viii) |
| Use of report limitations | 4.3.b.10 | USPAP | 49 | 71 | | | | (a) (ii) |
| Intended users of the valuation | | USPAP | 52 | 71 | | | | (a) (i) |
| **Representations, disclosures, and certifications** | 4.3.b | USPAP | 51 | 71 | | 5.4 | 4.4 | (a) (xi) |
| Subsequent events in certain circumstances | | | 52 | 71 | | | | |
| Jurisdictional exception application | | USPAP | 52 | 71 | | | | Stated |
| Firm attestation engagement disclosure | | | 54 | | | | | |
| Tax preparer/client relationship disclosure | | | 55 | | | | | |
| Hypothetical conditions if any | | USPAP | 52 | 71 | 74 | 1.22 | 1.22 | (a) (x) |
| Extraordinary assumptions if any | | USPAP | | | | | | (a) (x) |
| Disclosure of not auditing, reviewing or compiling F/S | | | 56 | | | | | |
| The reports scope limitations | 4.3.b.8 | USPAP | 52 | 71 | | | | (a) (viii) |

*(continued)*

**Exhibit 4.2** (Continued)

| Standard | NACVA | ASA (Full) | AICPA (Full) | AICPA (Summary) | AICPA (Calculation) | IBA (Full) | IBA (Letter) | USPAP 10–20 (1) |
|---|---|---|---|---|---|---|---|---|
| Statement of independence | 4.3.b.12 | p18 III A | | | | | | (a) (xi) |
| If a specialist was used, a reliance use statement | | p18 III B | 52 | 71 | | | | (a) (xi) |
| Appraiser representations | | | 65 | 71 | | | | |
| Appraisal certification signed by appraiser | | USPAP | | 71 | 76 | 5.3 | | (a) (xi) |
| No obligation to update statement | | | | | 76 | | | |
| Conforms to organizations' standards | 4.3.c | p18 II(B) | 65 | | | 1.25 | 1.25 | (a) (xi) |
| Qualifications of the appraiser | | | | | | 1.26 | 1.26 | |

Footnotes:

(1) USPAP 10(a) the appraisal report; 10(b) the restricted use report

(2) General description of engagement and calculation procedures agreed upon.

(3) USPAP requires a cite of standard and premise of value.

(4) AICPA requires whether a site visit was made and to what extent.

(5) IBA requires disclosure if no site visit was made by the appraiser.

(6) NACVA refers to Revenue Ruling 59-60 tenets as "fundamental analysis"

(7) USPAP 10(a)(ix) requires that the appraiser summarize the information analyzed, the appraisal procedures followed, and the reasoning that supports the analyses, opinions, and conclusions; exclusion of the market approach, asset-based (cost) approach, or income approach must be explained; 10(b) (ix) requires that the appraiser state the appraisal procedures followed, state the value opinion(s) and conclusion(s) reached, and reference the work file; exclusion of the market approach, asset-based (cost) approach, or income approach must be explained.

(8) ASA includes form of organization, history, products and/or services, markets and customers, management, major assets, both tangible and intangible, and major liabilities, sensitivity to seasonal or cyclical factors, competition and "such other factors"

(9) AICPA refers to nature, background and history, facilities, organizational structure, management team, classes of equity ownership interest and rights attached thereto, products and/or services, geographical markets, key customers and suppliers, competition and business risks.

(10) IBA includes the form of the organization and if incorporated, the state of incorporation, together with a description, adequate to the assignment, of all classes of securities outstanding and a list of shareholders whose interest should, in the appraiser's judgment be specified. If a partnership, the type and the state of filing, together with a list of those partners, whether general or limited, whose interest should, in the appraiser's judgment, be specified.

including USPAP's reporting Standard 10. In addition, the ASA allows for a report to be "less comprehensive" so long as the appraiser is in compliance with Standard 10. Preliminary communications of the results to a client, reporting on the valuation calculations, or other engagements that do not result in a conclusion of value are not subject to the ASA's reporting standards, including USPAP's Standard 10.

## IBA

The IBA provides for three different types of written reports: the Formal Written Report, the Letter Form Written Report, and the Preliminary Report. The Preliminary Report has not been included in Exhibit 4.2 and must be clearly identified as a "limited" opinion of value and include a "Statement of Departure" that reiterates that this limited report is preliminary and that the conclusion of value is subject to changes that could be material.

As stated in section 4.0, the IBA Letter Form Written Appraisal Report is "intended by the parties to reduce the normal burden of writing a comprehensive report, and thereby allow the client to realize some economic benefit." The appraiser, however, must still perform the same level of appraisal analysis as he or she would have performed for a comprehensive formal report.

## AICPA

With the emphasis on disclosure in its other professional standards, it should be of little surprise that the AICPA valuation standards were written with the CPA appraiser in mind. As mentioned earlier, the standards are more detailed than those of other organizations.

The reporting standards permit three types of written reports-detailed, summary, and calculation-which are included in Exhibit 4.2. This is the only set of standards that developed reporting standards for a calculation-only engagement.

Exhibit 4.2, Report Standard Comparative Chart, compares the reporting standards of NACVA, ASA, AICPA, IBA, and TAF (USPAP). Where the reporting standard is applicable, its page or section reference is listed.

## SAMPLE INTANGIBLE ASSET VALUATION REPORT LANGUAGE AND EXAMPLE 1[6]

Disclaimer: Caution for Using Report Example Language

Following is a sample valuation report of a purchase price allocation that reflects the valuation of the intangible assets shown in the Chapter 3 Case Study 1. This sample report language and structure is included only as an example of the type of information a typical analyst may include. Tailoring of this report example is necessary based on the appropriate valuation standards (see the Business Valuation Standards section of this chapter), influences of the business and legal environments, and the specific facts and circumstances of each valuation or engagement.

This sample intangible asset valuation report example and language is considered a minimalist report that is still in conformity with valuation standards. The facts and circumstances of each valuation, assignment, or engagement and sometimes the preferences of the valuation analyst, will dictate the scope and length of the report. The language examples presented here are a tool that is subordinate to the judgment of the valuation professional in charge of the engagement.

This language should not be used unless the valuation professional understands each term and phrase and has verified that the facts of an engagement were properly captured.

Readers who choose to use some or all of this report example ***must*** have an attorney review the terms of these report language examples to make sure they reflect the particular needs of each firm. James Hitchner, Michael Mard, Steven Hyden, David Ellner, Financial Valuation Solutions, LLC, FVG Holdings, LC, and The Financial Valuation Group assume no responsibility for any errors in the language, use of the language, or reliance on the language and shall not be liable for any indirect, special, or consequential damages. Use at your own risk.

This report example is designed only to provide some guidance to valuation analysts, auditors, and company management but is not to be used as a substitute for professional judgment. These procedures must be altered to fit each assignment. The practitioner takes sole responsibility for implementation of this guide. The implied warranties of merchantability and fitness of purpose and all other warranties, whether expressed or implied, are excluded from this transaction and shall not apply to this guide.

---

**FVA&M, LLC Appraisal and Appraisal Report of the Fair Value of the Identified Intangible Assets of Target Company as of December 31, 2006**

April 12, 2007

Mr. Iam Rich
Chief Financial Officer
Acquirer Corp.
900 West Main Road
Providence, RI 91367

Re: Valuation of the Identified Intangible Assets of Target Corporation

Dear Mr. Rich:

At your request, FVA&M, LLC (FVAM) was retained to assist you in the appraisal analysis pertaining to the fair value of the identified intangible assets of Target Company (Target or the Company) by Acquirer Corporation (Acquirer). It is our understanding that our analysis will be used by management of Acquirer in their determination of the value of identifiable assets solely to assist them in their allocation of the purchase price related to the acquisition of Target consummated on December 31, 2006 (the Valuation Date). This purchase price allocation was performed for financial statement reporting purposes only. Our work was performed subject to the assumptions and limiting conditions described in the Appendix of this report.

---

*(continued)*

The accompanying appraisal report presents the data, assumptions, and methodologies employed in developing our recommended values. Our report and analysis are in conformance with the Uniform Standards of Professional Appraisal Practice (USPAP) issued by The Appraisal Foundation. The Appraisal Foundation was authorized by Congress as the source of appraisal standards and appraiser qualifications. The standards deal with the procedures and reporting requirements to be followed in the preparation of an appraisal, analysis, or opinion. Standards 9 and 10 address the guidelines for developing and communicating business appraisals.

We have estimated the fair values of the intangible assets of the Company for purposes of assisting Acquirer in the allocation of the total purchase price solely for financial statement reporting. The premise of value is Going Concern. The intangible assets for which estimates of fair value were developed are summarized below. See Exhibit 4.16 for the complete allocation of purchase price.

| Identifiable Intangible Assets | Fair Value | Remaining Useful Life (In Years) |
|---|---|---|
| Acquired Computer Software | $7,120,000 | 4 |
| Technology | 16,560,000 | 5 |
| In-process Research and Development | 4,530,000 | N/A |
| Trade Name | 12,660,000 | N/A |
| Customer Base | 7,090,000 | 7 |
| Noncompete Agreement | 2,720,000 | 3 |
| Total Identified Intangible Assets | $50,680,000 | |

Our analysis and conclusions, which are to be used only in their entirety, are for the use of Acquirer and its attorneys and accountants solely for financial reporting purposes. They are not to be used for any other purpose, or by any other party for any purpose, without our express written consent.

The approaches and methodologies used in our work did not comprise an examination in accordance with generally accepted accounting principles, the objective of which is an expression of an opinion regarding the fair presentation of financial statements or other financial information, whether historical or prospective, presented in accordance with generally accepted accounting principles.

We express no opinion and accept no responsibility for the accuracy and completeness of the financial information or other data provided to us by others. We assume that the financial and other information provided to us is accurate and complete, and we have relied upon this information in performing our valuation.

If you have any questions concerning this valuation, please contact Barry Good Appraiser at (XXX) XXX–XXXX.

Very truly yours,

FVA&M, LLC

By: Barry Good Appraiser, ASA, CBA, CPA/ABV, CVA

(*continued*)

**TABLE OF CONTENTS**

**PURPOSE OF ENGAGEMENT**

According to the Financial Accounting Standards Board (FASB) Statement of Financial Accounting Standards (SFAS) No. 141, *Business Combinations*, all business combinations completed on or after June 30, 2001, are to be accounted for exclusively by the purchase method. Under purchase accounting, all assets acquired, including goodwill and other intangible assets, should be stated on the financial statements at fair value (see "Standard of Value" discussion below).

FASB Statement No. 141 requires that intangible assets be recognized as assets apart from goodwill if they meet one of two criteria: (1) the contractual-legal criterion or (2) the separability criterion. The Statement also requires the allocation of the purchase price paid to the assets acquired and the liabilities assumed by major balance-sheet caption.

An intangible asset shall be recognized as an asset apart from goodwill if it arises from contractual or other legal rights (regardless of whether those rights are transferable or separable from the acquired entity or from other rights and obligations). If an intangible asset does not arise from contractual or other legal rights, it shall be recognized as an asset apart from goodwill only if it is separable; that is, it is capable of being separated or divided from the acquired entity and sold, transferred, licensed, rented, or exchanged (regardless of whether there is an intent to do so). An intangible asset that cannot be sold, transferred, licensed, rented, or exchanged individually is considered separable if it can be sold, transferred, licensed, rented, or exchanged in combination with a related contract, asset, or liability.

*(continued)*

The excess of the cost of an acquired entity over the net of the amounts assigned to assets acquired and liabilities assumed is referred to as goodwill. An acquired intangible asset that does not meet the criterion mentioned above shall be included in the amount recognized as goodwill.

According to the definition in Appendix F of FASB Statement No. 141, the standard of value to be used in the application of purchase accounting rules is *fair value*. *Fair value* is defined as:

> The amount at which that asset (or liability) could be bought (or incurred) or sold (or settled) in a current transaction between willing parties, that is, other than in a forced or liquidation sale.[1]

The premise of value is Going Concern, defined as:

> An ongoing operating business enterprise.[2]

Going Concern Value is defined as:

> The value of a business enterprise that is expected to operate into the future. The intangible elements of Going Concern Value result from factors such as having a trained workforce, an operational plant, and the necessary licenses, systems, and procedures in place.[3]

## SCOPE OF SERVICES

We were engaged by the management of Acquirer to assist in their estimate of the fair values of the identified intangible assets of Target Company as of December 31, 2006.

- We understand that Acquirer will use our analysis in allocating the acquisition purchase price to fair values of the identified intangible assets of Target solely for financial reporting purposes in accordance with SFAS No. 141 and SFAS No. 142.
- Our analysis and conclusions are based on our discussions with the managements of Acquirer and Target, and a review of key transaction documents and records, including:
  - Agreement and Plan of Merger by and among Acquirer Corp. and Target Company, dated December 31, 2006
  - Audited Financial Statements for the Years Ended December 31, 2003, 2004, 2005, and 2006. Prepared by Stump & Dewey.
  - Business plan developed by Target, dated July 26, 2006
  - Transaction Analysis prepared by Acquirer's accountants, Stump & Dewey, dated August 15, 2006
  - Preliminary Due Diligence Draft Report, dated August 15, 2006, prepared by Stump & Dewey and signed by Forrest Stump, partner-in-charge
  - Target Due Diligence Report prepared by John Shire, Acquirer, dated March 27, 2006
  - Target Legal Due Diligence Memorandum prepared by Clue & Clue, dated June 15, 2006
  - Target Preliminary Information, Due Diligence Package by Flotsom & Jetsom, dated March 2006
  - Target Multiyear Plan (Projections) for the next five fiscal years, beginning 2007
  - Target and Vendor Technology Licensing Agreements, 2000–2006
- We also relied upon publicly available information from sources on capital markets, including industry reports, and various databases of publicly traded companies and news.

*(continued)*

In performing our analysis, we interviewed the following members of the Acquirer and Target:

- Acquirer
  - Carl Stiffer, Chief Architect
  - Iam Rich, CFO
  - Ivan Outbard, Vice President of Sales
  - Bruce Gender, Vice President of Operations
  - Samuel Hock, Vice President of Human Resources
- Target
  - Doug Noon, Chief Executive Officer
  - Marshall Fox, Chief Financial Officer
  - Gregory Ball, Chief Operations Officer
  - Luis Gerig, Vice President of Sales
  - Martha L. Litsey, Vice President of Technology
  - Robert Garcia, Vice President of Human Resources

**CERTIFICATION**

I certify that, to the best of my knowledge and belief:

- The statements of fact contained in this report are true and correct.
- The reported analyses, opinions, and conclusions are limited only by the reported assumptions and limiting conditions and are my personal, impartial, and unbiased professional analyses, opinions, and conclusions.
- I have no (or the specified) present or prospective interest in the property that is the subject of this report, and I have no (or the specified) personal interest with respect to the parties involved.
- I have no bias with respect to the property that is the subject of this report or to the parties involved with this assignment.
- My engagement in this assignment was not contingent upon developing or reporting predetermined results.
- My compensation for completing this assignment is not contingent upon the development or reporting of a predetermined value or direction in value that favors the cause of the client, the amount of the value opinion, the attainment of a stipulated result, or the occurrence of a subsequent event directly related to the intended use of this appraisal.
- My analyses, opinions, and conclusions were developed, and this report has been prepared, in conformity with the Uniform Standards of Professional Appraisal Practice. [State other standards if applicable, e.g., AICPA, ASA, NACVA, IBA]
- No one provided significant business and/or intangible asset appraisal assistance to the person signing this certification. [If there are exceptions, the name of each individual providing significant business and/or intangible asset appraisal assistance must be stated.]

Barry Good Appraiser, ASA, CBA, CPA/ABV, CVA
FVA&M, LLC

*(continued)*

## EXECUTIVE SUMMARY — IDENTIFIABLE INTANGIBLE ASSETS RECOGNIZED APART FROM GOODWILL

| Identifiable Intangible Asset | Description of Asset | Valuation Methodology | Estimated Fair Value | Estimated Remaining Useful Life (years) |
|---|---|---|---|---|
| Acquired Computer Software | Internally developed by Company; written in a sophisticated language | Cost Approach— Replacement cost new less obsolescence | $7,120,000 | 4 |
| Technology | Includes Target's completed construction accounting software | Income Approach— Multiperiod Excess Earnings Method | 16,560,000 | 5 |
| In-process Research and Development | Includes Target's in-process research and development; this is "brand-new" and "stand-alone" architectural software | Income Approach— Multiperiod Excess Earnings Method | 4,530,000 | N/A |
| Trade Name | The trade name "XXX" under which all Target's products are sold and services provided | Income Approach— Relief from royalty method | 12,660,000 | N/A |
| Customer Base | Includes the Company's total network of distributors and large and midsize retail outlets | Income Approach— Multiperiod Excess Earnings Method | 7,090,000 | 7 |
| Noncompete Agreement | Includes the noncompete agreements of the Company's top executive(s) | Income Approach— Difference in "with" and "without" competition | 2,720,000 | 3 |
| TOTAL | | | $50,680,000 | |

(*continued*)

## INTRODUCTION—TRANSACTION OVERVIEW

Acquirer acquired all of the outstanding shares of Target Company (Target or the Company) on December 31, 2006:

- The purchase price of the acquisition was $209 million, which included $150 million in cash plus $59 million in assumption of liabilities.

In our discussions with Acquirer management and review of key transaction documents, several reasons were cited for the acquisition of Target, including:

- The profitability of the Target business. Acquirer expects this profitability to impact its bottom line immediately.
- Target's product and service offerings complement Acquirer's, thus allowing Acquirer to advance its business strategy. Acquirer is seeking to further penetrate the software architectural market, and management believes that Target offers the technology for this market.
- The intellectual property of Target offers great opportunity in the marketplace.

*Sources:* Press Release, "Acquirer Corp. to Acquire Target Company" dated December 4, 2006.

## COMPANY OVERVIEWS

*Acquiring Company*

Acquirer uses its technological advanced accounting software products to provide highly technological services to a network of publicly held distributors and Fortune 500 companies requiring state-of-the-art accounting software products.

- Acquirer operates in the following two segments:
  1. Distribution networks of publicly held companies that provide Acquirer's products and services to small to midsize companies.
  2. Direct sales and services to Fortune 500 companies.
- Acquirer's accounting software provides its customers with the ability to monitor every facet of their accounting cycle in real time.
- Acquirer currently markets its products to the United States, Europe, and Asia.
- Acquirer is headquartered in San Francisco, California.
- Acquirer reported FY 2005 sales of approximately $800 million, and FY 2006 sales are expected to be approximately $1 billion.

*Target Company*

Target is a world leader in quality construction and architectural design.

- Target has a reputation for providing state-of-the-art construction design that offers unparalleled reliability and software support.
- Target's software integrates with its customer inventory systems in real time to deliver maximum inventory level efficiency.
- Target utilizes the finite element method to solve linear and nonlinear construction-related problems.
- Target serves clients in all construction industries.
- Target has 65 employees, 3 regional offices, and a network of technically advanced distributors throughout the United States.
- Target is headquartered in North Kingstown, Rhode Island, and was founded in 1992.

*Sources:* Press Release, Monopolies, "Acquirer Corp. to Acquire Target Company to Create Next-Generation Software for the Construction and Architectural industries," dated December 4, 2006.

*(continued)*

**ECONOMIC OVERVIEW**

The economy continued to grow, although at a slightly slower pace, in 2006. Price inflation accelerated a bit, largely due to increasing energy prices, although food prices also rose in 2006. Consumer spending continued to fuel growth, although spending on durable goods such as cars slowed considerably from the 2005 level. The employment situation was improving in 2006. Consumers showed confidence in present conditions at the end of 2006, while future expectations were less optimistic.

In September 2006, consumer confidence fell by the largest single-month amount in 15 years, due in large part to hurricanes on the Gulf Coast and their effects on the economy. The most obvious effect was on energy prices, which increased over 100% in the third quarter, although prices had moderated somewhat by the end of the year. Housing remained a positive factor in the economy in 2006, although forecasters continued to warn that the housing boom was slowing and would likely be unable to power the economy in 2007, as it did in the prior several years. The Fed increased interest rates by 1.5% during 2006. Economic growth, as measured by the real gross domestic product (GDP), was expected to slow only slightly in 2007 (3.4%). Likewise, inflation, as measured by the consumer price index (CPI), was forecasted to decelerate in 2007, with prices expected to increase 2.9% for the year.

A summary of major points concerning the nation's economic condition as of December 31, 2006, follows:

- For the year 2006, real GDP increased 3.5%, compared to 4.2% for the year in 2005. Consumer spending, equipment and software, and residential fixed investment contributed to the increase in GDP. Exports increased in 2006, but imports (which are a subtraction in the calculation of GDP) increased more, resulting in a negative contribution to GDP from trade. Growth was expected to slow somewhat in 2007 and 2008.
- In 2006, energy prices rose significantly, by the largest annual increase since 1990. Energy prices accounted for about 40% of the overall advance in the CPI, with petroleum-based energy accounting for about half of that advance. Core inflation in 2006 was unchanged from the previous year. Inflation at both the consumer and producer levels was expected to slow in 2007 and 2008.
- Consumer spending on durable goods increased by 4.4% in 2006, a slower rate than in the previous year. Nondurable goods spending and spending on services increased by 4.4% and 2.9%, respectively-about the same rates as in 2005. Consumer confidence rose slightly in 2006, as consumers reacted to a resilient economy, improving employment conditions, and lower energy prices at the end of the year.
- Market-driven interest rates fluctuated in 2006, with short-term rates rising sharply while long-term rates fell slightly from the year-earlier rates. The discount and federal funds rates were 5.25% and 4.25%, respectively, in December 2006. Long-term rates were expected to rise in 2007 and 2008, while short-term rates were expected to rise in the first half of 2007 and then level off through 2008.
- Financial markets remained near year-earlier levels in 2006 due in part to rising energy prices and low future expectations by consumers. Forecasters expected stock prices to increase steadily in 2007 and 2008, although at a slower pace than previously forecasted.
- Housing remained strong in 2006. Multifamily housing began to moderate, while single-family construction increased for the year. The average annual mortgage rates were essentially unchanged from a year earlier. Rates were expected to rise through 2007. It was anticipated that rising rates would cause housing starts and sales to slow somewhat.

*(continued)*

- Forecasters predicted that the economy would continue to strengthen in 2007, although at a slightly slower pace.

_Source:_ The Financial Valuation Group, Inc., 2006 4th Quarter Economic Review and 2007 Outlook.
[Note: The length and detail of an economic outlook section is based on the availability of information and the decision of the analyst.]

## INDUSTRY OVERVIEW

2006 Revenue in the Construction and Architectural Software (CAD) market is projected to finish the year at $10.6 billion, 11% higher than 2005 revenue. Several key trends factor into this recent growth:

- Construction and architectural firms are more receptive to the benefits of CAD software.
  - Contractors are moving away from cost-cutting measures and toward innovation, which can only benefit software companies and the CAD market.
  - CAD makes data available at the beginning of the project cycle, which provides the contractor with more complete and accurate design information early in the project development.
  - CAD software and tools continue to evolve and improve.
- The strong foreign currencies boost the data when reported in U.S. dollars.
- All segments of the CAD market performed above expectations in 2005 and are expected to do well again in 2006.
- Revenues in the CAD market are expected to grow 9% annually over the next four years.

_Adapted from:_ Datatech, Inc, "CAD Market Projected to Top $10.6 Billion in 2006, up 11 percent," dated April 27, 2006.

The growth in the CAD market is expected to be the main driver of growth in the Accounting software industry as a whole. Acct-Tech expects revenue in this market to grow at 12% per year through 2011.

- This growth can be attributed to several trends in this industry:
  - The software is becoming increasingly easier to implement and use.
  - Higher performance computing is now available and affordable, which results in better CAD software.
  - Contractors are beginning to recognize the benefits of CAD technology.
- In 2006, approximately 25.0% of the CAD investments will come from this industry.
- Acct-Tech says that growth should be even higher than the forecasted 12% because:
  - CAD software results in higher quality, better design, in less time for a lower price. In short, CAD technology can be a major competitive advantage for contractors. Therefore, more companies should be switching to the CAD software, but this is not yet the case because:
    - Contractors are hesitant about using software systems.
    - CAD is taking a back seat to other significant issues.

_(continued)_

- Once the software developers find a way to communicate the ease and effectiveness of the CAD software to contractors, the growth in this industry should rise even higher than its current rate.

*Adapted from:* Acct-Tech, Inc, "Acct-Tech Forecasts Digital Simulation Market to Top $2.1 Billion in 2005, up 12 percent," dated August 4, 2005.
[Note: The length and detail of an industry overview section is based on the availability of information and the decision of the analyst.]

## VALUATION METHODOLOGY

The appraisal of any asset can be broadly classified into one of three approaches, namely, the asset-based (i.e., cost), market, and income approaches. In any appraisal analysis, all three approaches must be considered, and the approach or approaches deemed most relevant will then be selected for use in the fair value analysis of that asset.

### Cost Approach

This is a general way of determining a fair value indication of a business, business owner-ship interest, security, or intangible asset by using one or more methods based on the value of the assets net of liabilities.[4]

The cost approach establishes value based on the cost of reproducing or replacing the property, less depreciation from physical deterioration and functional and economic obso-lescence, if present and measurable.

### Market Approach

This is a general way of determining a fair value indication of a business, business owner-ship interest, security, or intangible asset by using one or more methods that compare the subject to similar businesses, business ownership interests, securities, or intangible assets that have been sold.[5]

However, intangible assets are typically transferred only as part of the sale of a going concern, not in piecemeal transactions. Furthermore, because intangible assets are often unique to a particular business entity, comparison among entities can be difficult to make even if the data were available. Consequently, the market approach is often of limited use in the valuation of many intangible assets.

### Income Approach

This is a general way of determining a fair value indication of a business, business owner-ship interest, security, or intangible asset by using one or more methods that convert anticipated benefits into a present value amount.[6]

In the income approach, an economic benefit stream of the asset under analysis is selected, usually based on historical and/or forecasted cash flow. The focus is to determine a benefit stream that is reasonably reflective of the asset's most likely future benefit stream. This selected benefit stream is then discounted to present value with an appropriate risk-adjusted discount rate. Discount rate factors often include general market rates of return at the valuation date, business risks associated with the industry in which the company operates, and other risks specific to the asset being valued.

*(continued)*

In the valuation of intangible assets, elements of the income approach and the market approach are sometimes used simultaneously. For example, in the valuation of a trademark, a market investigation could establish a current fair royalty rate, and this rate could then be used as the basis for a projection of royalty savings to be discounted to present value.

*Valuation of Intangible Assets*

We have concluded to the fair values of the identifiable assets acquired in the purchase of Target. Based on our analysis and discussions with management, the following intangible assets were identified as having value:

>   Acquired Computer Software
>   Technology
>   In-process Research and Development
>   Trade Name
>   Customer Base
>   Assembled Workforce
>   Noncompete Agreement

Assembled workforce is not an identifiable intangible asset under SFAS No. 141. As part of our calculation of contributory asset charges, we were required to calculate a value for the assembled workforce. The value of the assembled workforce is included within the value of residual goodwill.

## DETERMINATION OF DISCOUNT RATE

Two approaches were used to estimate the Company's weighted average cost of capital (WACC). In our first approach, we relied on the business enterprise projections and value based on the acquisition of Target to arrive at an implied discount rate, which is the rate that, if used to discount the projected cash flows, would result in a present value equal to the actual amount paid for the invested capital. The discount rate implied by an arm's-length transaction is often a reliable indicator of the acquired company's WACC.

In our second approach, we developed Target's cost of equity capital and cost of debt capital based on data and factors relevant to the economy, the industry, and the Company as of the valuation date. These costs were then weighted in terms of a typical or market participant industry capital structure to arrive at the Company's estimated WACC.

*Analysis of Transaction*

This valuation engagement was precipitated by the acquisition of Target by Acquirer. The asset purchase price for Target included cash of $150,000,000 and the assumption of debt of $59,000,000, for a total cost of $209,000,000. Deducting for non-interest-bearing current liabilities assumed of $25,000,000 implied a business enterprise (invested capital) value of $184,000,000. Management provided us with a financial forecast. The financial projections are provided in the schedule on the following page. Provided below is a brief description of the major assumptions.

*Major Assumptions*

- Management provided a five-year financial forecast. Through discussions with management, this forecast was extended an additional five years. According to management,

(*continued*)

the revenue growth rate and cost structure of the Company are expected to stabilize. We evaluated management's projections by comparing profit margins and growth rates from various sources (e.g., public companies, benchmark data, industry and economic data) to determine what they would be from the view of market participants. We determined that the forecast reasonably represented the assumptions of market participants.

- Sales are forecast to increase 15% from $60 million in 2006 to $69 million in year 1 of the forecast due to conversions, upgrades, new customers, and price increases. Sales are expected to increase 15% in year 2 as one of the Company's key markets is expected to grow. The growth rate of that key market is expected to decline after year 2. The sales growth forecast by year is as follows: 15% in year 1 through year 2, 12.5% in year 3, 10% in year 4 through year 5, and 7.5% in year 6 through year 10. The 10-year compound annual growth rate is 9.96%.
- Cost of sales are 40% in year 1 and are expected to improve to 39% thereafter.
- Operating expenses are 30% in year 1 and are expected to improve to 29% thereafter. These margins do not consider depreciation and amortization.
- Debt-free working capital requirements were forecast at 15% of sales, based on the company's historical working capital position, expected needs, and industry benchmarks.
- Capital expenditures are forecast at 1% of net sales. This level of capital expenditures is considered adequate to support future levels of sales.
- Tax amortization of total intangible asset value is based on Section 197 of the Internal Revenue Code. The amortization acts as a tax shield and is added back to cash flow.
- The combined federal and state tax rate is estimated at 40%.
- The residual perpetual growth rate is 5%, based on discussions with management and an analysis of the industry.

Based on these projections, the implied WACC is approximately 16%.
See Exhibits 4.3 and 4.4 for our projections and reconciliation of the business enterprise value.

*Development of Weighted Average Cost of Capital (WACC)*

We also considered market and industry data to develop the weighted average cost of capital[7] for Target.

The traditional formula for calculating the WACC is:

$$\text{WACC} = (k_e \times W_e) + (k_p \times W_p) + (k_{d(pt)}[1 - t] \times W_d)$$

Where:
WACC = Weighted average cost of capital
$k_e$ = Cost of common equity capital
$W_e$ = Percentage of common equity in the capital structure, at market value
$k_p$ = Cost of preferred equity
$W_p$ = Percentage of preferred equity in the capital structure, at market value
$k_{d(pt)}$ = Cost of debt (pretax)
$t$ = Tax rate
$W_d$ = Percentage of debt in the capital structure, at market value[8]

*(continued)*

Based on an analysis of Target's industry, we relied on a capital structure of 35% debt and 65% equity. Using the estimates of the cost of equity and cost of debt, and weighting them based on the assumed capital structure resulted in a WACC as follows:

$$
\begin{aligned}
\text{WACC} &= (22.00\% \times 65.00\%) + (9.25\%[1 - 40.00\%] \times 35.00\%) \\
&= (14.30\%) + (5.55\% \times 35.00\%) \\
&= (14.30\%) + (1.94\%) \\
&= 16.24\% \\
&\text{Rounded to, } 16\%
\end{aligned}
$$

*Concluded Discount Rate*   The discount rate conclusion from the development of the WACC reconciles with the discount rate implied by the transaction.

The indicated WACC is 16.0%.

*Development of Cost of Equity*

We considered three alternative methods to calculate the cost of equity of Target, including the modified capital asset pricing model, build-up model and build-up model with a combined market and size risk premium. These three methods are considered some of the more common methods.[9]

*Modified Capital Asset Pricing Model*   The modified capital asset pricing model ("MCAPM"), as applied to a closely held company such as Target can be summarized as follows:

$$
\begin{aligned}
\text{ke} &= \text{Rf} + (\text{RPm}) * \beta + \text{RΠσ} + \text{RΠθ φηερε} \\
\text{ke} &= \text{Cost of equity} \\
\text{Rf} &= \text{Rate of return on } a \text{ risk-free security} \\
\text{RPm} &= \text{Equity risk premium for the market} \\
\beta &= \text{Beta (Systematic risk; industry risk relative to the market)} \\
\text{Rps} &= \text{Size premium} \\
\text{Rpu} &= \text{Company specific (unsystematic) risk}
\end{aligned}
$$

*Build-Up Method*   The build-up approach can be summarized as follows[10]:

$$
\begin{aligned}
\text{ke} &= \text{Rf} + \text{RPm} + \text{RPs} + \text{RPu} + \text{RPl} \text{ where} \\
\text{ke} &= \text{Cost of equity} \\
\text{Rf} &= \text{Rate of return on a risk-free security} \\
\text{RPm} &= \text{Equity risk premium for the market} \\
\text{Rps} &= \text{Size premium} \\
\text{Rpu} &= \text{Company specific (unsystematic)risk} \\
\text{RPl} &= \text{Industry specific risk}
\end{aligned}
$$

*Risk Free Return (Rf).*   The rate of return on a risk-free security was found by looking at the yields of United States Treasury securities. Ideally, the duration of the security used as an indication of the risk-free rate should match the horizon of the projected cash flows that are being discounted (which is into perpetuity in the present case). We relied on the 20-year Treasury rate of 4.91% as of December 29, 2006.

*(continued)*

*Market Equity Premium (rpm ) and Size Risk Premium (RPs).*   The risk premium for the equity market and risk premium for small stocks can be calculated based upon figures provided in Stocks, Bonds, Bills and Inflation, published by Ibbotson Associates.[11] The risk premium for the market can be calculated by subtracting the mean return for long-term government bonds from the mean return for large-company stocks. Based on the Ibbotson data, we relied on a market risk premium (RPm) of 7.1%.

The size risk premium for small stocks (over the risk premium for the market) can be calculated by subtracting the estimated return in excess of the riskless rate from the realized return in excess of the riskless rate of companies. In the case of Target, we applied the size premium return in excess of CAPM of companies the 10th decile of the NYSE. Once again we relied on the studies performed by Ibbotson Associates as reflected in their Stocks, Bonds, Bills, and Inflation: 2006 Yearbook. The indicated small-stock risk premium (RPs) was 6.36%.

Another alternative method relies on the Standard & Poor's (now Duff & Phelps) study published by Ibbotson Associates to calculate the combined market risk premium and size premium.[12] The study identifies the combined equity risk premium for a company based on certain characteristics, including market-invested capital, book and market value of equity, historical earnings and number of employees. Based on this data, we estimated a combined (market and size) equity risk premium of approximately 13%.

*Beta (β).*   In the MCAPM formula, Beta is a measure of the systematic risk of a particular investment relative to the market for all investment assets. We obtained betas for six identified publicly traded guideline companies (ABC Corp, DEF Inc., GHI Inc, JKL Corp, MNO Inc., PQR Inc.). The identified betas were unlevered to remove the effects of financial leverage on the indication of relative risk provided by the beta, and relevered at the optimal industry capital structure. The median guideline company unlevered beta was 0.95, and when relevered to the company's capital structure, the indicated beta was 1.26.

*Industry Risk Premium.*   Ibbotson publishes industry risk premiums based on an analysis of betas for public companies identified by SIC codes. The risk premiums calculated by Ibbotson generally include a larger sample size than the beta analysis calculated from our guideline public company analysis. The data for the guideline companies is a more targeted sample of companies that are more similar to Target. The Ibbotson industry risk premium for SIC 7373: computer integrated system design included a sample size of 140 companies. The indicated risk premium was 6.34%.

*Firm Specific (UNSYSTEMATIC) Risk (RPu).*   The risk premium for unsystematic risk attributable to the specific company is designed to account for additional risk factors specific to the Company.

Firm specific risk factors may include the following:

• Competition
• Customer Concentration
• Size
• Poor Access to Capital
• Thin Management
• Lack of Diversification

(*continued*)

- Environmental
- Litigation
- Distribution Channels
- Old Technology
- Company Outlook

We considered the factors above in determining the company specific risk premium to apply to the cost of equity of Target. We applied a 0% company specific risk premium to the cost of equity of Target.

*Cost of Equity Conclusion*    The MCAPM implied a cost of equity for Target of 20.22%. The build-up model implied a cost of equity of 24.71% (Exhibit 4.5). The build-up model relying on the Duff & Phelps risk premium study combined size specific equity risk premium indicated a cost of equity of 24.25% (Exhibit 4.6). Based on the indicated range of values, we selected a cost of equity for Target of 22.00%.

## VALUATION OF IDENTIFIED INTANGIBLE ASSETS

This section describes the valuation methodologies used to value the identified intangible assets of Target:

| Asset | Valuation Approach |
|---|---|
| Acquired Computer Software | Cost Approach—Replacement cost new less obsolescence |
| Assembled Workforce | Cost Approach—Replacement cost new |
| Trade Name | Income Approach—Relief from royalty method |
| Noncompete Agreement | Income Approach—Difference in "with" and "without" competition |
| Technology | Income Approach—Multiperiod excess earnings method |
| In-process Research and Development | Income Approach—Multiperiod excess earnings method |
| Customer Base | Income Approach—Multiperiod excess earnings method |
| Goodwill | Residual |

## VALUATION ANALYSIS—ACQUIRED COMPUTER SOFTWARE

*Description*

- Target's computer software was internally developed by Target and is not commercially available. The company's software system comprises 20 modules. The software is written in a very sophisticated programming language.

*Valuation Methodology*

- Cost Approach—Replacement cost new less obsolescence
  - Management provided a report detailing the number of lines of code per program and/or module.

*(continued)*

- Management assessed a productivity rate of 1 to 3. A rating of 1 indicates code could be programmed at a rate of four lines per hour; a rating of 2 indicates three lines per hour; and a rating of 3 indicates two lines per hour. The code ratings encompass completely debugged program statements.
- We divided the lines of code for each module by the coding rate to determine the number of hours to re-create the program/module.
- We multiplied the sum of the hours by the blended hourly rate.
- We applied an obsolescence factor of 25% to recognize the fact that the acquired software was not new.
- We adjusted the replacement cost for taxes and added an amortization benefit factor to reflect the additional value accruing to the asset due to the deduction of tax amortization over the 15-year tax life of the asset.

*Major Assumptions*

- Per discussions with management, we determined the total lines of code of each of the 20 modules.
- Productivity ratings of 1 through 3, as assessed by management, were determined at rates commensurate with the complexity of code.
- A fully burdened hourly rate of $119 per hour was determined to re-create the software based on a project team of ten individuals consisting of a project manager, two system analysts, one technical writer, four programmers, and two support persons.
- Per discussions with management regarding the capabilities of the software, an obsolescence factor of 25% was determined to be appropriate based on the number of lines of redundant/extraneous code, effective age, and remaining economic life of the system.
- We utilized a discount rate of 17%.
- Contributory Asset Charges
  - No contributory or supporting assets are applicable.

*Conclusion of Fair Value of Asset:*

- See Exhibit 4.7 for detailed calculations.
- Concluded value was $7,120,000.

### VALUATION ANALYSIS—ASSEMBLED WORKFORCE

*Description*

- Target has an assembled and trained workforce. As such, Acquirer does not have to expend time, effort, and money to recruit, select, and train employees with comparable skills and expertise.

*Valuation Methodology*

- Cost Approach—Replacement cost new
  - Based on information from and discussions with management, we estimated the anticipated salaries a market participant would pay for each of the 65 employees of Target.
  - We determined the hiring cost associated with replacing Target's workforce. Hiring costs are based on cost to recruit.

(*continued*)

- We determined the cost to train a replacement workforce. Training costs are based on estimates of inefficiency while the new workforce is trained and a fully burdened weekly salary of each employee.
- Next, we determined the anticipated cost to interview the replacement workforce. Interview costs are based on the class of the employee and the typical number of hours to interview each replacement employee.
- The summation of the hiring cost, training cost, and interview costs is the cost to replace Target's workforce.
- We adjusted the replacement cost for taxes and added an amortization benefit factor to reflect the additional value accruing to the asset due to the deduction of tax amortization over the 15-year tax life of the asset.

*Major Assumptions*

- Recruiting Costs
  - Per discussions with management, the average recruiting cost is 27.5% of starting salaries, which includes fees to employment agencies, advertising, and other recruitment-related expenses.

- Training and Supervisory Costs
  - Training costs were estimated by determining the amount of time a new employee would be "inefficient" in performing his or her duties within the organization.
  - Training and supervisory costs were estimated by multiplying the fully burdened weekly salary of each employee by the average rate of inefficiency incurred during the training period of 33.3%.
  - The training periods varied with each employee classification, Employee classifications are defined in Exhibit 4.8.

- Interview Costs
  - Interview costs per management are estimated at a fully burdened interview rate of $75 per hour.
  - The workforce was separated into three classes based on the anticipated number of hours to interview each class. The anticipated number of interview hours for class 1 is 5 hours, class 2 is 10 hours, and class 3 is 20 hours.

- Contributory Asset Charges
  - No contributory or supporting assets are applicable.
  - The value of the assembled workforce is determined so that a contributory charge may be applied in determining the value of technology and customer base. However, the fair value of assembled workforce is included in goodwill in the final allocation of the purchase price, not as a separate asset.
- Other
  - We utilized a discount rate 16%.

*Conclusion of Fair Value of Asset*

- See Exhibit 4.8 for detailed calculations.
- Concluded value was $1,790,000.

**VALUATION ANALYSIS–TRADE NAME**

*Description*

- All products and services by Target are sold under the trade name "*XXX*".

(*continued*)

*Valuation Methodology:*

- Income Approach—Relief from royalty method
  - We relied on revenue projections utilized in determining the business enterprise value of the company and as provided by management. Revenue projections were provided for the ten-year projection period beginning in 2007. We also relied on a revenue projection for the residual year.
  - We determined the appropriate royalty rate based on a review of publicly available data on trademark/trade name licensing transactions and a comparison of the name recognition between "XXX" and the guideline royalties.
  - We multiplied this pretax royalty rate to the forecast revenue over the ten-year forecast period and the residual year revenue projection.
  - We applied a tax rate of 40% to the projected trade name cash flows.
  - Next, we determined the present value of the after-tax cash flow of the trade name over the ten-year forecast period and added the present value of the residual at the end of the ten-year period.
  - Finally, we added the amortization benefit factor.

*Major Assumptions*

- A pretax royalty rate of 2% was determined based on discussions with management and an analysis of The Financial Valuation Group's proprietary database. Information from this database documented a range of royalty rates for trademarks to be from 1% to 10%. The median royalty rate was 4%.
- Acquirer has the right to use the name "XXX" in perpetuity; therefore, the trade name is an indefinite life asset.
- We utilized a discount rate of 16%.
- Contributory Asset Charges
  - No contributory or supporting assets are applicable.

*Conclusion of Fair Value of Asset*

- See Exhibit 4.9 for detailed calculations.
- Concluded value was $12,660,000

## VALUATION ANALYSIS—NONCOMPETE AGREEMENT

*Description*

- Paragraph 10.1 of Article X of the Acquirer/Target purchase agreement identifies the three-year noncompete agreement, which commences at the purchase transaction date.

*Valuation Methodology*

- Income Approach—Difference in cash flows "with" and "without" competition
  - We held discussions with management to determine what impact the seller would have on the financial prospects of the Company if the seller were able to compete.
  - We started with the projections as provided by management that we utilized in verifying the cost of capital and in determining the cash flows of other identifiable intangible assets.
  - We determined the indicated company cash flow based on management's projections assuming that the noncompete agreement was in place.

*(continued)*

- We determined the indicated cash flow of the company, making changes to the initial projections based on management's indications as to how the projections would differ if the noncompete agreement did not exist and the seller were able to compete.
- We determined the difference in the cash flows with and without the noncompete agreement in place.
- We calculated the annual implied differential and discounted those cash flows to present value at the estimated rate of return of the noncompete agreement.
- Next, we determined the probability that the seller would compete, based on conversations with management and economic and industry factors.
- The present value of the noncompete agreement was reduced by the probability that the seller would not compete.
- Finally, we added the amortization benefit factor.

*Major Assumptions*

We relied on a cash flow forecast as provided by management

- Forecast

  - We utilized initial projections provided by management as described in the analysis of the transaction section of the determination of the WACC.
  - Management has projected that if the seller were free to compete, he would be able to take a total of approximately 10% of revenue in 2007, 20% in 2008, and 10% the next year. Management believes that after the third year, the seller would not take any of the company's projected revenues.
  - Expense percentages for COGS and operating expense percentages would not be affected by competition for the seller.
- Other
  - We utilized a discount rate of 16%.

*Conclusion of Fair Value of Asset*

- See Exhibits 4.10a, 4.10b and 4.10c for detailed calculations.
- Concluded value was $2,720,000.

## VALUATION ANALYSIS–TECHNOLOGY (CONSTRUCTION ACCOUNTING SOFTWARE)

*Description*

- Construction accounting software providing state-of-the-art real-time access.

*Valuation Methodology*

- Income Approach—Multiperiod excess earnings method
  - We used the business enterprise value as a starting point. We relied on pretax earnings attributable to the technology that existed at the valuation date.
  - We applied contributory charges to the technology cash flow to represent the use of contributory assets employed to support the technology-based and customer based assets and help generate revenue (Exhibit 4.11).
  - We discounted the surviving residual cash flow to present value using the discount rate of the asset.
  - Finally, we deducted an income tax charge and added the amortization benefit factor.

*(continued)*

*Major Assumptions*

We relied on a cash flow forecast as provided by management.

- Forecast
  - Revenue is estimated at 2006 levels, which are expected to decline over time as the technology becomes obsolete and competitors increasingly impact sales.
  - Deductions are made for cost of goods sold (40% of revenue attributable to existing technology in 2007 and 39% thereafter).
  - Deductions are made for operating expenses (20% of revenue in 2007 and then 19% after deducting estimated development expenses of 10% from the operating expense base to reflect the fact that the developed technology should not be burdened by expenses of developing new technology).
- Other
  - We utilized a discount rate of 18%.
- Contributory Asset Charges
  - Contributory charges were made for supporting or contributory assets employed to support the Company's existing technology and assist in the generation of revenues.
  - Contributory charges after tax are directly related to the analyst's assessment of the risk inherent in each asset. Contributory asset charges are as follows:

| | |
|---|---|
| Net Working Capital | 5.0% |
| Land and Building | 7.0% |
| Machinery and Equipment, net | 8.0% |
| Computer Software | 17.0% |
| Trade Name | 16.0% |
| Noncompete Agreement | 16.0% |
| Assembled Workforce | 16.0% |
| Customer Base | 17.0% |

- Contributory charges are allocated between existing and in-process technology based on relative revenues.

*Conclusion of Fair Value of Asset*

- See Exhibit 4.12 for detailed calculations.
- Concluded value was $16,560,000.

**VALUATION ANALYSIS–IN-PROCESS RESEARCH AND DEVELOPMENT**

*Description*

- Architectural Accounting Development (AAD) Software— This new technology is stand-alone technology not supported by the base or core technology.

*Valuation Methodology*

- Income Approach–Multiperiod excess earnings method
  - We used the business enterprise value as a starting point. As such, we relied on pretax cash flows attributable to the technology that was in-process at the valuation date.
  - We applied contributory charges to the new technology cash flow to represent the use of contributory assets employed.

*(continued)*

- We discounted the residual cash flow to present value using the discount rate of the asset.
- Finally, we deducted an income tax charge and added the amortization benefit factor.

*Major Assumptions*

We relied on a cash flow forecast as provided by management.

- Forecast
  - Per management, IPR&D will be complete in early 2007 and will produce sales of $7.2 million. Revenue will increase in year 2, then decline in subsequent years.
  - Cost of sales are estimated at 40% in 2007 and 39% thereafter.
  - Operating expenses are estimated at 20% [excluding synergies] in 2007 and 19% thereafter, net of development costs.
- Other
  - IPR&D is projected to contribute for a period of six years.
  - We utilized a discount rate of 20% to reflect the additional risk of the unproven technology.
- Contributory Asset Charges
  - Contributory charges were made for supporting or contributory assets employed to support the Company's new technology and assist in the generation of revenues.
  - Contributory charges are directly related to the analyst's assessment of the risk inherent in each asset.

*Conclusion of Fair Value of Asset*

- See Exhibit 4.13 for detailed calculations.
- Concluded value was $4,530,000.

**VALUATION ANALYSES—CUSTOMER BASE**

*Description*

- Target has a long, uninterrupted business relationship with its network of distributors and its large to midsize clients that have remained loyal to Target.

*Valuation Methodology*

The acquisition of the customer base has allowed Acquirer to avoid the cost of having to build up the customer base through years of expenditures. The cost approach can be utilized to determine the value of this asset as the analyst, with management's assistance, can estimate the cost to re-create this asset. However, when possible, it is often more appropriate to consider the cash flow contributed by the customer base when determining value. In such a case, you must also consider contributory charges of other assets utilized.

- Income Approach-Multiperiod excess earnings method
  - We used the business enterprise value as a starting point. As such, we relied on pretax cash flows attributable to the customer base at the valuation date.
  - We applied contributory charges to the customer base cash flow to represent the use of contributory assets employed.
  - Next, we multiplied the surviving cash flows by a projected survivorship of the customer base based on a survivor curve of seven years.

(*continued*)

- We discounted the surviving residual cash flow to present value using the discount rate of the asset.
- Finally, we deducted an income tax charge and added the amortization benefit factor.

*Major Assumptions*

- We relied on the cash flow forecast as provided by management.
- Forecast
  - Per management, revenue is estimated at 2006 levels plus growth rate commensurate with inflation and some real growth of 5% per year.
  - Cost of sales are estimated at 40% in 2007 and 39% thereafter.
  - Operating expenses are estimated at 30% [excluding synergies] in 2007 and 29% thereafter, less expenses of 7% for the solicitation of potential customers.
- Other
  - The average life of a customer relationship is projected to be seven years based on an analysis of prior relationships and discussions with management. The survivor curve of the customer base is projected on a straight-line basis.
  - We utilized a discount rate of 17% to reflect the additional risk of this asset.
- Contributory Asset Charges
  - Contributory charges were made for supporting or contributory assets employed to support the Company's customer base and assist in the generation of revenues.
  - Contributory charges are directly related to the analyst's assessment of the risk inherent in each asset.

*Conclusion of Fair Value of Asset*

- See Exhibit 4.14 for detailed calculations.
- Concluded value was $7,090,000.

## ALLOCATION OF PURCHASE PRICE AND THE VALUE OF RESIDUAL GOODWILL

The allocable purchase price is $209,000,000. From that amount we subtracted the value of current assets of $41,500,000, tangible assets of $41,000,000, and identifiable intangible assets of $50,680,000. As shown in Exhibit 4.15 the residual amount of goodwill (including assembled workforce) is $75,820,000. See Exhibit 4.16 for the full allocation of purchase price.

## RECONCILIATION OF WEIGHTED AVERAGE COST OF CAPITAL (WACC) TO THE WEIGHTED AVERAGE RATE OF RETURN (WARR)

The WACC was estimated to be 16%. We also selected different discount rates for each asset based on the risk of that asset. Typically, current assets have a lower discount rate than tangible assets, and tangible assets have a lower discount rate than intangible assets. The stratification of discount rates for intangible assets is again based on the risk of that asset, with IPR&D and goodwill typically at the high end of the range and assembled workforce and trade names typically at the lower end of the range. We used the Company's WACC as a starting point and selected discount rates accordingly. This was based on discussions with management, industry information, and perceived risk. The individual returns of all assets, both tangible and intangible, were then aggregated into a single rate, the WARR. Based on the selected individual discount rates, the WARR of 16.28% was very close to the WACC of 16.00% (see Exhibit 4.16).

*(continued)*

**Exhibit 4.3**  Target Company Business Enterprise Analysis—Assumptions as of December 31, 2006 ($000s)

| | Actual | Forecast | | | | | | | | | |
|---|---|---|---|---|---|---|---|---|---|---|---|
| | 2006 | 2007 | 2008 | 2009 | 2010 | 2011 | 2012 | 2013 | 2014 | 2015 | 2016 |
| **1. SALES** | | | | | | | | | | | |
| Sales Growth Percentage | | 15.0% | 15.0% | 12.5% | 10.0% | 10.0% | 7.5% | 7.5% | 7.5% | 7.5% | 7.5% |
| Net Sales | $60,000 | $69,000 | $79,350 | $89,269 | $98,196 | $108,015 | $116,116 | $124,825 | $134,187 | $144,251 | $155,070 |
| **2. EXPENSES** | | | | | | | | | | | |
| Cost of Sales | $24,000 | $27,600 | $30,947 | $34,815 | $38,296 | $42,126 | $45,285 | $48,682 | $52,333 | $56,258 | $60,477 |
| Cost of Sales Percentage | 40.0% | 40.0% | 39.0% | 39.0% | 39.0% | 39.0% | 39.0% | 39.0% | 39.0% | 39.0% | 39.0% |
| Operating Expenses | $18,000 | $20,700 | $23,012 | $25,888 | $28,477 | $31,324 | $33,674 | $36,199 | $38,914 | $41,833 | $44,970 |
| Operating Expenses Percentage | 30.0% | 30.0% | 29.0% | 29.0% | 29.0% | 29.0% | 29.0% | 29.0% | 29.0% | 29.0% | 29.0% |
| Depreciation (MACRS) | $1,750 | $3,097 | $5,171 | $3,961 | $3,120 | $2,544 | $2,649 | $2,762 | $2,011 | $1,246 | $1,551 |
| Other Income (Expense), Net Percentage | 0.0% | 0.0% | 0.0% | 0.0% | 0.0% | 0.0% | 0.0% | 0.0% | 0.0% | 0.0% | 0.0% |
| **3. CASH FLOW** | | | | | | | | | | | |
| Capital Expenditures | | $690 | $794 | $893 | $982 | $1,080 | $1,161 | $1,248 | $1,342 | $1,443 | $1,551 |
| Capital Expenditures Percentage | 1.0% | 1.0% | 1.0% | 1.0% | 1.0% | 1.0% | 1.0% | 1.0% | 1.0% | 1.0% | 1.0% |
| Projected Working Capital as Percent of Sales | 15.0% | | | | | | | | | | |
| (1) Projected Working Capital Balance | $16,500 | $10,350 | $11,903 | $13,390 | $14,729 | $16,202 | $17,417 | $18,724 | $20,128 | $21,638 | $23,260 |
| Projected Working Capital Requirement | | (6,150) | 1,553 | 1,488 | 1,339 | 1,473 | 1,215 | 1,306 | 1,404 | 1,510 | 1,623 |

**4. OTHER**

| | |
|---|---|
| Effective Tax Rate | 40.0% |
| Required Rate of Return | 16.0% |
| Residual Growth Rate | 5.0% |

**AMORTIZATION OF INTANGIBLES (TAX)**

Assumption: Intangibles receive 15-year tax life per Sec. 197

| | |
|---|---|
| Purchase Price | $150,000 |
| Plus: Liabilities Assumed | 59,000 |
| Adjusted Purchase Price | 209,000 |
| Less: Current and Tangible Assets | 82,500 |
| Amortizable Intangible Assets | $126,500 |
| Divide: Sec. 197 Amortization Period (Years) | 15 |
| Annual Amortization of Intangibles, Rounded | $8,433 |

Footnote:

(1) Balance at December 31, 2006 stated at fair value

Note: Some amounts may not foot due to rounding.

**Exhibit 4.4** Target Company Business Enterprise Analysis (Bea) - Cash Flow Forecast as of December 31, 2006 ($000s)

| | Actual | Forecast | | | | | | | | | |
|---|---|---|---|---|---|---|---|---|---|---|---|
| | 2006 | 2007 | 2008 | 2009 | 2010 | 2011 | 2012 | 2013 | 2014 | 2015 | 2016 |
| Sales Growth Percentage | | 15.0% | 15.0% | 12.5% | 10.0% | 10.0% | 7.5% | 7.5% | 7.5% | 7.5% | 7.5% |
| Net Sales | $60,000 | $69,000 | $79,350 | $89,269 | $98,196 | $108,015 | $116,116 | $124,825 | $134,187 | $144,251 | $155,070 |
| Cost of Sales | 24,000 | 27,600 | 30,947 | 34,815 | 38,296 | 42,126 | 45,285 | 48,682 | 52,333 | 56,258 | 60,477 |
| Gross Profit | 36,000 | 41,400 | 48,404 | 54,454 | 59,899 | 65,889 | 70,831 | 76,143 | 81,854 | 87,993 | 94,593 |
| Operating Expenses | 18,000 | 20,700 | 23,012 | 25,888 | 28,477 | 31,324 | 33,674 | 36,199 | 38,914 | 41,833 | 44,970 |
| Depreciation (MACRS) | 1,750 | 3,097 | 5,171 | 3,961 | 3,120 | 2,544 | 2,649 | 2,762 | 2,011 | 1,246 | 1,551 |
| Amortization of Intangibles (Tax) | 0 | 8,433 | 8,433 | 8,433 | 8,433 | 8,433 | 8,433 | 8,433 | 8,433 | 8,433 | 8,433 |
| Total Operating Expenses | 19,750 | 32,230 | 36,615 | 38,282 | 40,030 | 42,302 | 44,756 | 47,395 | 49,358 | 51,512 | 54,955 |
| Taxable Income | 16,250 | 9,170 | 11,788 | 16,171 | 19,870 | 23,587 | 26,075 | 28,749 | 32,496 | 36,481 | 39,638 |
| Income Taxes  40.0% | 6,500 | 3,668 | 4,715 | 6,469 | 7,948 | 9,435 | 10,430 | 11,499 | 12,998 | 14,593 | 15,855 |
| Net Income | $9,750 | $5,502 | $7,073 | $9,703 | $11,922 | $14,152 | $15,645 | $17,249 | $19,497 | $21,889 | $23,783 |
| Net Cash Flow | | | | | | | | | | | |
| Net Income | | $5,502 | $7,073 | $9,703 | $11,922 | $14,152 | $15,645 | $17,249 | $19,497 | $21,889 | $23,783 |
| Capital Expenditures | | (690) | (794) | (893) | (982) | (1,080) | (1,161) | (1,248) | (1,342) | (1,443) | (1,551) |
| Change in Working Capital | | 6,150 | (1,553) | (1,488) | (1,339) | (1,473) | (1,215) | (1,306) | (1,404) | (1,510) | (1,623) |
| Depreciation | | 3,097 | 5,171 | 3,961 | 3,120 | 2,544 | 2,649 | 2,762 | 2,011 | 1,246 | 1,551 |
| Amortization of Intangibles (Tax) | | 8,433 | 8,433 | 8,433 | 8,433 | 8,433 | 8,433 | 8,433 | 8,433 | 8,433 | 8,433 |
| Net Cash Flow | | $22,492 | $18,331 | $19,717 | $21,154 | $22,577 | $24,351 | $25,890 | $27,195 | $28,616 | $30,594 |
| (1) Present Value Factor, where | 16.0% | 0.9285 | 0.8004 | 0.6900 | 0.5948 | 0.5128 | 0.4421 | 0.3811 | 0.3285 | 0.2832 | 0.2441 |
| Discount Rate | | | | | | | | | | | |
| Present Value of Net Cash Flow | | $20,884 | $14,672 | $13,605 | $12,582 | $11,577 | $10,765 | $9,867 | $8,934 | $8,104 | $7,468 |

*(continued)*

**Exhibit 4.4** (Continued)

|  | Actual | Forecast | | | | | | | | | |
|---|---|---|---|---|---|---|---|---|---|---|---|
|  | 2006 | 2007 | 2008 | 2009 | 2010 | 2011 | 2012 | 2013 | 2014 | 2015 | 2016 |
| 2016 Taxable Income |  | $39,638 |  |  |  |  |  |  |  |  |  |
| Plus: Intangible Asset Amortization |  | 8,433 |  |  |  |  |  |  |  |  |  |
|  |  |  |  |  |  |  | 2017 | 2018 | 2019 | 2020 | 2021 |
| 2016 Adjusted Taxable Income |  | 48,071 | Amortization of Intangibles (Pretax) |  |  |  | $8,433 | $8,433 | $8,433 | $8,433 | $8,433 |
| Less: Income Taxes | 40.0% | 19,228 |  |  |  |  |  |  |  |  |  |
|  |  |  | Tax Benefit of Amortization 40.0% |  |  |  | $3,373 | $3,373 | $3,373 | $3,373 | $3,373 |
| 2016 Adjusted Net Income |  | $28,843 | (1) Present Value Factor |  |  |  | 0.2105 | 0.1814 | 0.1564 | 0.1348 | 0.1162 |
| 2017 Adjusted Net Income, Growth | 5.0% | $30,285 | Present Value of Tax Benefit |  |  |  | $710 | $612 | $528 | $455 | $392 |
| Less: 2017 Working Capital Provision |  | (1,163) |  |  |  |  |  |  |  |  |  |
| 2017 Adjusted Cash Flow |  | $29,122 | Sum = Present Value of Tax Benefit |  |  |  | $2,697 |  |  |  |  |
| Residual Cap. Rate, Perpetual Growth | 5.0% | 11.00% |  |  |  |  |  |  |  |  |  |
| Residual Value, 2017 |  | $264,745 |  |  |  |  |  |  |  |  |  |
| (1) Present Value Factor |  | 0.2441 |  |  |  |  |  |  |  |  |  |
| Present Value of Residual Cash Flow |  | $64,624 |  |  |  |  |  |  |  |  |  |
| Present Value of Net Cash Flow, 2007-2016 |  | $118,458 |  |  |  |  |  |  |  |  |  |
| Present Value of Residual Cash Flow |  | 64,624 |  |  |  |  |  |  |  |  |  |
| Present Value of Amortization Tax Benefit, 2017-2021 |  | 2,697 |  |  |  |  |  |  |  |  |  |
| **Total Invested Capital, Rounded** |  | **$186,000** |  |  |  |  |  |  |  |  |  |

Footnote:
(1) Based on mid-period assumption
Note: Some amounts may not foot due to rounding.

**Exhibit 4.5**   Target Company Weighted Average Cost of Capital as of December 31, 2006

**MCAPM, Cost of Equity: Ke = Rf + RPm + RPs + RPu**

| | | | |
|---|---|---|---|
| (1) | Risk-Free Rate (Rf) | | 4.91% |
| (2) | Beta (β) | 1.26 | |
| (3) | Market Premium (RPm) | 7.10% | 8.95% |
| (4) | Size Premium (RPs) | | 6.36% |
| (5) | Company Specific Risk Premium (RPu) | | 0.00% |
| | | **ke =** | **20.22%** |

**Build-Up Method, Cost of Equity: Ke = Rf + RPm + RPs + RPu**

| | | |
|---|---|---|
| (1) | Risk-Free Rate (Rf) | 4.91% |
| (6) | Industry Risk Premium | 6.34% |
| (3) | Market Premium (RPm) | 7.10% |
| (4) | Size Premium (RPs) | 6.36% |
| (5) | Company Specific Risk Premium (RPu) | 0.00% |
| | **ke =** | **24.71%** |

**Based on Duff & Phelps Risk Premium Study Report on Size Characteristics**

| | | |
|---|---|---|
| | Risk-Free Rate (Rf) | 4.91% |
| (6) | Size Specific Equity Risk Premium | 13.00% |
| (7) | Industry Risk Premium | 6.34% |
| | Company Specific Risk Premium (RPu) | 0.00% |
| | **ke =** | **24.25%** |
| | Range ke   = | **20.22%**   to   **24.71%** |
| | Concluded Cost of Equity   = | **22.00%** |

**After-tax Cost of Debt: kd = Kb(1-t)**

| | | |
|---|---|---|
| (8) | Borrowing Rate (Kb) | 9.25% |
| (9) | Estimated Tax Rate (t) | 40.00% |
| | **kd =** | **5.55%** |

**Weighted Average Cost of Capital (WACC)**

| | Capital Structure [10] | Cost | Weighted Cost |
|---|---|---|---|
| Debt | 35.00% | 5.55% | 1.94% |
| Equity | 65.00% | 22.00% | 14.30% |
| | | **WACC =** | **16.24%** |
| | | **Rounded =** | **16.00%** |

Footnotes:

(1) Based on 20-year U.S. Treasury at December 29, 2006 as published in the *Federal Reserve Statistical Release*.

(2) Beta estimated from analysis of betas of guideline public companies relevered at industry capital structure.

(3) Ibbotson: *Stocks, Bonds, Bills, and Inflation Yearbook 2006 Valuation Edition*

(4) Ibbotson: *SBBI: Valuation Edition 2006 Yearbook* (Long-term Returns in Excess of CAPM Estimations for Decile Portfolios of the NYSE/AMEX/NASDAQ -10th Decile)

(5) Based on financial position and risks associated with cash flows.

(6) Size specific equity risk premiums are based on comparison of Target to risk premium groups presented in the Duff & Phelps Study (Exhibit 4.6).

(7) SIC 7373, Computer Integrated Systems Design from Ibbotson Associates *Stocks, Bonds, Bills and Inflation Valuation Edition 2006 Yearbook*

(8) Prime + 100 basis points. Prime was 8.25% as of December 29, 2006.

(9) Estimated effective corporate tax rate.

(10) Based on analysis of Target's industry

**Exhibit 4.6**   Target Company Estimated Weighted Average Cost of Capital Comparison to Historical Equity Risk Premiums by Characteristic Based on the 2006 Duff & Phelps, LLC Risk Premium Report Published by Ibbotson Associates

| Characteristic | Implied Category | Smoothed Ave. Premium |
|---|---|---|
| Market Value of Equity | 25 | 13.74% |
| Book Value of Equity | 25 | 12.34% |
| 5-Year Ave. Net Income | 25 | 13.10% |
| Market Value of Invested Capital | 25 | 13.36% |
| Total Assets | 25 | 12.72% |
| 5-Year Ave. EBITDA | 25 | 12.93% |
| Sales | 25 | 12.21% |
| Number of Employees | 25 | 12.57% |
| | Min | 12.21% |
| | Max | 13.74% |
| | Mean | 12.87% |
| | Median | 12.83% |
| | Selected | 13.00% |

**Exhibit 4.7**   Target Company Valuation of Acquired Software as of December 31, 2006

All software was developed internally by Target Company for its own use. Rights to the software were transferred at acquisition. The software is written in a very sophisticated programming language. Valuation is based on cost to replace less obsolescence. Costs are based on internally developed Company metrics for software development productivity. Source: Leonard Riles, Director of Product Development

| In Place | Lines of Code | Productivity Assesment | (1) Rate | Hours to Recreate |
|---|---|---|---|---|
| Module 1 | 26,400 | 2 | 3.0 | 8,800 |
| Module 2 | 32,600 | 3 | 2.0 | 16,300 |
| Module 3 | 46,000 | 1 | 4.0 | 11,500 |
| Module 4 | 8,480 | 3 | 2.0 | 4,240 |
| Module 5 | 12,000 | 3 | 2.0 | 6,000 |
| Module 6 | 12,500 | 2 | 3.0 | 4,167 |
| Module 7 | 2,000 | 2 | 3.0 | 667 |
| Module 8 | 32,000 | 2 | 3.0 | 10,667 |
| Module 9 | 3,000 | 2 | 3.0 | 1,000 |
| Module 10 | 3,000 | 2 | 3.0 | 1,000 |
| Module 11 | 3,000 | 2 | 3.0 | 1,000 |
| Module 12 | 13,000 | 2 | 3.0 | 4,333 |
| Module 13 | 6,000 | 2 | 3.0 | 2,000 |
| Module 14 | 10,000 | 2 | 3.0 | 3,333 |
| Module 15 | 5,000 | 2 | 3.0 | 1,667 |
| Module 16 | 6,000 | 2 | 3.0 | 2,000 |
| Module 17 | 5,000 | 3 | 2.0 | 2,500 |
| Module 18 | 8,000 | 1 | 4.0 | 2,000 |
| Module 19 | 7,000 | 2 | 3.0 | 2,333 |
| Module 20 | 54,000 | 3 | 2.0 | 27,000 |

| Total Number of Lines | 294,980 | | | |
|---|---|---|---|---|
| Total Number of Hours to Recreate | | | | 112,507 |
| Times: Blended Hourly Rate (see below) | | | | $119 |

|  |  |  |
|---|---|---|
| Reproduction Cost | | $13,388,333 |
| (2) Less: Obsolescence | 25.0% | (3,347,083) |
| | | |
| Replacement Cost | | 10,041,250 |
| Less: Taxes | 40.0% | (4,016,500) |
| After-tax Value Before Amortization Benefit | | 6,024,750 |
| Amortization | | |
| Benefit | | |
|   Discount Rate | 17.0% | |
|   Tax Rate | 40.0% | |
|   Tax Amortization Period (Years) | 15 | |
| | | |
| Amortization | | 1,093,112 |
| Benefit | | |
| **Fair Value of Software, Rounded** | | **$7,120,000** |

### SOFTWARE DEVELOPMENT COSTS—ESTIMATED PROJECT TEAM

| Function | Number | Burdened Hourly Rate |
|---|---|---|
| Project Manager | 1 | $200.00 |
| Systems Analyst | 2 | 150.00 |
| Technical Writer | 1 | 125.00 |
| Programmer | 4 | 115.00 |
| Support | 2 | 50.00 |
| | | |
| Blended Hourly Rate, Rounded | | $119.00 |

Footnotes:

(1) Lines of code per hour, based on productivity assessment for average module of programming

(2) Estimate based on number of lines of redundant/extraneous code, effective age, and remaining economic life of system. Remaining useful life of this asset is four years.

Note: Some amounts may not foot due to rounding.

**Exhibit 4.8**  Target Company Valuation of Assembled Workforce as of December 31, 2006

| NO. | Job Title | Salary | 20% Benefits | Total | (1) Train. per. Cl. | Yrs. | 33.3% Cost | (2) 27.5% RECRUIT. | Interview & H.R. | Total |
|---|---|---|---|---|---|---|---|---|---|---|
| 1 | Member of Technical Staff | $90,000 | $18,000 | $108,000 | 1 | 0.125 | $4,496 | $24,750 | $375 | $29,621 |
| 2 | Member of Technical Staff | 80,250 | 16,050 | 96,300 | 2 | 0.375 | 12,025 | 22,069 | 750 | 34,844 |
| 3 | Member of Technical Staff | 60,000 | 12,000 | 72,000 | 2 | 0.375 | 8,991 | 16,500 | 750 | 26,241 |
| 4 | Member of Technical Staff | 44,953 | 8,991 | 53,944 | 1 | 0.125 | 2,245 | 12,362 | 375 | 14,982 |
| 5 | Member of Operations Staff | 71,641 | 14,328 | 85,969 | 1 | 0.125 | 3,578 | 19,701 | 375 | 23,654 |
| 6 | Account Executive | 91,170 | 18,234 | 109,404 | 1 | 0.125 | 4,554 | 25,072 | 375 | 30,001 |
| 7 | Member of Technical Staff | 107,888 | 21,578 | 129,466 | 2 | 0.375 | 16,167 | 29,669 | 750 | 46,586 |
| 8 | Member of Technical Staff | 33,244 | 6,649 | 39,893 | 1 | 0.125 | 1,661 | 9,142 | 375 | 11,178 |
| 9 | Vice President | 142,000 | 28,400 | 170,400 | 2 | 0.375 | 21,279 | 39,050 | 750 | 61,079 |
| 10 | Member of Technical Staff | 83,647 | 16,729 | 100,376 | 2 | 0.375 | 12,535 | 23,003 | 750 | 36,288 |
| 11 | Member of Operations Staff | 104,700 | 20,940 | 125,640 | 1 | 0.125 | 5,230 | 28,793 | 375 | 34,398 |
| 12 | Chief Architect | 155,500 | 31,100 | 186,600 | 3 | 0.750 | 46,603 | 42,763 | 1,500 | 90,866 |
| 13 | Director of Development | 135,000 | 27,000 | 162,000 | 2 | 0.375 | 20,230 | 37,125 | 750 | 58,105 |
| 14 | Member of Technical Staff | 77,772 | 15,554 | 93,326 | 2 | 0.375 | 11,654 | 21,387 | 750 | 33,791 |
| 15 | Account Executive | 94,950 | 18,990 | 113,940 | 1 | 0.125 | 4,743 | 26,111 | 375 | 31,229 |
| 16 | Member of Technical Staff | 81,300 | 16,260 | 97,560 | 1 | 0.125 | 4,061 | 22,358 | 375 | 26,794 |
| 17 | Chief Executive Officer | 250,000 | 50,000 | 300,000 | 1 | 0.125 | 12,488 | 68,750 | 375 | 81,613 |
| 18 | Member of Marketing Staff | 99,000 | 19,800 | 118,800 | 1 | 0.125 | 4,945 | 27,225 | 375 | 32,545 |
| 19 | Member of Technical Staff | 82,000 | 16,400 | 98,400 | 2 | 0.375 | 12,288 | 22,550 | 750 | 35,588 |
| 20 | Member of Technical Staff | 57,460 | 11,492 | 68,952 | 1 | 0.125 | 2,870 | 15,802 | 375 | 19,047 |
| 21 | Account Executive | 106,400 | 21,280 | 127,680 | 2 | 0.375 | 15,944 | 29,260 | 750 | 45,954 |
| 22 | Member of Technical Staff | 107,867 | 21,573 | 129,440 | 2 | 0.375 | 16,164 | 29,663 | 750 | 46,577 |
| 23 | Member of Technical Staff | 110,000 | 22,000 | 132,000 | 3 | 0.750 | 32,967 | 30,250 | 1,500 | 64,717 |
| 24 | Vice President of American Sales | 135,000 | 27,000 | 162,000 | 2 | 0.375 | 20,230 | 37,125 | 750 | 58,105 |
| 25 | Member of Technical Staff | 71,892 | 14,378 | 86,270 | 2 | 0.375 | 10,773 | 19,770 | 750 | 31,293 |
| 26 | Member of Technical Staff | 96,343 | 19,269 | 115,612 | 2 | 0.375 | 14,437 | 26,494 | 750 | 41,681 |
| 27 | Member of Technical Staff | 114,500 | 22,900 | 137,400 | 1 | 0.125 | 5,719 | 31,488 | 375 | 37,582 |
| 28 | Member of Technical Staff | 47,028 | 9,406 | 56,434 | 1 | 0.125 | 2,349 | 12,933 | 375 | 15,657 |
| 29 | Account Executive | 90,660 | 18,132 | 108,792 | 1 | 0.125 | 4,528 | 24,932 | 375 | 29,835 |
| 30 | Member of Technical Staff | 63,329 | 12,666 | 75,995 | 1 | 0.125 | 3,163 | 17,415 | 375 | 20,953 |
| 31 | Member of Operations Staff | 131,000 | 26,200 | 157,200 | 1 | 0.125 | 6,543 | 36,025 | 375 | 42,943 |
| 32 | Chief Financial Officer | 150,000 | 30,000 | 180,000 | 1 | 0.125 | 7,493 | 41,250 | 375 | 49,118 |
| 33 | Member of Technical Staff | 100,210 | 20,042 | 120,252 | 2 | 0.375 | 15,016 | 27,558 | 750 | 43,324 |
| 34 | Member of Technical Staff | 87,372 | 17,474 | 104,846 | 2 | 0.375 | 13,093 | 24,027 | 750 | 37,870 |
| 35 | Member of Technical Staff | 108,000 | 21,600 | 129,600 | 2 | 0.375 | 16,184 | 29,700 | 750 | 46,634 |
| 36 | Member of Technical Staff - Nonexempt | 22,326 | 4,465 | 26,791 | 1 | 0.125 | 1,115 | 6,140 | 375 | 7,630 |
| 37 | Member of Technical Staff | 70,000 | 14,000 | 84,000 | 1 | 0.125 | 3,497 | 19,250 | 375 | 23,122 |
| 38 | Director of Operations | 137,000 | 27,400 | 164,400 | 3 | 0.750 | 41,059 | 37,675 | 1,500 | 80,234 |
| 39 | Member of Technical Staff | 94,248 | 18,850 | 113,098 | 2 | 0.375 | 14,123 | 25,918 | 750 | 40,791 |
| 40 | Member of Operations Staff | 71,000 | 14,200 | 85,200 | 1 | 0.125 | 3,546 | 19,525 | 375 | 23,446 |
| 41 | Director of Marketing | 125,000 | 25,000 | 150,000 | 2 | 0.375 | 18,731 | 34,375 | 750 | 53,856 |
| 42 | Member of Technical Staff | 65,000 | 13,000 | 78,000 | 1 | 0.125 | 3,247 | 17,875 | 375 | 21,497 |
| 43 | Member of Technical Staff - Nonexempt | 42,950 | 8,590 | 51,540 | 1 | 0.125 | 2,145 | 11,811 | 375 | 14,331 |
| 44 | Member of Technical Staff | 90,000 | 18,000 | 108,000 | 1 | 0.125 | 4,496 | 24,750 | 375 | 29,621 |

| # | Title | | | | (1) | | | | | |
|---|---|---|---|---|---|---|---|---|---|---|
| 45 | Member of Technical Staff | 109,000 | 21,800 | 130,800 | 2 | 0.375 | 16,334 | 29,975 | 750 | 47,059 |
| 46 | Member of Technical Staff | 84,200 | 16,840 | 101,040 | 1 | 0.125 | 4,206 | 23,155 | 375 | 27,736 |
| 47 | Member of Technical Staff | 128,500 | 25,700 | 154,200 | 3 | 0.750 | 38,511 | 35,338 | 1,500 | 75,349 |
| 48 | Member of Technical Staff | 80,900 | 16,180 | 97,080 | 1 | 0.125 | 4,041 | 22,248 | 375 | 26,664 |
| 49 | Member of Technical Staff | 60,300 | 12,060 | 72,360 | 1 | 0.125 | 3,012 | 16,583 | 375 | 19,970 |
| 50 | Member of Technical Staff | 58,500 | 11,700 | 70,200 | 1 | 0.125 | 2,922 | 16,088 | 375 | 19,385 |
| 51 | Director Release and Customer Support | 116,000 | 23,200 | 139,200 | 2 | 0.375 | 17,383 | 31,900 | 750 | 50,033 |
| 52 | Executive Assistant | 35,000 | 7,000 | 42,000 | 1 | 0.125 | 1,748 | 9,625 | 375 | 11,748 |
| 53 | Member of Technical Staff | 113,400 | 22,680 | 136,080 | 2 | 0.375 | 16,993 | 31,185 | 750 | 48,928 |
| 54 | Member of Technical Staff | 112,041 | 22,408 | 134,449 | 2 | 0.375 | 16,789 | 30,811 | 750 | 48,350 |
| 55 | Member of Operations Staff | 70,000 | 14,000 | 84,000 | 1 | 0.125 | 3,497 | 19,250 | 375 | 23,122 |
| 56 | Member of Technical Staff | 77,000 | 15,400 | 92,400 | 2 | 0.375 | 11,538 | 21,175 | 750 | 33,463 |
| 57 | Member of Technical Staff | 107,000 | 21,400 | 128,400 | 3 | 0.750 | 32,068 | 29,425 | 1,500 | 62,993 |
| 58 | Director of International Operations | 150,000 | 30,000 | 180,000 | 1 | 0.125 | 7,493 | 41,250 | 375 | 49,118 |
| 59 | Member of Technical Staff | 110,000 | 22,000 | 132,000 | 2 | 0.375 | 16,484 | 30,250 | 750 | 47,484 |
| 60 | Vice President and General Manager of EMEA | 145,000 | 29,000 | 174,000 | 2 | 0.375 | 21,728 | 39,875 | 750 | 62,353 |
| 61 | Account Executive | 82,500 | 16,500 | 99,000 | 1 | 0.125 | 4,121 | 22,688 | 375 | 27,184 |
| 62 | Account Executive | 75,261 | 15,052 | 90,313 | 2 | 0.375 | 11,278 | 20,697 | 750 | 32,725 |
| 63 | Member of Technical Staff | 67,735 | 13,547 | 81,282 | 2 | 0.375 | 10,150 | 18,627 | 750 | 29,527 |
| 64 | Member of Technical Staff | 73,350 | 14,670 | 88,020 | 2 | 0.375 | 10,991 | 20,171 | 750 | 31,912 |
| 65 | Member of Technical Staff | 99,465 | 19,893 | 119,358 | 3 | 0.750 | 29,810 | 27,353 | 1,500 | 58,663 |
| Total 65 | | $6,134,752 | $1,226,950 | $7,361,702 | | | $770,302 | $1,687,060 | $41,625 | $2,498,987 |

Replacement Cost of Assembled Workforce    $2,498,987
Less: Taxes    40.0%    (999,595)

Costs Avoided, Net of Tax    1,499,392
Amortization Benefit
Rate of Return    16.0%
Tax Rate    40.0%
Tax Amortization Period (Years)    15

Amortization Benefit    285,879

**Fair Value of Assembled Workforce, Rounded**    **$1,790,000**

Footnotes:

(1) Qualified Replacement Training Months
1 = < 3 months
2 = 3-6 months
3 = 6-12 months

| Interview & H.R. Hours | Rate |
|---|---|
| 5 | $75.00 |
| 10 | $75.00 |
| 20 | $75.00 |

(2) Source: Karl Malloney, Recruiter

Note: Some amounts may not foot due to rounding.

**Exhibit 4.9**  Target Company Valuation of Trade Name as of December 31, 2006 ($000s)

|  |  | 2007 | 2008 | 2009 | 2010 | 2011 | 2012 | 2013 | 2014 | 2015 | 2016 |
|---|---|---|---|---|---|---|---|---|---|---|---|
| (1) Net Sales from Business Enterprise Analysis |  | $69,000 | $79,350 | $89,269 | $98,196 | $108,015 | $116,116 | $124,825 | $134,187 | $144,251 | $155,070 |
| Pretax Relief from Royalty | 2.0% | $1,380 | $1,587 | $1,785 | $1,964 | $2,160 | $2,322 | $2,497 | $2,684 | $2,885 | $3,101 |
| Income Tax Liability | 40.0% | 552 | 635 | 714 | 786 | 864 | 929 | 999 | 1,073 | 1,154 | 1,241 |
| After-tax Royalty |  | $828 | $952 | $1,071 | $1,178 | $1,296 | $1,393 | $1,498 | $1,610 | $1,731 | $1,861 |
| (2) Present Value Income Factor | 16.0% | 0.9285 | 0.8004 | 0.6900 | 0.5948 | 0.5128 | 0.4421 | 0.3811 | 0.3285 | 0.2832 | 0.2441 |
| Present Value Relief from Royalty |  | $769 | $762 | $739 | $701 | $665 | $616 | $571 | $529 | $490 | $454 |

Sum of Present Value Relief from Royalty, 2007-2016    $6,296

Residual Calculation:
2016 After-tax Royalty    $1,861

2017 After-tax Royalty, Assuming Growth of    5.0%    $1,954
Residual Capitalization Rate, Perpetual Growth    5.0%    11.0%

Residual Value, 2017    $17,764
(2) Present Value Factor    0.2441

Fair Market Value of Residual    4,336

Present Value of Trade Name Royalty Flows    10,632

Amortization Benefit
Discount Rate    16.0%
Tax Rate    40.0%
Tax Amortization Period (Years)    15

Amortization Benefit    2,027

**Fair Value of Trade Name, Rounded    $12,660**

Footnotes:
(1) Figures shown from Business Enterprise Analysis (BEA) - Cash Flow Forecast (Exhibit 4.4)
(2) Based on mid-period assumption
Note: Some amounts may not foot due to rounding.

**Exhibit 4.10a**   Target Company Valuation of Noncompete Agreement as of December 31, 2006 ($000s)

| Comparison: Scenario I & Scenario II | For the Years Ended December 31, | | | | |
|---|---|---|---|---|---|
| | 2007 | 2008 | 2009 | 2010 | 2011 |
| Net Cash Flow | | | | | |
| (1) With Restrictive Covenant (Exhibit 3.9b) | $14,992 | $18,329 | $19,717 | $21,154 | $22,577 |
| (2) Without Restrictive Covenant (Exhibit 3.9c) | 14,733 | 16,370 | 16,881 | 19,815 | 22,577 |
| Reduction in Debt-free Net Cash Flow | $259 | $1,959 | $2,836 | $1,339 | $0 |
| Present Value Period | 1 | 2 | 3 | 4 | 5 |
| (3) Present Value Factor | 0.9285 | 0.8004 | 0.6900 | 0.5948 | 0.5128 |
| Present Value of Cash Flow | $241 | $1,568 | $1,957 | $796 | $0 |

| | |
|---|---|
| Sum, Present Value of Cash Flows | $4,562 |
| Amortization Benefit | |
|     Discount Rate | 16.0% |
|     Tax Rate | 40.0% |
|     Tax Amortization Period (Years) | 15 |
| Amortization Benefit | 870 |
| Raw Value of Noncompete Agreement | $5,432 |
| (4) Probability of Competing | 50% |
| **Fair Value of Noncompete Agreement, Rounded** | **$2,720** |

Footnotes:
(1) See Projected Cash Flows Over Competitive Time Horizon, Scenario 1: With Noncompete Agreement With Seller In Place (Exhibit 4.10b).
(2) Year 4 cash flow reflects adjustment to working capital provision under the assumption of competition starting in Year 4. See Projected Cash Flows Over Competitive Time Horizon, Scenario 2: Without Noncompete Agreement With Seller In Place (Exhibit 4.10c).
(3) Based on mid-period assumption
(4) Based on discussions with management
Note: Some amounts may not foot due to rounding

**Exhibit 4.10b**   Target Company Projected Cash Flows Over Competitive Time Horizon
Scenario 1: With Noncompete Agreement with Seller in Place Discounted Cash Flow Analysis
($000s)

| Assumptions | 2007 | 2008 | 2009 | 2010 | 2011 |
|---|---|---|---|---|---|
| Cost of Goods Sold | 40.0% | 39.0% | 39.0% | 39.0% | 39.0% |
| Operating Expenses | 30.0% | 29.0% | 29.0% | 29.0% | 29.0% |
| Capital Expenditures Percent of Sales | 1.0% | 1.0% | 1.0% | 1.0% | 1.0% |
| Estimated Effective Tax Rate | 40.0% | 40.0% | 40.0% | 40.0% | 40.0% |
| Debt-free Net Working Capital Percent of Revenues | 15.0% | 15.0% | 15.0% | 15.0% | 15.0% |

| | | | | | |
|---|---|---|---|---|---|
| Base Year Revenues 2006 | $60,000 | | | | |

| | For the Years Ended December 31, | | | | |
|---|---|---|---|---|---|
| | 2007 | 2008 | 2009 | 2010 | 2011 |
| (1) Total Revenues | $69,000 | $79,350 | $89,269 | $98,196 | $108,015 |
| Cost of Goods Sold | 27,600 | 30,947 | 34,815 | 38,296 | 42,126 |
| Operating Expenses | 20,700 | 23,012 | 25,888 | 28,477 | 31,324 |
| EBITDA | $20,700 | $25,391 | $28,566 | $31,423 | $34,565 |
| *EBITDA Margin* | *30.0%* | *32.0%* | *32.0%* | *32.0%* | *32.0%* |
| Depreciation (MACRS) | $3,097 | $5,171 | $3,961 | $3,120 | $2,544 |
| Amortization | 8,433 | 8,433 | 8,433 | 8,433 | 8,433 |
| EBIT | $9,170 | $11,787 | $16,171 | $19,870 | $23,588 |
| *EBIT Margin* | *13.3%* | *14.9%* | *18.1%* | *20.2%* | *21.8%* |
| Income Taxes | $3,668 | $4,715 | $6,468 | $7,948 | $9,435 |
| Debt-free Net Income | $5,502 | $7,072 | $9,703 | $11,922 | $14,153 |
| *Debt-free Net Income Margin* | *8.0%* | *8.9%* | *10.9%* | *12.1%* | *13.1%* |
| Plus: Depreciation | $3,097 | $5,171 | $3,961 | $3,120 | $2,544 |
| Plus: Amortization | 8,433 | 8,433 | 8,433 | 8,433 | 8,433 |
| Less: Capital Expenditures | (690) | (794) | (893) | (982) | (1,080) |
| (2) Less: Incremental Working Capital | (1,350) | (1,553) | (1,488) | (1,339) | (1,473) |
| Debt-free Cash Flow | $14,992 | $18,329 | $19,717 | $21,154 | $22,577 |

Footnotes:
(1) Based on Business Enterprise Analysis (BEA) - Cash Flow Forecast (Exhibit 4.4)
(2) Incremental Working Capital in Year 1 reflects a lower provision than shown in the Business Enterprise
    Analysis (BEA) - Cash Flow Forecast (Exhibit 4.4) because the BEA provision normalizes from an actual
    balance, while the provision for the noncompete agreement only accounts for the incremental amount
    necessary based on the growth of revenues.
Note: Some amounts may not foot due to rounding.

**Exhibit 4.10c**    Target Company Projected Cash Flows Over Competitive Time Horizon Scenario 2: Without Noncompete Agreement with Seller in Place Discounted Cash Flow Analysis ($000s)

| Assumptions | 2007 | 2008 | 2009 | 2010 | 2011 |
|---|---|---|---|---|---|
| Cost of Goods Sold | 40.0% | 39.0% | 39.0% | 39.0% | 39.0% |
| Operating Expenses | 30.0% | 29.0% | 29.0% | 29.0% | 29.0% |
| Capital Expenditures Percent of Sales | 1.0% | 1.0% | 1.0% | 1.0% | 1.0% |
| Estimated Effective Tax Rate | 40.0% | 40.0% | 40.0% | 40.0% | 40.0% |
| Debt-free Net Working Capital Percent of Revenues | 15.0% | 15.0% | 15.0% | 15.0% | 15.0% |
| Base Year Revenues 2006 | $60,000 | | | | |

| | For the Years Ended December 31, | | | | |
| | 2007 | 2008 | 2009 | 2010 | 2011 |
|---|---|---|---|---|---|
| (1) Total Revenues | $69,000 | $79,350 | $89,269 | $98,196 | $108,015 |
| Decline in Revenues Caused by Competition of Seller | 10% | 20% | 10% | 0% | 0% |
| Decline in Revenues | $6,900 | $15,870 | $8,927 | $0 | $0 |
| | | | | | |
| Adjusted Base Revenues | 62,100 | 63,480 | 80,342 | 98,196 | 108,015 |
| Cost of Goods Sold | 24,840 | 24,757 | 31,333 | 38,296 | 42,126 |
| Operating Expenses | 18,630 | 18,409 | 23,299 | 28,477 | 31,324 |
| | | | | | |
| EBITDA | $18,630 | $20,314 | $25,710 | $31,423 | $34,565 |
| *EBITDA Margin* | *30.0%* | *32.0%* | *32.0%* | *32.0%* | *32.0%* |
| (2) Depreciation | $2,795 | $4,126 | $3,535 | $3,120 | $2,544 |
| Amortization | 8,433 | 8,433 | 8,433 | 8,433 | 8,433 |
| | | | | | |
| EBIT | $7,402 | $7,755 | $13,742 | $19,870 | $23,588 |
| *EBIT Margin* | *11.9%* | *12.2%* | *17.1%* | *20.2%* | *21.8%* |
| Income Taxes | $2,961 | $3,102 | $5,497 | $7,948 | $9,435 |
| | | | | | |
| Debt-free Net Income | $4,441 | $4,653 | $8,245 | $11,922 | $14,153 |
| *Debt-free Net Income Margin* | *7.2%* | *7.3%* | *10.3%* | *12.1%* | *13.1%* |
| Plus: Depreciation | $2,795 | $4,126 | $3,535 | $3,120 | $2,544 |
| Plus: Amortization | 8,433 | 8,433 | 8,433 | 8,433 | 8,433 |
| Less: Capital Expenditures | (621) | (635) | (803) | (982) | (1,080) |
| (3) Less: Incremental Working Capital | (315) | (207) | (2,529) | (2,678) | (1,473) |
| | | | | | |
| Debt-free Net Cash Flow | $14,733 | $16,370 | $16,881 | $19,815 | $22,577 |

Footnotes:
(1) Based on Business Enterprise Analysis (BEA) - Cash Flow Forecast (Exhibit 4.4)
(2) Depreciation in this exhibit give effect to an estimated reduction due to reduced net sales, which it is assumed would result in reduced capital expenditures.
(3) Incremental Working Capital in Year 1 reflects a lower provision than shown in the Business Enterprise Analysis (BEA) - Cash Flow Forecast (Exhibit 4.4) because the BEA provision normalizes from an actual balance, while the provision for the noncompete agreement only accounts for the incremental amount necessary based on the growth of revenues. Incremental Working Capital in other years reflect different amounts than shown in the BEA (Exhibit 4.4) in order to fund working capital balances based on different revenue projections.
Note: Some amounts may not foot due to rounding.

**Exhibit 4.11**   Target Company Calculation of Contributory Asset Charges as of December 31, 2006 ($000s)

| Contributory Asset A. Asset Balances | | 2007 | 2008 | 2009 | 2010 | 2011 | 2012 | 2013 |
|---|---|---|---|---|---|---|---|---|
| Net Working Capital | | $13,425 | $11,126 | $12,646 | $14,060 | $15,466 | $16,810 | $18,071 |
| Land and Building | | 21,934 | 21,815 | 21,718 | 21,640 | 21,580 | 21,536 | 21,503 |
| Machinery and Equipment, net | | 17,849 | 14,551 | 10,900 | 8,348 | 6,582 | 5,125 | 3,631 |
| Software | | 7,120 | 7,120 | 7,120 | 7,120 | 7,120 | 7,120 | 7,120 |
| Trade Name | | 12,660 | 12,660 | 12,660 | 12,660 | 12,660 | 12,660 | 12,660 |
| Noncompete Agreement | | 2,720 | 2,720 | 2,720 | 0 | 0 | 0 | 0 |
| Assembled Workforce | | 1,790 | 1,790 | 1,790 | 1,790 | 1,790 | 1,790 | 1,790 |
| Technology | | 16,560 | 16,560 | 16,560 | 16,560 | 16,560 | 16,560 | 16,560 |
| IPR&D | | 4,530 | 4,530 | 4,530 | 4,530 | 4,530 | 4,530 | 4,530 |
| Customer Base | | 7,090 | 7,090 | 7,090 | 7,090 | 7,090 | 7,090 | 7,090 |

| | B. Total Returns | Rate | 2007 | 2008 | 2009 | 2010 | 2011 | 2012 | 2013 |
|---|---|---|---|---|---|---|---|---|---|
| (1) | Net Working Capital | 5.0% | $671 | $556 | $632 | $703 | $773 | $840 | $904 |
| | Land and Building | 7.0% | 1,535 | 1,527 | 1,520 | 1,515 | 1,511 | 1,507 | 1,505 |
| | Machinery and Equipment, net | 8.0% | 1,428 | 1,164 | 872 | 668 | 527 | 410 | 290 |
| | Software | 17.0% | 1,210 | 1,210 | 1,210 | 1,210 | 1,210 | 1,210 | 1,210 |
| | Trade Name | 16.0% | 2,026 | 2,026 | 2,026 | 2,026 | 2,026 | 2,026 | 2,026 |
| | Noncompete Agreement | 16.0% | 435 | 435 | 435 | 0 | 0 | 0 | 0 |
| | Assembled Workforce | 16.0% | 286 | 286 | 286 | 286 | 286 | 286 | 286 |
| | Technology | 18.0% | 2,981 | 2,981 | 2,981 | 2,981 | 2,981 | 2,981 | 2,981 |
| | IPR&D | 20.0% | 906 | 906 | 906 | 906 | 906 | 906 | 906 |
| | Customer Base | 17.0% | 1,205 | 1,205 | 1,205 | 1,205 | 1,205 | 1,205 | 1,205 |

| | C. Distribution of Revenues | 2007 | 2008 | 2009 | 2010 | 2011 | 2012 |
|---|---|---|---|---|---|---|---|
| (2) | Net Sales-Technology | $61,800 | $38,192 | $32,782 | $23,636 | $13,911 | |
| (3) | Projected Sales per BEA | 69,000 | 79,350 | 89,269 | 98,196 | 108,015 | |
| | Technology Percent of BEA | 89.57% | 48.13% | 36.72% | 24.07% | 12.88% | |
| (4) | Net Sales-IPR&D | $7,200 | $12,557 | $11,853 | $10,733 | $7,692 | $4,447 |
| (3) | Projected Sales per BEA | 69,000 | 79,350 | 89,269 | 98,196 | 108,015 | 116,116 |
| | IPR&D Percent of BEA | 10.43% | 15.82% | 13.28% | 10.93% | 7.12% | 3.83% |

| D. Allocated Returns-Technology | 2007 | 2008 | 2009 | 2010 | 2011 |
|---|---|---|---|---|---|
| Net Working Capital | $601 | $268 | $232 | $169 | $100 |
| Land and Building | 1,375 | 735 | 558 | 365 | 195 |
| Machinery and Equipment, net | 1,279 | 560 | 320 | 161 | 68 |
| Software | 1,084 | 583 | 444 | 291 | 156 |
| Trade Name | 1,814 | 975 | 744 | 488 | 261 |
| Noncompete Agreement | 390 | 209 | 160 | 0 | 0 |
| Assembled Workforce | 257 | 138 | 105 | 69 | 37 |
| Customer Base | 1,080 | 580 | 443 | 290 | 155 |
| Total | $7,880 | $4,048 | $3,006 | $1,833 | $972 |

| E. Allocated Returns-IPR&D | 2007 | 2008 | 2009 | 2010 | 2011 | 2012 |
|---|---|---|---|---|---|---|
| Net Working Capital | $70 | $88 | $84 | $77 | $55 | $32 |
| Land and Building | 160 | 242 | 202 | 166 | 108 | 58 |
| Machinery and Equipment, net | 149 | 184 | 116 | 73 | 37 | 16 |
| Software | 126 | 192 | 161 | 132 | 86 | 46 |
| Trade Name | 211 | 321 | 269 | 221 | 144 | 78 |
| Noncompete Agreement | 45 | 69 | 58 | 0 | 0 | 0 |
| Assembled Workforce | 30 | 45 | 38 | 31 | 20 | 11 |
| Customer Base | 126 | 191 | 160 | 132 | 86 | 46 |
| Total | $917 | $1,332 | $1,088 | $832 | $536 | $287 |

Footnotes:
(1) Used for Customer Base (Exhibit 4.14), except no return is taken on Customer Base asset.
(2) Based on Valuation of Technology (Exhibit 4.12)
(3) Based on Business Enterprise Analysis (BEA) - Cash Flow Forecast (Exhibit 4.4)
(4) Based on Valuation of In-Process Research and Development (Exhibit 4.13)
Note: Some amounts may not foot due to rounding.

## APPENDICES

*Statement of Assumptions and Limiting Conditions.* The primary assumptions and limiting conditions pertaining to the value estimate conclusion(s) stated in this report are summarized below. Other assumptions are cited elsewhere in this report.

The valuation may not be used in conjunction with any other appraisal or study. The value conclusion(s) stated in this appraisal are based on the program of utilization described in the report and may not be separated into parts. The appraisal was prepared solely for the purpose, function, and party so identified in the report. The appraisal report may not be reproduced, in whole or in part, and the findings of the report may not be utilized by a third party for any purpose, without the express written consent of FVA&M, LLC.

No change of any item in any of the appraisal report shall be made by anyone other than FVA&M, LLC, and we shall have no responsibility for any such unauthorized change.

Unless otherwise stated in the appraisal, the valuation of the business has not considered or incorporated the potential economic gain or loss resulting from contingent assets, liabilities, or events existing as of the valuation date.

The working papers for this engagement are being retained in our files and are available for your reference. We would be available to support our valuation conclusion(s) should this be required. Those services would be performed for an additional fee.

Neither all nor any part of the contents of the report shall be disseminated or referred to the public through advertising, public relations, news or sales media, or any other public means of communication, or referenced in any publication, including any private or public offerings, including but not limited to those filed with the Securities and Exchange Commission or other governmental agency, without the prior written consent and approval of FVA&M, LLC.

Management is assumed to be competent, and the ownership to be in responsible hands, unless noted otherwise in this report. The quality of business management can have a direct effect on the viability and value of the business. The financial projections contained

(*continued*)

**Exhibit 4.12**   Target Company Valuation of Technology as of December 31, 2006 ($000s)

|  | Actual | Forecast | | | | |
|---|---|---|---|---|---|---|
|  | 2006 | 2007 | 2008 | 2009 | 2010 | 2011 |
| (1) Net Sales-Existing Technology | $60,000 | $61,800 | $38,192 | $32,782 | $23,636 | $13,911 |
| Cost of Sales | 24,000 | 24,720 | 14,895 | 12,785 | 9,218 | 5,425 |
| Gross Profit | 36,000 | 37,080 | 23,297 | 19,997 | 14,418 | 8,486 |
| (2) Operating Expenses | 12,000 | 12,360 | 7,256 | 6,229 | 4,491 | 2,643 |
| (3) Depreciation | 1,750 | 2,774 | 2,489 | 1,455 | 751 | 328 |
| Total Operating Expenses | 13,750 | 15,134 | 9,745 | 7,684 | 5,242 | 2,971 |
| Taxable Income | 22,250 | 21,946 | 13,552 | 12,313 | 9,176 | 5,515 |
| Income Taxes            40.0% | 8,900 | 8,778 | 5,421 | 4,925 | 3,670 | 2,206 |
| Net Income | $13,350 | 13,168 | 8,131 | 7,388 | 5,506 | 3,309 |

(4) Residual Cash Flow Attributable to Technology
    Less: Returns on

|  |  | Actual | Forecast | | | |
|---|---|---|---|---|---|---|
| Net Working Capital | 5.0% | 601 | 268 | 232 | 169 | 100 |
| Land and Building | 7.0% | 1,375 | 735 | 558 | 365 | 195 |
| Machinery and Equipment, net | 8.0% | 1,279 | 560 | 320 | 161 | 68 |
| Software | 17.0% | 1,084 | 583 | 444 | 291 | 156 |
| Trade Name | 16.0% | 1,814 | 975 | 744 | 488 | 261 |
| Noncompete Agreement | 16.0% | 390 | 209 | 160 | 0 | 0 |
| Assembled Workforce | 16.0% | 257 | 138 | 105 | 69 | 37 |
| Customer Base | 17.0% | 1,080 | 580 | 443 | 290 | 155 |
| Sum of Returns |  | 7,880 | 4,048 | 3,006 | 1,833 | 972 |
| After-tax Residual Cash Flows |  | $5,288 | $4,083 | $4,382 | $3,673 | $2,337 |
| (5) 18.0% Present Value Factor for | | 0.9206 | 0.7801 | 0.6611 | 0.5603 | 0.4748 |
| Residual Cash Flow |  |  |  |  |  |  |
| Present Value of Residual Cash Flows |  | $4,868 | $3,185 | $2,897 | $2,058 | $1,110 |

| Sum of Present Values, 2007-2011 |  | $14,118 |
|---|---|---|
| Amortization Benefit |  |  |
| Discount Rate | 18.0% |  |
| Tax Rate | 40.0% |  |
| Tax Amortization Period (Years) | 15 |  |
| Amortization Benefit |  | 2,443 |
| **Fair Value of Technology, Rounded** |  | **$16,560** |

Footnotes:
(1) Sales attributable to the existing technology, which are 100% of company sales in 2006, are projected to decline over time as the technology becomes obsolete and competitors increasingly impact sales.
(2) Excludes development expenses of 10% to reflect that developed technology should not be burdened by the expense of developing new technology.
(3) MACRS depreciation per Business Enterprise Analysis (BEA) - Cash Flow Forecast (Exhibit 4.4) allocated by relative net sales between Technology and IPR&D
(4) See Calculation of Contributory Asset Charges (Exhibit 4.11)
(5) Based on mid-period assumption
Note: Some amounts may not foot due to rounding.

**Exhibit 4.13**    Target Company Valuation of In-Process Research and Development (IPR&D) as of December 31, 2006 ($000s)

| | | Forecast | | | | | |
|---|---|---|---|---|---|---|---|
| | | 2007 | 2008 | 2009 | 2010 | 2011 | 2012 |
| (1) Net Sales-IPR&D | | $7,200 | $12,557 | $11,853 | $10,733 | $7,692 | $4,447 |
| Cost of Sales | | 2,880 | 4,897 | 4,623 | 4,186 | 3,000 | 1,734 |
| Gross Profit | | 4,320 | 7,660 | 7,230 | 6,547 | 4,692 | 2,713 |
| (2) Operating Expenses | | 1,440 | 2,386 | 2,252 | 2,039 | 1,461 | 845 |
| (3) Cost to Complete | | 750 | 0 | 0 | 0 | 0 | 0 |
| (4) Depreciation | | 323 | 818 | 526 | 341 | 181 | 101 |
| Total Operating Expenses | | 2,513 | 3,204 | 2,778 | 2,380 | 1,642 | 946 |
| Taxable Income | | 1,807 | 4,456 | 4,452 | 4,167 | 3,050 | 1,767 |
| Income Taxes | 40.0% | 723 | 1,782 | 1,781 | 1,667 | 1,220 | 707 |
| Net Income | | 1,084 | 2,674 | 2,671 | 2,500 | 1,830 | 1,060 |
| Residual Cash Flow Attributable to IPR&D | | | | | | | |
| (5) Less: Returns on | | | | | | | |
| Debt-free Net Working Capital | 5.0% | 70 | 88 | 84 | 77 | 55 | 32 |
| Land and Building | 7.0% | 160 | 242 | 202 | 166 | 108 | 58 |
| Machinery and Equipment, net | 8.0% | 149 | 184 | 116 | 73 | 37 | 16 |
| Software | 17.0% | 126 | 192 | 161 | 132 | 86 | 46 |
| Trade Name | 16.0% | 211 | 321 | 269 | 221 | 144 | 78 |
| Noncompete Agreement | 16.0% | 45 | 69 | 58 | 0 | 0 | 0 |
| Assembled Workforce | 16.0% | 30 | 45 | 38 | 31 | 20 | 11 |
| Customer Base | 17.0% | 126 | 191 | 160 | 132 | 86 | 46 |
| Sum of Returns | | 917 | 1,332 | 1,088 | 832 | 536 | 287 |
| After-tax Residual Cash Flows | | $167 | $1,342 | $1,583 | $1,668 | $1,294 | $773 |
| (6) 20.0% Present Value Factor for Residual Cash Flow | | 0.9129 | 0.7607 | 0.6339 | 0.5283 | 0.4402 | 0.3669 |
| Present Value of Residual Cash Flows | | $152 | $1,021 | $1,004 | $881 | $570 | $284 |
| Sum of Present Values, 2007–2012 | | $3,911 | | | | | |
| Amortization Benefit | | | | | | | |
| Discount Rate | 20.0% | | | | | | |
| Tax Rate | 40.0% | | | | | | |
| Tax Amortization Period (Years) | 15 | | | | | | |
| Amortization Benefit | | 619 | | | | | |
| **Fair Value of IPR&D, Rounded** | | **$4,530** | | | | | |

Footnotes:

(1) Based on Management's forecast

(2) Excludes development expenses of 10% to reflect no future development costs relative to this technology.

(3) The cost to complete is typically known with certainty and cannot be avoided. With IPR&D, one often does not know if the project will be successful until the amounts are spent. Thus, some practitioners separately calculate the present value of inflows and the present value of outflows. We have elected to present the single calculation here, for simplicity and because the alternative treatment does not result in a materially different conclusion of value.

(4) MACRS depreciation per Business Enterprise Analysis (BEA) - Cash Flow Forecast (Exhibit 4.4) allocated by relative net sales between Technology and IPR&D

(5) See Calculation of Contributory Asset Charges (Exhibit 4.11)

(6) Based on mid-period assumption

Note: Some amounts may not foot due to rounding.

**Exhibit 4.14**   Target Company Valuation of Customer Base as of December 31, 2006 ($000s)

| Cash Flows | Actual | Projections | | | | | | |
|---|---|---|---|---|---|---|---|---|
| | 2006 | 2007 | 2008 | 2009 | 2010 | 2011 | 2012 | 2013 |
| (1) Net Sales-Existing Customers | $60,000 | $63,000 | $66,150 | $69,458 | $72,931 | $76,578 | $80,407 | $84,427 |
| Cost of Sales | 24,000 | 25,200 | 25,799 | 27,089 | 28,443 | 29,865 | 31,359 | 32,927 |
| Gross Profit | 36,000 | 37,800 | 40,352 | 42,369 | 44,488 | 46,713 | 49,048 | 51,500 |
| (2) Operating Expenses | 12,000 | 14,490 | 14,553 | 15,281 | 16,045 | 16,847 | 17,690 | 18,574 |
| Depreciation (MACRS) | 1,750 | 3,097 | 5,171 | 3,961 | 3,120 | 2,544 | 2,649 | 2,762 |
| Total Operating Expenses | 13,750 | 17,587 | 19,724 | 19,242 | 19,165 | 19,391 | 20,338 | 21,336 |
| Taxable Income | 22,250 | 20,213 | 20,628 | 23,127 | 25,323 | 27,321 | 28,710 | 30,164 |
| Income Taxes         40.0% | 8,900 | 8,085 | 8,251 | 9,251 | 10,129 | 10,929 | 11,484 | 12,066 |
| Net Income | $13,350 | 12,128 | 12,377 | 13,876 | 15,194 | 16,393 | 17,226 | 18,099 |

Residual Cash Flow Attributable to Existing Customer Base

| (3) Less: Returns on | | | | | | | | |
|---|---|---|---|---|---|---|---|---|
| Debt-free Net Working Capital 5.0% | | 671 | 556 | 632 | 703 | 773 | 840 | 904 |
| Land and Building | 7.0% | 1,535 | 1,527 | 1,520 | 1,515 | 1,511 | 1,507 | 1,505 |
| Machinery and Equipment, net 8.0% | | 1,428 | 1,164 | 872 | 668 | 527 | 410 | 290 |
| Software | 17.0% | 1,210 | 1,210 | 1,210 | 1,210 | 1,210 | 1,210 | 1,210 |
| Trade Name | 16.0% | 2,026 | 2,026 | 2,026 | 2,026 | 2,026 | 2,026 | 2,026 |
| Noncompete Agreement | 16.0% | 435 | 435 | 435 | 0 | 0 | 0 | 0 |
| Assembled Workforce | 16.0% | 286 | 286 | 286 | 286 | 286 | 286 | 286 |
| Technology | 18.0% | 2,981 | 2,981 | 2,981 | 2,981 | 2,981 | 2,981 | 2,981 |
| IPR&D | 20.0% | 906 | 906 | 906 | 906 | 906 | 906 | 906 |
| Sum of Returns | | 11,479 | 11,092 | 10,869 | 10,295 | 10,220 | 10,167 | 10,108 |
| After-tax Residual Cash Flows | | $649 | $1,285 | $3,008 | $4,899 | $6,173 | $7,059 | $7,990 |
| (4) Survivorship of Customer Base, Rounded | | 92.9% | 78.6% | 64.3% | 50.0% | 35.7% | 21.4% | 7.1% |
| Surviving Excess Cash Flows | | $603 | $1,010 | $1,934 | $2,450 | $2,204 | $1,511 | $567 |
| (5) 17.0% Present Value Factor for Residual Cash Flow | | 0.9245 | 0.7902 | 0.6754 | 0.5772 | 0.4934 | 0.4217 | 0.3604 |
| Present Value of Surviving Residual Cash Flows | | $557 | $798 | $1,306 | $1,414 | $1,087 | $637 | $204 |

| | | |
|---|---|---|
| Sum of Present Values, 2007-2013 | | $6,004 |
| Amortization Benefit | | |
| Discount Rate | 17.0% | |
| Tax Rate | 40.0% | |
| Tax Amortization Period (Years) | 15 | |
| Amortization Benefit | | 1,089 |

**Fair Value of Customer Base, Rounded $7,090**

Footnotes:

(1) Assumes existing sales to existing customers will increase at a rate of 5% (to account for inflation and some real growth), before considering attrition.

(2) Excludes expenses of 7% for the solicitation of potential new customers to reflect that existing customers should not be burdened by the expense of developing new customers.

(3) See Calculation of Contributory Asset Charges (Exhibit 4.11)

(4) Assumes 7-year life, straight line (survivorship analysis per management)

(5) Based on mid-period assumption

Note: Some amounts may not foot due to rounding.

**Exhibit 4.15**   Target Company Valuation of Goodwill as of December 31, 2006 ($000s)

| | |
|---|---:|
| Cash and Acquisition Costs | $150,000 |
| Debt-free Current Liabilities | 25,000 |
| Current Maturities of Long-term Debt | 4,000 |
| Long-term Debt | 30,000 |
| Adjusted Purchase Price | 209,000 |
| Less: Fair Value of Current Assets | (41,500) |
| Less: Fair Value of Tangible Assets | (41,000) |
| Less: Fair Value of Intangible Assets | |
| Software | (7,120) |
| Technology | (16,560) |
| In-process Research and Development | (4,530) |
| Trade Name | (12,660) |
| Customer Base | (7,090) |
| Noncompete Agreement | (2,720) |
| (1) **Residual Goodwill** | **$75,820** |

Footnote:
(1) Residual Goodwill includes the value of Assembled Workforce of $1.790 million.

Note: Some amounts may not foot due to rounding.

in the valuation assume both responsible ownership and competent management unless noted otherwise. Any variance from this assumption could have a significant impact on the final value estimate.

Unless otherwise stated, no effort has been made to determine the possible effect, if any, on the subject business due to future federal, state, or local legislation, including any environmental or ecological matters or interpretations thereof.

Events and circumstances frequently do not occur as expected, and there will usually be differences between prospective financial information and actual results, and those differences may be material. Accordingly, to the extent that any of the information used in this analysis and report requires adjustment, the resulting fair value would be different.

Any decision to purchase, sell, or transfer any interest or asset in Acquirer or Target, or any portion thereof, shall be solely your responsibility, as well as the structure to be utilized and the price to be accepted.

The selection of the price to be accepted requires consideration of factors beyond the information we will provide or have provided. An actual transaction involving the subject business or assets might be concluded at a higher value or at a lower value, depending on the circumstances of the transaction and the business, and the knowledge and motivations of the buyers and sellers at that time.

All facts and data set forth in our letter report are true and accurate to the best of the valuator's knowledge and belief.

No investigation of legal fees or title to the property has been made, and the owner's claim to the property has been assumed valid. No consideration has been given to liens or

(*continued*)

**Exhibit 4.16**    Target Company Valuation Summary as of December 31, 2006 ($000s)

| Asset Name | Fair Value | Return | Percent to Purchase Price | Weighted return |
|---|---|---|---|---|
| Current Assets | $41,500 | | | |
| Debt-free Current Liabilities | 25,000 | | | |
| Net Working Capital | 16,500 | 5.00% | 9.0% | 0.45% |
| Land and Buildings | 22,000 | 7.00% | 12.0% | 0.84% |
| Machinery and Equipment, net | 19,000 | 8.00% | 10.3% | 0.83% |
| TOTAL NET WORKING CAPITAL AND TANGIBLE ASSETS | $57,500 | | | |
| Software | $7,120 | 17.00% | 3.9% | 0.66% |
| Technology | 16,560 | 18.00% | 9.0% | 1.62% |
| In-process Research and Development | 4,530 | 20.00% | 2.5% | 0.49% |
| Trade Name | 12,660 | 16.00% | 6.9% | 1.10% |
| Customer Base | 7,090 | 17.00% | 3.9% | 0.66% |
| Assembled Workforce | 1,790 | 16.00% | 1.0% | 0.16% |
| Noncompete Agreement | 2,720 | 16.00% | 1.5% | 0.24% |
| TOTAL INTANGIBLE ASSETS | $52,470 | | | |
| (1) GOODWILL (excluding assembled workforce) | $74,030 | 23.00% | 40.2% | 9.25% |
| TOTAL | $184,000 | | | 16.28% |

Footnote:

(1) For financial reporting purposes, the fair value of goodwill includes the fair value of assembled workforce for a total fair value of residual goodwill of $75.820 million.

Note: Some amounts may not foot due to rounding.

encumbrances that may be against the property except as specifically stated in the valuation executive summary report.

All recommendations as to fair value are presented as the valuator's conclusion based on the facts and data set forth in this report.

During the course of the valuation, we have considered information provided by management and other third parties. We believe these sources to be reliable, but no further responsibility is assumed for their accuracy.

We have conducted interviews with the current management of Acquirer concerning the past, present, and prospective operating results of Acquirer.

Any projections of future events described in this report represent the general expectancy concerning such events as of the evaluation date. These future events may or may not occur as anticipated, and actual operating results may vary from those described in our report.

This valuation study is intended solely for use by the management of Acquirer in connection with financial reporting relating to SFAS No. 141 and should not be used for any other purpose or distributed to third parties, in whole or in part, without the express written consent of FVA&M, LLC.

*(continued)*

We have used financial projections approved by management. We have not examined the forecast data or the underlying assumptions in accordance with the standards prescribed by the American Institute of Certified Public Accountants and do not express an opinion or any other form of assurance on the forecast data and related assumptions. The future may not occur as anticipated, and actual operating results may vary from those described in our report. In the case that the forecast data differ from the actual future events, our recommendations as to the indication of value may be materially affected.

We have no responsibility or obligation to update this report for events or circumstances occurring subsequent to the date of this report.

Our report is based on historical and/or prospective financial information provided to us by management and other third parties. This information has not been audited, reviewed, or compiled by us, nor has it been subjected to any type of audit, review, or compilation procedures by us, nor have we audited, reviewed, or compiled the books and records of the subject company. Had we audited, reviewed, or compiled the underlying data, matters may have come to our attention that would have resulted in our using amounts that differ from those provided; accordingly, we take no responsibility for the underlying data presented or relied upon in this report.

We have relied upon the representations of the owners, management, and other third parties concerning the value and useful conditions of all equipment, real estate, investments used in the business, and any other assets of the business are free and clear of liens and encumbrances, or that the Company has good title to all assets.

Our valuation judgment, shown herein, pertains only to the subject assets, the stated value standard (fair value), as at the stated valuation date, and only for the stated valuation purpose (financial reporting).

The various estimates of value presented in this report apply to the valuation report only, and may not be used out of the context presented herein.

In all matters that may be potentially challenged by the Securities and Exchange Commission, a Court, the Internal Revenue Service, or other governmental and/or regulatory body, we do not take responsibility for the degree of reasonableness of contrary positions that others may choose to take, nor for the costs or fees that may be incurred in the defense of our recommendations against challenge(s). We will, however, retain our supporting work papers for your matter(s), and will be available to assist in active defense of our professional positions taken, at our then current rates, plus direct expenses at actual, and according to our then current Standard Professional Agreement.

## ENDNOTES

1. The authors wish to thank Donald P. Wisehart, ASA, CPA/ABV, CVA, MST, for his contribution to this section.
2. Revenue Ruling 59–60 lists eight factors for the appraiser to consider: (1) The nature of the business and the history of the enterprise from its inception, (2) the economic outlook in general and the condition and outlook of the specific industry in particular, (3) the book value of the stock and the financial condition of the business, (4) the earning capacity of the company, (5) the dividend-paying capacity, (6) whether or not the enterprise has goodwill

or other intangible value, (7) sales of the stock and the size of the block to be valued, and (8) the market price of stock of corporations engaged in the same or a similar line of business having their stocks actively traded in a free and open market, either on an exchange or over-the-counter. Note: Revenue Ruling 59–60 does not contain any reporting requirements.

3. USPAP Standard 10, p. 74.

4. Ibid.

5. The Scope of Work section of USPAP replaced the Departure Rule section effective July 1, 2006.

6. The authors wish to thank David Ellner, CPA/ABV, for his assistance with this section.

# REPORT FOOTNOTE

1. This definition differs from SFAS No. 157, *Fair Value Measurements,* which is, "The price that would be received to sell an asset or paid to transfer a liability in an orderly transaction between market participants at the measurement date." The SFAS No. 141 definition presumes the perspective of an entry price while SFAS No. 157 presumes an exit price. For purposes of this sample report, we assume the two definitions are materially consistent.

2. *International Glossary of Business Valuation Terms,* jointly published by the American Institute of Certified Public Accountants, the American Society of Appraisers, the Canadian Institute of Chartered Business Valuators, the National Association of Certified Public Accountants, and The Institute of Business Appraisers (2000).

3. Ibid.

4. Refer to the *International Glossary of Business Valuation Terms,* published in January 2000 as a joint project by the American Institute of Certified Public Accountants, American Society of Appraisers, Canadian Institute of Chartered Business Valuators, National Association of Certified Fair Value Measurement Analysts, and the Institute of Business Appraisers.

5. Ibid.

6. Ibid.

7. For an explanation of the development of the weighted average cost of capital, refer to *Financial Valuation: Applications and Models, 2nd edition,* (Hoboken, NJ: John Wiley & Sons, Inc., 2006).

8. James R. Hitchner, *Financial Valuation: Applications and Models, 2nd edition,* (Hoboken, NJ: John Wiley & Sons, Inc., 2006), p. 1182.

9. Ibid, pp. 153, 164, 186.

10. Ibid, p.164.

11. *Stocks, Bonds, Bills and Inflation Edition 2006 Yearbook,* Ibbotson Associates (March 2006).

12. James R. Hitchner, *Financial Valuation: Applications and Models, 2nd edition,* (Hoboken, NJ: John Wiley & Sons, Inc., 2006), p. 180.

# Chapter 5

# Implementation Aids

The SEC is concerned that financial statements properly reflect acquired assets at their fair values. It is safe to assume that they will place a similar level of emphasis on nonamortizable assets as they have on in-process research and development, and will be looking for instances of overvaluation of nonamortizable intangible assets. Management should be aware that the overvaluation of nonamortizable assets increases the potential of later having to recognize impairment charges on such assets. If impairment losses become commonplace, investors may begin to question management's ability to make successful acquisitions. Therefore, it is vital that purchase price allocations and impairment testing be done by a qualified professional.

Management may conduct impairment testing internally *only if company personnel can meet the criteria of Statement on Auditing Standards (SAS) 73, Using the Work of a Specialist.* Auditors will be reviewing management's qualifications and work product to ensure that the requirements of SAS 73 and SFAS Nos. 141, 142 and 157 are met. Most auditors are interpreting the new independence standards as not allowing the auditor to perform SFAS Nos. 141, 142 and 157 services.

The services of an independent valuation specialist are usually required in estimating the fair value of assets acquired in a business combination. Some entities employ valuation specialists in their organizations; others will find it necessary to engage the services of an external valuation specialist. Regardless of who performs the valuation, the auditor should determine that the specialist has the requisite skills and expertise to develop a valuation of the acquired assets in conformity with GAAP.

A review of the qualifications of the appraiser should be at the same high level as that for any critical professional. These qualifications should focus on the appraiser's skill, education, and experience and may include:

- Specialized training in business valuation
- Specialized training in valuing intangible assets
- Audit experience or exposure to comprehend the audit environment for the valuation
- Recognized business valuation designations
- Postgraduate education
- Professional leadership activities at the state or national level
- Unique professional activity such as serving on task forces or committees for organizations like the SEC, SFAS, or AICPA on these issues
- Knowledge of the elements of SFAS Nos. 141, 142 and 157, including critically related SFAS Nos. 144 (impairment) and 131 (segment reporting), as well as others

- Experience in rendering opinions related to intangible assets
- Experience defending valuation opinions (e.g., SEC)

So, what steps should companies take when they are faced with implementing SFAS Nos. 141, 142 and 157? We recommend that companies:

- Consider creating new accounts to capture adjustments that may be needed to effectively provide the information necessary for goodwill impairment testing
- Clarify management's role in data gathering
- Get the auditors involved as soon as possible
- Select appraisers and involve them as soon as possible
- Clearly define the scope of the engagement and the responsibilities and expectations of each of the involved parties (i.e., company management, auditors, and appraisers)
- Promptly complete financial statements before the due dates

The steps outlined in *Procedures for the Valuation of Intangible Assets* (Exhibit 5.1 at the end of the chapter) are provided to assist auditors, management, and valuers in compiling operational information that will aid in assigning values to intangible assets acquired in a business combination. These procedures will also assist in determining the appropriate valuation approach for each intangible asset (i.e., cost, market, income). The *Valuation Information Request—Intangible Assets* (Exhibit 5.2 at the end of the chapter) can be used with these procedures to assist in gathering necessary information.

A portion of the purchase price in a purchase business combination may be allocated to In-Process Research and Development (IPR&D), but IPR&D is particularly common in acquisitions of software, electronic devices, and pharmaceutical companies. This model audit program outlines audit procedures that should be considered when an entity has consummated a purchase business combination that may involve IPR&D.

The *Model Audit Program* procedures focus on the software, electronic devices, and pharmaceutical industries. Further tailoring of the recommended procedures may be necessary upon review of the specific circumstances of each acquisition. These modifications may be influenced by the business, legal, and regulatory environments of both the acquiring company and the acquiree. Hence in tailoring the recommended procedures to each acquisition, the auditors should apply their professional judgment in correlation with the knowledge of the environments of the acquiring company and the acquiree.

---

**Exhibit 5.1:** Procedures for the Valuation of Intangible Assets

---

**Business Name** **Valuation Date**

---

The definition of intangible asset should include current and non-current assets (excluding financial instruments) that lack physical substance. An intangible asset acquired in a business combination shall be recognized as an asset apart from goodwill if that asset arises from contractual or other legal rights. If an intangible asset does not arise from contractual or other legal rights, it shall be recognized as an asset apart from goodwill only if it is separable, that is, it is capable of being separated or divided from the acquired enterprise and sold, transferred, licensed, rented, or exchanged (regardless of whether there is an intent to do so). For GAAP purposes, an intangible asset that cannot be sold, transferred, licensed, rented, or exchanged individually is considered separable if it can be sold, transferred, licensed, rented, or exchanged with a related contract, asset, or liability. However, the value of an assembled workforce of at-will employees acquired in a business combination shall be included in the amount recorded as goodwill regardless of whether it meets the criteria for recognition apart from goodwill.

The purpose of this checklist is to guide the analyst in the valuation of intangible assets. For each item, the analyst should indicate completion, or check the item N/A.

**Completed**

**N/A**

| | | Valuation |
|---|---|---|
| ☐ | ☐ | 1. Determine the standard of value: |

    a. Fair market value

    b. Fair value

    c. Investment value

    d. Intrinsic value or fundamental value

    e. Other: _____

☐ ☐ 2. State the purpose of the valuation:

☐ ☐ 3. Determine the premise of value:

    a. Value in use, as part of a going concern (This premise contemplates the contributory value to an income producing enterprise of the intangible asset as part of a mass assemblage of tangible and intangible assets.)

    b. Value in place, as part of an assemblage of assets (This premise contemplates that the intangible asset is fully functional, is part of an assemblage of assets that is ready for use but is not currently engaged in the production of income.)

*(continued)*

Completed

N/A

    c.  Value in exchange, in an orderly disposition (This premise contemplates that the intangible asset will be sold in its current condition, with normal exposure to its appropriate secondary market, but without the contributory value of any associated tangible or intangible assets.)

    d.  Value in exchange, in a forced liquidation (This premise contemplates that the intangible
asset is sold piecemeal, in an auction environment, with an artificially abbreviated exposure to its secondary market.)

**Intangible Asset Description**

☐  ☐   4.  Is the intangible asset subject to specific identification or a recognizable description?

☐  ☐   5.  Categorize the intangible asset as:

    a.  Marketing related

    b.  Customer related

    c.  Artistic related

    d.  Contract related

    e.  Technology related

☐  ☐   6.  Determine and list the intangible assets eligible for appraisal

☐  ☐   7.  Describe fully the intangible asset identified. Attach necessary contracts, drawings, patents, listings, and so on to fully identify the intangible asset.

**History of the Asset**

☐  ☐   8.  Describe the legal existence and protection associated with the intangible asset.

☐  ☐   9.  Is the transferability of the ownership restricted? Explain.

☐  ☐  10.  Describe the susceptibility of the asset being destroyed.

☐  ☐  11.  Describe the inception of the intangible asset (attach a list providing start dates for all customer or client lists).

☐  ☐  12.  To what degree is the revenue associated with these intangible assets due to the day-to-day efforts of the owner? Explain.

(*continued*)

Completed

N/A

| | | **History of the Asset (Continued)** |
|---|---|---|
| ❑ | ❑ | 13. Provide isolated financial results directly related to the asset, such as: |

    a.  Historical cost to create the asset

    b.  Annual cost to maintain the asset

    c.  Specific cash flow related to the asset

❑  ❑   14. Provide a description of the history of the asset, including year(s) created.

❑  ❑   15. Provide all contracts or agreements.

❑  ❑   16. Provide all strategic, marketing and business plans related to the asset.

### Industry and Market

❑  ❑   17. Provide all market or industry surveys or studies related to the asset.

❑  ❑   18. Describe the competitive environment related to the asset.

❑  ❑   19. Describe the general economic environment related to the asset.

### Financial Information

❑  ❑   20. Describe the specific industry environment related to the asset.

❑  ❑   21. Provide all previous valuation reports related to the asset

❑  ❑   22. Provide all financial projections including unit sales.

❑  ❑   23. Provide all budgets/forecasts.

❑  ❑   24. Determine associated cost of capital related directly to the asset.

### Life Cycle

❑  ❑   25. At what stage in its life cycle is the asset?

❑  ❑   26. Please describe the product life cycle.

### Valuation Approaches

❑  ❑   27. Determine valuation approach:

    a.  **Cost Approach** - The cost approach is based on the principle of substitution. A prudent investor would not pay more for an intangible asset than it would cost to replace that intangible asset with a ready-made comparable substitute. Some intangible assets likely to be valued using the

*(continued)*

Completed

N/A

cost approach include computer software, automated databases, technical drawings and documentation, blueprints and engineering drawings, laboratory notebooks, technical libraries, chemical formulations, food and other product recipes, and so on.

b.  **Market Approach** - The market approach compares the subject intangible asset with similar or comparable intangible assets that have been sold or listed for sale in the appropriate primary or secondary market. Correlations must be extrapolated.

c.  **Income Approach** - The income approach measures future economic benefits, discounted to a present value. Different measures of economic income may be relevant to the various income approach methodologies. Given the different measures of economic income that may be used in the income approach, an essential element in the application of this valuation approach is to ensure that the discount rate or the capitalization rate used is derived on a basis consistent with the measure of economic income used.

**Cost Approach**

❑  ❑  28.  Determine the appropriate cost method

a.  Reproduction cost (The cost at current prices to construct an exact duplicate or replica of the subject intangible asset. This duplicate would be created using the same materials, standards, design, layout and quality of workmanship used to create the original intangible asset.)

b.  Replacement cost (The cost to create at current prices an asset having equal utility to the intangible asset. Replacement cost utilizes modern methods and standards, state of the art design and layout and the highest available quality of workmanship.)

❑  ❑  29.  Determine the appropriate adjustment for obsolescence.

a.  Physical deterioration (The reduction from cost due to physical wear and tear resulting from continued use.)

b.  Functional obsolescence (The reduction due to the inability to perform the function or yield the periodic utility for which the asset was originally designed.)

c.  Technological obsolescence (The reduction due to improvements in technology that make an asset less than an ideal replacement for itself, generally resulting in improvements in design or engineering technology and resulting in greater standardized measure of utility production.)

d.  Economic obsolescence (The reduction due to the effects, events or conditions that are not controlled by, and thus external to, the current use or condition of the subject asset.)

*(continued)*

Completed

N/A

| | | **Cost Approach (Continued)** |
|---|---|---|
| ☐ | ☐ | 30. Determine the number of employees involved in creating the intangible asset. |
| ☐ | ☐ | 31. Categorize the employees by salary level. |
| ☐ | ☐ | 32. Capture the associated employer cost related to each hour of salary level. |
| ☐ | ☐ | 33. Determine the number of hours per employee salary level utilized to develop the asset. |
| ☐ | ☐ | 34. Extend the number of hours per salary level by the salary and associated employer cost for an estimate of reproduction costs new. |
| ☐ | ☐ | 35. Adjust reproduction cost new for associated deterioration or obsolescence. |
| ☐ | ☐ | 36. Compare net result of reproduction cost with replacement cost new. |
| ☐ | ☐ | 37. Complete the cost approach analysis. |

| | | **Market Approach** |
|---|---|---|
| ☐ | ☐ | 38. Determine the market served by the guideline or comparable asset. |
| ☐ | ☐ | 39. Complete a primary and secondary market search for similar guideline assets, including an analysis of available public data specific to royalty rates and intellectual property transactions. |
| ☐ | ☐ | 40. Determine the historical return on the investment earned by the subject intangible asset. |
| ☐ | ☐ | 41. Determine the income generating capacity of the subject intangible asset. |
| ☐ | ☐ | 42. Determine the expected prospective return on the investment earned by the guideline asset. |
| ☐ | ☐ | 43. Determine the expected prospective return by the subject intangible asset. |
| ☐ | ☐ | 44. Determine the historical age and expected remaining useful life of the guideline or comparable intangible asset. |
| ☐ | ☐ | 45. Determine the historical age and the remaining useful life of the subject intangible asset. |

(*continued*)

Completed

N/A

**Market Approach (Continued)**

☐  ☐  46. Analyze the terms of the sale of the guideline or the comparable intangible
        asset including:

    a.  The time of the sale
    b.  The price paid
    c.  The payout terms
    d.  Other related terms (including special seller financing and earn out
        agreement, non-compete agreement and so on)

☐  ☐  47. Determine the degree of adjustment necessary to the guideline or
        comparable intangible asset related to:

    a.  Physical deterioration
    b.  Functional obsolescence
    c.  Technological obsolescence
    d.  Economic obsolescence

☐  ☐  48. Determine the degree of adjustment necessary to the subject intangible
        asset related to:

    a.  Physical deterioration
    b.  Functional obsolescence
    c.  Technological obsolescence
    d.  Economic obsolescence

☐  ☐  49. Complete extrapolation of market approach correlation.

**Income Approach**

☐  ☐  50. Determine the economic income related to the identified intangible asset for
        the following:

    a.  Net income before tax
    b.  Net income after tax
    c.  Net operating income
    d.  Gross rental income
    e.  Gross royalty or license income (actual or hypothetical if a relief from
        royalties method is employed, in which case should include an analysis
        of available public data specific to royalty rates and intellectual property
        transactions)
    f.  Gross or operating cash flow
    g.  Net or free cash flow

(*continued*)

Completed

N/A

**Income Approach (Continued)**

☐ ☐ 51. Determine the direct cost associated with maintaining the identified intangible asset. These costs should include cost of operating the asset, storing the asset (facilities), and managing a return from the asset (staff expenses). Pay particular attention to any anticipated unusual costs (such as renewing a patent).

☐ ☐ 52. Determine specific cash flow to the intangible asset by taking an economic return on contributory assets that are part of the initial cash flow stream. Contributory assets include:

    a.  Working capital

    b.  Fixed assets

    c.  Other intangible assets

☐ ☐ 53. Determine an appropriate discount rate reflecting a fair return on the investment by considering:

    a.  The opportunity cost of capital

    b.  The term period of the investment (including consideration of the expected remaining life of the subject intangible asset)

    c.  The systematic risk of the investment

    d.  The unsystematic risk of the investment

    e.  The time value of money

    f.  Growth (utilized for computing terminal value)

☐ ☐ 54. Obtain the necessary data to complete the actuarial retirement rate methodology including:

    a.  Inception dates for all active files

    b.  Inception dates and retirement dates for all inactive files comprising the subject intangible asset (five year history desirable)

☐ ☐ 55. In absence of hard data for No. 54 above, obtain management's representations as to:

    a.  Average age of all active files

    b.  Average remaining life of all active files

    c.  "Estimate the number of visits per file"

☐ ☐ 56. Complete the actuarial retirement rate methodology by:

    a.  Observing the data

    b.  Determine the curve fitting using appropriate statistical tools (S-curve, O-curve, L-curve, R-curve)

*(continued)*

Completed   N/A

## Income Approach (Continued)

❑ ❑   57. Match the actuarial retirement rate curve with the actual data.

❑ ❑   58. Determine the probable life curve.

❑ ❑   59. Determine the remaining useful life and survivorship percentages.

❑ ❑   60. Apply the survivorship percentages to the discounted cash flow.

❑ ❑   61. Complete income approach methodology.

## Relief from Royalties Method

❑ ❑   62. How is the licensed product unique? What are the competitive advantages of the licensed product including the scope and remaining life of any patents related to the products.

❑ ❑   63. Analyze the markets in which the licensee will sell the licensed products, including:

    a. Market size

    b. Growth rates

    c. Extent of competition

    d. Recent developments

❑ ❑   64. Determine the degree of complexity in the sale of the licensed product.

❑ ❑   65. Determine the extent of customization in customer-specific applications. (Note: Royalty rates are generally inversely related to the level of complexity and licensee customization.)

❑ ❑   66. Determine the size of the licensed territory, including any restrictions or exclusivity. (Note: Exclusivity is directly correlated to higher royalty rates.)

❑ ❑   67. Determine the length of the initial license term and provisions for renewal. (Note: Royalty rates will increase if the provisions for renewal are favorable for licensing.)

❑ ❑   68. What are the provisions for termination? (Note: The conditions for unilateral license termination generally protect the licensor from a material breach committed by the licensee. These terms should be identified.)

❑ ❑   69. Does a minimum royalty rate exist?

*(continued)*

| Completed | N/A | |
|---|---|---|

**Relief from Royalties Method (Continued)**

☐ ☐ 70. Analyze the licensee's ability to assign the license to a third party, either directly or indirectly (for instance through the purchase of stock ownership).

☐ ☐ 71. What is the licensor's presence within its own markets.

☐ ☐ 72. What is the licensor's financial viability.

☐ ☐ 73. What is the licensor's size and market share.

☐ ☐ 74. What is the licensor's depth of senior management and stability.

☐ ☐ 75. What is the licensor's depth of technical knowledge.

☐ ☐ 76. What is the licensor's business plan related to the licensed products, including R&D funding and market analysis.

☐ ☐ 77. To what extent and timeliness does the licensor offer to support the licensee including:

    a.  Technical product advice

    b.  Assisting the licensee with sales

    c.  Assisting the licensee with marketing efforts in the defined territory

☐ ☐ 78. Determine the licensee's available profit percentage available for the royalty (25%?, 50%?) dependent upon the following:

    a.  Available profitability as compared with the industry

    b.  The nature of the long-term competitive advantage of the product

    c.  The degree the license terms are favorable to the licensee

    d.  The degree of support and market share offered by the licensor

    e.  The degree of any noncash value offered by the licensee to the licensor

    f.  The degree the licensee is required to purchase certain components used in the manufacturing of licensed products from the licensor (mandatory supply arrangement)

    g.  The degree of foreign exchange risk borne by either the licensee or the licensor (the risk of future devaluation).

**Exhibit 5.2:**    Valuation Information Request – Intangible Assets

**Business Name**                                                    **Valuation Date**

This is a generalized information request. Some items may not pertain to your company, and some items may not be readily available to you. In such cases, indicate N/A or notify us if other arrangements can be made to obtain the data. Items already provided are indicated. If you have any questions on the development of this information, please call.

Provided   N/A

### Patent

☐ ☐   1.   Provide a summary of patents held by the Company.

☐ ☐   2.   Provide copies of patent applications and patent abstracts.

☐ ☐   3.   Distinguish which patents have commercial applications (i.e., are producing or are reasonably forecast to produce revenue in the future).

☐ ☐   4.   If available, provide historical cost records documenting development of the patent(s):

       a.   person hours to develop;
       b.   various technical levels of persons working on the assignment;
       c.   pay scales for individuals in 4b; and
       d.   information to determine overhead rate.

☐ ☐   5.   Identify patents and associated products that now have or are expected to have commercial viability.

       a.   prepare forecast or projection of revenues related to patent over the life of the patent; and
       b.   project direct expenses associated with producing revenue in 5a

☐ ☐   6.   Comment on the possibility of extending patent protection beyond statutory life of patent.

☐ ☐   7.   Are you licensing in or out any patents? If yes, provide details.

### Copyrights

☐ ☐   1.   Provide a list of all copyrighted registrations.

☐ ☐   2.   Provide a list of works (articles, books, painting, etc.).

☐ ☐   3.   Identify copyright names that are associated with products and/or services (such as software or report templates).

*(continued)*

| Provided | N/A | |
|---|---|---|

**Copyrights (Continued)**

☐ ☐ 4. Identify historical sale of products and/or services employing the works for the last five years.

☐ ☐ 5. Provide projection of products and/or services that will employ the works for the next five years.

☐ ☐ 6. Are you licensing in or out any copyrighted works? If yes, provide details.

**Trademark/Trade Name**

☐ ☐ 1. Provide a list of all trademark/trade name registrations.

☐ ☐ 2. Provide a list of trademark/trade names that are not registered.

☐ ☐ 3. Identify trademarks/trade names that are associated with products and/or services.

☐ ☐ 4. Identify historical sale of products and/or services employing trademarks/trade names for the last five years.

☐ ☐ 5. Provide projection of products and/or services that employ the trademarks/trade names for the next five years.

☐ ☐ 6. Are you licensing in or out any trademarks/trade names? If yes, provide details.

**Proprietary Processes/Products Technology**

☐ ☐ 1. Describe the proprietary process/product technology.

☐ ☐ 2 Describe competitive advantages and disadvantages of the proprietary process/product technology.

☐ ☐ 3. Describe industry trends and competitive pressures that may affect the useful life of the proprietary process/product technology.

☐ ☐ 4. In light of 2 and 3 above, what is the estimated useful life of the proprietary process/product technology support?

☐ ☐ 5. If available, please provide historical cost records documenting development of the process/product technology:

    a.  Person hours to develop
    b.  Various technical levels of persons working on the assignment
    c.  Pay scales for individuals in 5b
    d.  Information to determine overhead rate

(*continued*)

Provided

N/A

| Proprietary Processes/Products Technology (Continued) |

❑ ❑ 6. In the absence of historical cost records, estimate effort to recreate the process/product technology if it were to be developed from scratch:

    a. Who would work on the assignment (employees and consultants)
    b. Pay rates for individuals in 6a
    c. Information to determine overhead rate

❑ ❑ 7. Identify historical sale of products and/or services employing process/ product technology for the last five years.

❑ ❑ 8. What products or services employ the proprietary process/product technology?

❑ ❑ 9. Provide projection of products and/or services that employ the process/ product technology for the next five years.

    a. Project revenues including licensing income for the lifespan of process/product technology.
    b. Project direct expenses associated with producing revenue in 9a.
    c. Obtain or develop indirect expenses (i.e., overhead).

❑ ❑ 10. Are you licensing in or out any technology? If yes, provide details.

| In Process Research and Development |

❑ ❑ 1. Describe the in-process research and development.

❑ ❑ 2. Describe competitive advantages and disadvantages of the in-process research and development.

❑ ❑ 3. Describe industry trends and competitive pressures that may affect the useful life of the in-process research and development.

❑ ❑ 4. In light of 2 and 3 above, what is the estimated useful life of the in-process research and development support?

❑ ❑ 5. If available, please provide cost records documenting development of the in-process research and development:

    a. person hours to develop;
    b. various technical levels of persons working on the assignment;
    c. pay scales for individuals in 5b; and
    d. information to determine overhead rate.

*(continued)*

Provided

N/A

### In Process Research and Development (Continued)

☐ ☐ 6. In the absence of cost records, estimate effort to create the in-process research and development:

    a. who would work on the assignment (employees and consultants);
    b. pay rates for individuals in 6a; and
    c. information to determine overhead rate.

☐ ☐ 7. What products or services will employ the in-process research and development?

☐ ☐ 8. Provide projections of products and/or services that will employ the in-process research and development for the next five years.

    a. Project revenues including licensing income for the lifespan of the in-process research and development.
    b. Project direct expenses associated with producing revenue in 8a.
    c. Obtain or develop indirect expenses (i.e., overhead).

### Know-How

☐ ☐ 1. Describe know-how, including competitive advantages and disadvantages.

☐ ☐ 2. Describe industry trends and competitive pressures that may affect the useful life of the know-how.

☐ ☐ 3. In light of 1 and 2 above, what is the estimated useful life of the know-how?

☐ ☐ 4. What products or services employ the know-how?

☐ ☐ 5. If available, provide historical cost records documenting development of the know-how:

    a. person hours to develop;
    b. various technical levels of persons working on the assignment;
    c. pay scales for individuals in 5b; and
    d. information to determine overhead rate.

☐ ☐ 6. In the absence of historical cost records, estimate corporate effort to recreate the know-how if it were to be developed from scratch:

    a. who would work on the assignment (employees and consultants);
    b. pay rates for individuals in 6a; and
    c. information to determine overhead rate.

*(continued)*

**Provided**  
**N/A**

**Know-How (Continued)**

☐ ☐ 7. Identify historical sale of revenues for products and/or services employing know-how for the last five years.

☐ ☐ 8. Know-how associated with products and/or services:

    a. provide projection of products and/or services that employ the know-how for the next five years;  
    b. project direct expenses associated with producing revenue in 8a; and  
    c. obtain or develop indirect expenses (i.e., overhead).

☐ ☐ 9. Are you licensing in or out any know-how? If yes, provide details.

**Software**

☐ ☐ 1. Describe the function of the software.

☐ ☐ 2. If available, provide historical cost records documenting development of the software:

    a. Person hours to develop  
    b. Various technical levels of persons working on the assignment  
    c. Pay scales for individuals in 2b  
    d. Information to determine overhead rate

☐ ☐ 3. In the absence of historical cost records, estimate effort to recreate the software if it were to be developed from scratch:

    a. Who would work on the assignment (employees and consultants)  
    b. Pay rates for individuals in 3a  
    c. Information to determine overhead rate

☐ ☐ 4. What was the expected useful life at inception and at valuation date. Obtain support for estimate:

    a. When was software actually placed in use  
    b. Describe internal development that may extend life  
    c. Describe internal development of replacement software that might shorten life  
    d. Describe external factors that may affect life

☐ ☐ 5. Obtain historical revenues applicable to software

☐ ☐ 6. Provide projection of revenues applicable to the software for the next five years:

    a. Project revenues including licensing income for lifespan of software

*(continued)*

**Provided**

**N/A**

### Software (Continued)

    b.  Project direct expenses associated with producing revenue in 6a

    c.  Obtain or develop indirect expenses (i.e., overhead)

### Customer Relationships

❑  ❑  1.  Provide customer sales history for the last five years for the top ten customers.

❑  ❑  2.  Provide complete customer history for the last five years (this would be for lifing).

❑  ❑  3.  Provide financial data representing annual costs for the last five years associated with developing/soliciting new customers.

❑  ❑  4.  Provide schedule of new customers gained in each of the last five years with sales.

❑  ❑  5.  For the last five years, how many customers in a given year failed to purchase in the following year? Provide those customers' sales for the prior year.

### General Information

❑  ❑  1.  Financial statements for fiscal years ending FIVE YEARS (order of preference: audited, reviewed, compiled, and internal).

❑  ❑  2.  Interim financial statements for the month-end DATE OF VALUATION and one year prior.

❑  ❑  3.  Financial projections, if any, for the current year and the next three years. Include any prepared budgets and/or business plans.

❑  ❑  4.  Federal and State Corporate Income Tax Returns and supporting schedules for fiscal years ending FIVE YEARS.

❑  ❑  5.  Explanation of significant nonrecurring and/or nonoperating items appearing on the financial statements in any fiscal year if not detailed in footnotes.

❑  ❑  6.  Copies of any appraisals of the stock of the business made during the last three years.

❑  ❑  7.  Copies of any appraisals of real estate or personal property owned by the business.

❑  ❑  8.  Summary of major covenants or agreements binding on the business (e.g., union contracts, capital leases, employment contracts, service contracts, product warranties, etc.).

*(continued)*

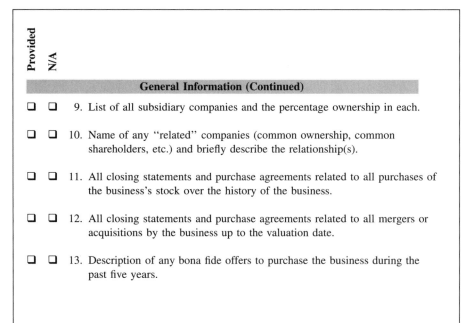

Provided | N/A

**General Information (Continued)**

☐ ☐   9. List of all subsidiary companies and the percentage ownership in each.

☐ ☐   10. Name of any "related" companies (common ownership, common shareholders, etc.) and briefly describe the relationship(s).

☐ ☐   11. All closing statements and purchase agreements related to all purchases of the business's stock over the history of the business.

☐ ☐   12. All closing statements and purchase agreements related to all mergers or acquisitions by the business up to the valuation date.

☐ ☐   13. Description of any bona fide offers to purchase the business during the past five years.

---

**Exhibit 5.3**    Model Audit Program – In-Process Research and Development[1]

---

**General**

The procedures focus on the software, electronic devices, and pharmaceutical industries; however, further tailoring of the recommended procedures may be necessary in response to the specific circumstances of each acquisition. The nature and extent of the needed tailoring may be influenced by the business, legal, and regulatory environments in which both the acquiring company and the acquiree operate. Accordingly, auditors should use their knowledge of those environments and their professional judgment in tailoring the recommended procedures to each acquisition.

The services of a valuation specialist are usually required in estimating the amount of the purchase price allocated to IPR&D. Some entities employ valuation specialists in their organizations; others will find it necessary to engage the services of an external valuation specialist. Regardless of who performs the valuation, the auditor should determine that the specialist has the requisite skills and expertise to develop a valuation of the acquired IPR&D in conformity with generally accepted accounting principles. In gathering audit evidence as to the appropriateness of the IPR&D valuation, the auditor may also require the assistance of a valuation specialist. That specialist may be an employee of the auditor's firm or may be an external valuation specialist engaged by the auditor to assist in evaluating the reasonableness of the IPR&D valuation.

**Procedures**

1. Obtain an understanding of the acquisition.

   a. Inquire of appropriate client personnel as to the nature and business purpose of the acquisition and whether special terms or conditions may exist. Persons of whom inquiry might be made include the CEO, the CFO, and appropriate personnel from marketing, business development, research and development, and technology departments. The auditor should become familiar with the types of products and services sold by the acquiree, and its production, marketing, distribution, and compensation methods. The auditor should also become aware of significant matters and trends affecting the industry, including economic conditions, changes in technology, government regulations, and competition.

   b. Obtain and read the acquisition agreements, due diligence reports prepared by client personnel or other parties engaged by the client, analyst's reports, acquiree prospectuses or offering memoranda, and other industry analyses pertinent to the acquisition.

   c. Obtain and read presentations to the board of directors and any press releases concerning the acquisition.

2. Ascertain the identity and affiliation of the valuation specialist. Arrange to meet with the valuation specialist and discuss the following:

   a. The objectives and scope of the valuation study.

---

[1] Randy J. Larson, et al, Assets *Acquired in a Business Combination to be Used in Research and Development Activities: A Focus on Software, Electronic Devices, and Pharmaceutical Industries,* (New York: AICPA, 2001), Appendix D.

(*continued*)

b. Whether the valuation specialist has any relationships with the client that might impair the valuation specialist's objectivity.

c. The valuation specialist's understanding of the requirements of GAAP as they relate to the valuation.

d. The types and sources of information to be provided by the acquiring company to the valuation specialist.

e. The methods and significant assumptions used in the valuation.

f. The consistency of methods and assumptions with previous valuations.

g. The scope and nature of the conclusions included in the valuation report.

3. Ascertain the following:

a. The professional competence of the valuation specialist as evidenced by accreditation or certification, licensure or recognition by a recognized professional organization.

b. The professional reputation of the valuation specialist as viewed by his or her peers and others familiar with his or her capabilities or performance.

c. The experience of the valuation specialist in the industry or in the valuation of tangible and intangible assets, including acquired IPR&D.

4. Inquire of client personnel regarding any relationship between the valuation specialist and the client.

a. The auditor should evaluate any relationship between the valuation specialist and the client to ascertain whether the client has the ability-through employment, ownership, contractual rights, family relationship or otherwise-to directly or indirectly control or significantly influence the valuation specialist's work, The valuation report should identify such relationships.

5. With respect to the valuation report:

a. Determine whether the valuation methodology used reconciles to the AICPA Practice Aid, Assets Acquired in a Purchase Business Combination to be Used in Research and Development Activities.

b. Review the reconciliation of the valuation to the purchase price paid. This information is normally found in the "valuation analysis" section of the valuation report.

c. Consider whether other intangibles exist to which a portion of the purchase has not been allocated. The report should identify and value all intangibles acquired (when several specialists are used to value intangibles, there may be more than one report, but identifiable intangibles should be valued).

6. If the income approach to valuation is used, review the cash flow forecasts and consider whether the significant assumptions applied to the projects in process are unreasonable.

Among the more significant assumptions are the following:

• Potential for introduction of new technologies that may obsolete the acquired technology

(*continued*)

- Likelihood of project completion
- Estimates of stage of completion and time to completion
- Cost to complete
- Product life cycle and technology development strategies
- Expected sales volumes, product pricing, and expected revenues (exclusive of amounts attributable to contributory assets and core technology)
- Production and other costs (exclusive of the effects of buyer synergies)
- Discount rates
- Competitors' expected prices

7. Test the data furnished to the valuation specialist as follows:

   a. Assess the relative importance of IPR&D to the acquisition by considering the materials reviewed during the planning procedures as well as other materials, such as presentations to the Board, white papers, and due diligence working papers.

   b. Test the mathematical accuracy of the forecasts furnished to the specialist.

   c. Determine whether cash flow estimated were developed using "market participant" assumptions. With respect to "market participant" assumptions, paragraph 1.1.16 of the AICPA Practice Aid states:

   For purposes of assigning cost to the assets acquired in accordance with APB Opinion 16, the amount of the purchase price allocated to an acquired identifiable intangible asset would not include any entity-specific synergistic value. Fair value does not include strategic or synergistic value resulting from expectations about future events that are specific to a particular buyer because the value associated with those components are unique to the buyer and seller and would not constitute market-based assumptions. As such, entity-specific value associated with strategic or synergistic components would be included in goodwill. Fair value would incorporate expectations about future events that affect market participants. If the acquiring company concludes that the discounted cash flow method best approximates the fair value of an acquired identifiable intangible asset, the discounted cash flows would incorporate assumptions that market participants would use in their estimates of future revenues and future expenses.

   (A footnote to paragraph 1.1.16 refers readers to current developments in accounting related to market participant assumptions.)

   d. Consider the amounts of R&D costs expended to date and estimated remaining completion costs for reasonableness.

   e. Review descriptions of the milestones achieved and compare the status with the actual costs incurred and projected remaining costs.

   f. Consider whether IPR&D is related to products that will be marketed externally.

   g. Inquire of appropriate client personnel whether IPR&D has achieved technological feasibility (or the equivalent) and has no alternative future use.

*(continued)*

8. Evaluate the overall results of the valuation. Consider:

   a. Whether the size of the IPR&D charge is consistent with the overall nature of the business and management's purchase rationale.

   b. The size of the existing base (or core) technology value relative to the IPR&D value is reasonable.

   c. The reasonableness of the IPR&D value with respect to the extent of completion efforts remaining.

   d. Whether the IPR&D value will be realizable and whether both the buyer and seller are compensated considering the risks.

   e. Major milestones achieved in the IPR&D project as of the purchase date and their consistency with the valuation.

   f. The entire purchase price allocation reflects the acquiring company's technology, industry position, age, reputation, and strategic plan.

9. Obtain a representation letter from the client that includes the following:

   a. Management agrees with the findings of the valuation specialist.

   b. The IPR&D assets have substance, are incomplete, and have no alternative future use.

   c. The historical financial data provided to the valuation specialist was prepared on a basis consistent with the audited financial statements.

   d. Forecasts and other estimated provided to the valuation specialist are consistent with those developed for other parties or for internal use. The forecasts of future cash flows used in the valuation represent management's best estimate of future conditions consistent with the assumptions specified in the specialist's valuation using market participant assumptions rather that those that are entity specific (see the footnote to paragraph 1.1.16 of the AICPA Practice Aid).

   e. Under the traditional approach, the discount rate applied to estimated future net cash flows appropriately reflects the nature and complexity of the remaining development effort and the amount and timing of estimated expenditures necessary to complete the development of the IPR&D projects.

10. Determine that information requiring separate disclosure in the financial statements is properly identified in the working papers and presented in the financial statements, including the disclosures identified in paragraph 4.2.11 of the AICPA Practice Aid.

## CONCLUSION

Based on the procedures performed, we are satisfied that our working papers appropriately document that acquired IPR&D does not contain any material misstatements, in relation to the financial statements taken as a whole. Exceptions are attached or stated below.

# Index